*Yale Publications in Religion, 14*

*"Unica Christianorum gloria est
in solo Christo . . ."* (WA 13, 570, 16)

# Martin Luther's Doctrine of Christ

by Jan D. Kingston Siggins

Yale University Press New Haven and London 1970

# Acknowledgments

The genesis, progress, and completion of this work are immeasurably indebted to the following people, my mentors, friends, and critics, in degrees which they will each recognize. For their wisdom, clarity, and humanity, I make this more than formal act of gratitude. In approximately chronological order, they are: at Melbourne Grammar School, Geoffrey Fell; at the University of Melbourne, R. M. Crawford, K. S. Inglis (now of Adelaide), and the Reverend George M. Yule; at Yale University, Dr. Lorraine D. Siggins, Roland H. Bainton, Robert L. Calhoun, George A. Lindbeck, Nils A. Dahl, Paul L. Holmer, Jaroslav Jan Pelikan, Sydney E. Ahlstrom, and Heinz S. Bluhm (now of Boston College); at the Church Divinity School of the Pacific, the Reverend Professor Francis I. Andersen; and at Yale University Press, Wayland Schmitt and Mrs. June Guicharnaud. I am also indebted for support to the University of Melbourne, for funds to begin postgraduate research in Luther; to the U.S. Government, for a Fulbright Travel Grant to Yale; to the Lutheran World Federation, for subsidizing my participation in the Third International Congress of Luther Research in Järvenpää, Finland; and to Lorraine Siggins, for food, shelter, and tender care.

Ian D. Kingston Siggins
Jonathan Edwards College
Yale University

*New Haven, October 1969*

# Contents

# Abbreviations

Luther is cited throughout the text from the Weimar Edition of his works (*WA*). For the title and date of composition of each work refer to the register of citations at the end of the volume. The first, italic, number in each reference indicates the volume, the second indicates the page, and the third indicates the line. Several volumes of the Weimar Edition consist of two or more separate fascicles: this has been indicated by a slash (/) after the volume number.

The same method is used for Luther's German Bible (*DB*), and for his correspondence (*Br*). In the case of the Table Talk (*Tr*), however, the third number indicates not the line but the item.

### LUTHER'S WORKS

| | |
|---|---|
| *WA* | *Luthers Werke, Kritische Gesamtausgabe* (Weimar, 1883– ) |
| *Br* | *Briefwechsel* (Luther's *Letters* in the Weimar Edition) |
| *DB* | *Deutsche Bibel* (Luther's *German Bible* in the Weimar Edition) |
| *Tr* | *Tischreden* (Luther's *Table Talk* in the Weimar Edition) |

### OTHER COLLECTIONS

| | |
|---|---|
| MPG | J.-P. Migne, *Patrologia cursus completus, Series graeca* (Paris, 1857–1912) |
| MPL | J.-P. Migne, *Patrologia cursus completus, Series latina* (Paris, 1844–1890) |

SCG        Thomas Aquinas, *Summa contra Gentiles* (5 vols. New
           York, 1955)
ST         Thomas Aquinas, *Summa theologiae*, in *Sancti Thomae
           opera omnia* (25 vols. New York, 1948–50)

PERIODICALS

ARG        *Archiv für Reformationsgeschichte*
ThLZ       *Theologische Literaturzeitung*
ZKG        *Zeitschrift für Kirchengeschichte*

*Martin Luther's Doctrine of Christ*

# Introduction

"This should be the Christian's only skill, to learn Christ aright," Luther said.[1] Our object here is to be instructed in this skill by Martin Luther's own precept and example.

The method by which the study seeks this high goal requires some explanation, if not justification. In large measure it is an inductive examination of Luther's own ways of preaching Christ. It proceeds by identifying first the vocabulary, then the themes, of his christological doctrine. While this task is carried out as thoroughly as possible, the result may be frustrating if the reader expects exhaustive treatment of all the classical questions of Christology, since Luther does not address them all. What may appear as glaring omissions or tantalizing loose ends will be the result of Luther's choices and interests, not mine; that, at least, is my intention, however imperfectly realized.

Such omissions, of course, are themselves significant: they are not necessarily defects. In other words, the choice of this methodology is quite deliberate. I hope to exhibit only and all of Luther's own approaches to the doctrine of Christ, and in his own terminology. (As a corollary, I hope the account also illuminates some features of Luther's style.) What is called in question by such inductive study is whether Luther "has a Christology" at all in the sense of an abstract conceptual account of the hypostatic union. We shall find, I think, that his thorough-going intention to espouse the orthodox dogma proceeds in virtual isolation from the vital themes of his preaching Christ, and that he is less comfortable (and less clear) when he moves from the concrete to the abstract, from the historical to the ideal, from the

1. 45, 511, 4.

practical to the theoretical. For need I say that to Luther theology is an urgently practical, not a theoretical, discipline?

My method, then, is prompted first and foremost by the character of the material. It attempts to be faithful to Luther's own logic. Luther does not intend to provide systematic definitions or theoretical accounts of christological terms. In the nominalist logic, which he espoused, whereas concepts are univocal, terms that stand for concepts in language vary flexibly with the nature of the discourse. As a result, the correct hermeneutical order, he insists, is from the subject matter to the grammar, and not vice versa.[2] In order to understand the grammar of theological terms, one must learn the language of faith, since the subject matter is God's promise in Christ. The meanings of christological terms are accordingly not univocal but a matter of family resemblance, patterned after Scripture and traditional usage in all their richness and variety. By constant demonstration of these usages, Luther wishes to teach us the language of faith—to teach us that *usus passionis* which is faith.

Like the apostolic church itself, Luther's characteristic mode of exploiting the nuances of the doctrine of Christ is the application of titles and names to the person and work of Jesus. "God does not trifle with empty names," he says.[3] Indeed, it is the name of Christ by which we must be saved; for God will not be known except in the Son Whom He gave, yet "faith cannot see what He gives, nor grasp or perceive it with the senses—it apprehends no more than the name, the oral Word, heard with the ears."[4] We shall be representing Luther accurately, then, if we concern ourselves especially with the names he gives to Christ, and in which he constantly couches his doctrine of consolation.

This attempt to see Luther's doctrine in its own terms, however, may provoke another reasonable objection. It has the effect of isolating Luther somewhat both from the tradition to which he was heir and from the tradition of Luther interpretation to which he has given rise. This, too, is deliberate. The present direction of

2. *42*, 195, 3ff.; 272, 16; 358, 33; 597, 17; 43, 144, 9.
3. *45*, 548, 10.
4. *21*, 493, 26.

Luther scholarship is illuminating many lines of influence both backward and forward from Luther, and this is extremely fruitful material. Here, however, I have consciously refrained from pursuing this approach, in order to preserve the inductive character of the description. Where Luther's language is demonstrably and directly in debt to postbiblical tradition, this has been indicated in the notes; but by the nature of Luther's endeavor, this dependence is not pervasive. More unfashionably, I have given no résumé of the later accounts of Luther's Christology and have reduced to a minimum my discussion of the secondary literature. My object, of course, is to avoid posing questions of Luther's Christology which do not arise in Luther's frame of reference. The secondary literature is quite divergent in its interpretations, and in this instance (one can think of others!) the texts shed considerably more light on the commentaries than vice versa. Acquaintance with the secondary literature has convinced me that a fresh inductive description of the originals would be helpful. Clearly, it is only when Luther is accurately represented that he can adequately be set in relation to others.

The "Luther renaissance" is indeed one of the most pleasing features of modern theological scholarship—the more so now that it can be shared so fully between Protestant and Catholic scholars. It has given rise to a simply prodigious spate of invaluable study and reflection, and one would be churlish not to express one's debt to many magisterial works. Indebtedness to secondary opinion, however, does not absolve the scholar from exercising his independent judgment upon the original source materials; and where conflicts seem to occur, he is duty bound to voice his misgivings with received opinion. I have found myself harboring such misgivings in several areas of Luther scholarship. Let me sketch some of the concerns that led me to adopt this methodology.

My own intense interest in Luther studies began with the difference of opinion (it has since burgeoned into an open dispute) about the chronology of Luther's theological development. I was startled by the implications for Reformation history of the possibility that decisive theological shifts from Catholicism followed rather than preceded the indulgence controversy—a possibility raised afresh in a striking if rather simplistic way by Uuras Saarnivaara in *Luther Discovers the Gospel* (St. Louis, 1951). Saarnivaara indicated how widely earlier scholars had differed in their dating of the "tower discovery" of justification by faith, and insisted on theological grounds upon a date late in 1518, disputing the majority opinion most clearly represented by Erich Vogelsang (*Die Anfänge von Luthers Christologie*, Berlin and Leipzig, 1929) that Luther's mature doctrine was already present in the later Psalms lectures (1514–15) and the Romans commentary (1515–16). In the subsequent debate Saarnivaara's position has received its most forthright, subtle, and convincing exposition from Ernst Bizer (*Fides ex auditu*, Neukirchen, 1961). Even those who remain unconvinced by his careful argument have acknowledged how much Bizer illuminates the developing thought of these crucial years. Nevertheless, many Luther scholars, notably Heinrich Bornkamm,[5] do remain unconvinced. An attempt to resolve the issue at the Third International Luther Research Congress in Järvenpää, Finland, in August 1966 was inconclusive. Scholars on both sides continue to argue the importance of the continuities and discontinuities between the "young" and the "mature" Luther.

Much of the argument has concentrated on the famous autobiographical excursus in the 1545 *Preface to the Latin Writings* (54, 179–87), with its apparent implication that the "tower discovery" of the meaning of justification took place as late as 1518 or 1519. It is undeniable that a passive meaning of *iustitia dei* is already taught in the Psalms and Romans lectures (e.g. 3, 465, 1; 56, 97, 24). Yet it is quite consistent with Luther's account in the 1545 *Preface* to suppose that the tower discovery which "opened the gates of paradise" had already taken place and was reflected in his earliest lectures, and that nevertheless he underwent such decisive developments later that he felt obliged to warn his reader against virtually everything he had written before 1519.

---

5. Heinrich Bornkamm, "Zur Frage der Iustitia Dei beim jungen Luther," *ARG*, 52 (1961), 16–29; 53 (1962), 1–60. Cf. E. Gordon Rupp's review of Bizer in *ZKG*, 71 (1960), 351–55.

The very point of the *Preface* and its autobiographical excursus is to issue a *caveat lector* for a group of works which Luther was most reluctant to publish. He agreed to publication only because he felt it wiser to publish them himself with his own disclaimer than to have them published after his death without it. He appealed to the reader to use understanding and caution in approaching works which he himself called "my confused musings . . . a crude and inchoate muddle." [6]

Too much attention to the dating of the tower experience may have obscured what is really at issue here: What was it about these works which Luther in 1545 found confused and muddled? Are we entitled to accept as mature, positions which Luther himself regarded as crude and inchoate?

These questions deserve very serious answers in spite of the fact that the early lectures are distinctively works of budding genius, a breath of fresh air in the stale corridors of late medieval exposition. We may decide, with Professor Rupp, that "it is clear, in all essentials, his theology was in existence before the opening of the church struggle of 1517." [7] Or we may conclude, with Professor Cranz, that "the differences between the early and the mature works are so great that only confusion results from the assumption that we are dealing with a single, unified position." [8] In either case the answer makes an undeniable difference to the shape of Luther's doctrine. The highly influential school of Karl Holl has devoted itself to integrating the viewpoints of the "young" Luther with materials from the "mature" period, and the result has proved highly congenial to existentialist theologies in the present century. The formulations of justification in, say, the 1531 Galatians lectures are read as maintaining the highly paradoxical character of faith in the 1515–16 Romans lectures—a sort of courage to be in the face of God's apparent contradiction.

---

6. *54*, 179, 2–12: an allusion to Ovid, *Metamorphoses* I, 17: "chaos rudis indigestaque moles."

7. E. Gordon Rupp, *Luther's Progress to the Diet of Worms* (Greenwich, 1951), p. 39.

8. F. Edward Cranz, *An Essay on the Development of Luther's Thought on Justice, Law, and Society,* Harvard Theological Studies, 19 (Cambridge, Mass., 1959), p. xiv.

Every word of God may be law or gospel, depending on man's response, since faith is that existential word-event in which a man is, as it were, lifted out of himself to discover God's "yes!" hidden beneath His "no!" An experiential *theologia crucis* thus becomes the characteristic spirituality of all Luther's doctrine. If Luther's caveat is honored, however, this procedure is very suspect. He has warned that his early emphases, so far from having an all-important and integral place in Reformation theology, deserve to be distinguished from maturer positions and corrected by them. Then, however strong the strands of continuity between the "young" and the "mature" Luther (or even more importantly, between Luther and those Professor Oberman calls the "forerunners"),[9] the later emphases appear as self-conscious attempts to define his doctrine over against his own earliest evangelical positions. In this case salvation is outside us (*extra nos*) not because the word-event lifts us existentially out of ourselves when we justify God by our resignation to His absolute judgment; rather, it is outside us because it was achieved in historical occurrences quite apart from us—alien to us. God's "no!" is no longer transformed into His "yes!" by a movement of faith, but confusion between the law and the gospel reveals a fatal failure to distinguish a demand from a promise, two forms of address which are mutually exclusive and plainly distinct both in content and even in grammar. The characteristic quest of theology is not for a God Who remains the hidden God even in the moment of His revelation, but for the empirical discovery of who God really is in the history of the man Christ.

This is admittedly to present the dilemma in an extreme form. Proponents of the one school do not deny that Luther continued to adapt, refine, and develop his views throughout his career; nor do proponents of the other deny the large-scale persistence of certain themes from one end of the corpus to the other. Yet this unresolved conflict of interpretation still allows the most divergent schools of modern theology severally to claim Luther as their forebear. Moreover, it is a virtual requirement in Lutheran

9. Heiko A. Oberman, *Forerunners of the Reformation: The Shape of Late Medieval Thought Illustrated by Key Documents* (New York, 1966).

circles that one's theological stance be justified by citations from Luther (just as a psychoanalytic position is incomplete without the ritual obeisances to Freud), and a dispassionate resolution has been correspondingly more difficult. The present study is not an attempt to resolve the conflict; yet its method is designed to take account of the problem and perhaps even to shed some light on it, since it is obvious that the soteriological emphases in dispute have a very intimate connection with the doctrine of Christ. First, the inductive approach is an attempt to avoid unconsciously forcing Luther into the procrustean bed of concerns not his own. (It should perhaps be added that the author is not a Lutheran.) Secondly, in order to avoid begging the question—on the one hand, by omitting some of the material; on the other, by failing to handle it chronologically—I have drawn materials from all parts of Luther's corpus, but I have been careful to use works written before 1520 largely for purposes of comparison with later works. If I may anticipate the results of this method, it becomes clear, I believe, that Luther's convictions concerning the certainty of salvation, the biblical character of theology, and the Christocentric character of faith were already well established before the Reformation began, but that such extensive rethinking and reformulation took place in 1518–19 (and continued over the next several years) that Luther's grave misgivings about his early works are thoroughly justified and deserve to be heeded.

It is already apparent that this discussion has wide ramifications in other areas of central interest. One of the most valuable works of the Luther renaissance is Walther von Loewenich's *Luthers Theologia crucis* (München, 1933), a book whose influence is deservedly disproportionate to its slender size. It is beyond dispute that Luther's theology was from first to last a theology of the cross, set explicitly against any vain attempt at a theology of glory, *theologia maiestatis*. Von Loewenich has brilliantly described the sources and implications of this stance in Luther's emerging doctrine. Yet serious question needs to be raised about the common assumption that Luther's *theologia crucis* means the same thing throughout his career—the assumption that the form of this theme in the Heidelberg Disputation, for instance, remains normative for the knowledge of God in the later theology. Again, close comparison reveals that he never abandoned his insistence that God will be known only as the crucified God; but that the doctrine of the knowledge of God is dramatically recast by a later insistence that faith's knowledge of God in Christ is a knowledge of God fully as He is, with sweeping implications for Christology and for faith.

This observation, in turn, calls in question the whole problematic brought to Luther's doctrine of the knowledge of God by the Ritschlian school, who were fascinated by the concept of the *deus absconditus*. John Dillenberger has analyzed the fruits of their fascination in his *God Hidden and Revealed* (Philadelphia, 1953). The deep-seated dualism they imputed to Luther's doctrine of God widely affected German Luther-research through the influence of Karl Holl, but it appears to be based on a misconception. Scandinavian scholars have since proposed a rather less metaphysical but more pervasive version of dualism than the Ritschlians'. There, since Ragnar Bring's seminal essay *Dualismen hos Luther* (Lund, 1929), and under the guiding influence of Gustaf Aulén, it has been common to assume that deep religious dualism "is not another doctrine in Luther's theology; it is an intrinsic factor in every doctrine." [10] Accordingly, Scandinavian scholars have labored diligently to identify those pairs of antithetical principles which they assume to be the authentic mark of Luther's outlook. Their efforts have brought much needed clarity to many issues. Here, however, I have not approached the material in the expectation of finding such a pattern of couplets, in order to test inductively whether these dualistic motifs are indeed intrinsic and whether they are sufficiently flexible to accommodate Luther's extraordinary freedom and subtlety of exposition. To take the two simplest examples: even the familiar pairs law/gospel and the two kingdoms are distorted, and their usefulness truncated, unless they are kept in the closest connection with their exegetical basis in the historical succession of the covenants.

The last and greatest of my misgivings with received opinion is

10. Edgar M. Carlson, *The Reinterpretation of Luther* (Philadelphia, 1948), p. 57.

a conviction that Luther's doctrine of Christ has suffered from the common but erroneous assumption that Luther is a Paulinist, by which is meant that Paul's doctrine of justification by faith is the material norm of his theology and his "canon within the canon." This study attempts to redress the balance by paying careful attention to his exposition of Johannine materials, for reasons which must now appear.

Luther regarded St. John as "a master above all other evangelists."[11] St. John's he called "the one fine, true, and chief Gospel" and valued it "far, far above" the Synoptics.[12] With the exception of the mammoth ten-year lecture series on Genesis, in terms of sheer bulk Luther's Johannine expositions outweigh his attentions to any other part of Scripture, and only St. Matthew's Gospel equals St. John's as a subject for public preaching. Between 400 and 500 of his sermons on the Fourth Gospel have been recorded—209 individual sermons on various texts, 71 pericope-expositions from the Church and House Postils, and continuous serial expositions of chapters 1–4, 6–8, and 14–20. When the duplicates are subtracted, we are left with the remarkable total of between a fifth and a quarter of his recorded preaching. In addition, there are 23 extant sermons on the First Epistle of St. John, together with a complete exposition of the Epistle in 28 lectures (given in the University of Wittenberg in 1527 to a handful of students who remained behind when most of the University fled to Jena from an outbreak of plague). And since St. John provides the lion's share of the *loci classici* of christological debate, Luther's own handling of these texts aptly illuminates his relation to the Church's dogmatic tradition (before and since).

Moreover, we do not have to rely on mere quantity to justify giving an important role to St. John. Recently, various scholars have drawn attention to the central place of Johannine concepts in Luther's theology.[13] I hope the present study will confirm that

11. 33, 116, 26.

12. *DB*, 6, 10, 25.

13. Walter von Loewenich, *Luther und das johanneische Christentum* (München, 1935); Carl Stange, *Der johanneische Typus der Heilslehre Luthers* (Gütersich, 1949); James Atkinson, "Luthers Einschätzung des Johannesevangeliums," in Vilmos Vajta, ed., *Lutherforschung Heute* (Berlin, 1958), 49–56.

his way of teaching the faith is at least as much Johannine as it is Pauline. This is not to belittle the enormous importance for Luther of St. Paul's doctrine of righteousness from God and the cosmic setting of Christ's Lordship in the salvation-history. It is not hard to see why Luther has been traditionally regarded as a Paulinist. But the themes which return persistently in his doctrine of Christ are the themes of the unique and all-sufficient bearer of the Word of God, transcending Moses and all the prophets, Whose mission is to preach, and Who is Himself the object and content of His message, the ἐγώ εἰμι; of the knowledge of the only-begotten Son as the sole valid and proper knowledge of God; and of Christ's "going to the Father," His dynamic redemptive descent and ascent for the sake of His own, who now participate in His life and glory as they coinhere in Him and He in the Father. These are the rubrics of the Johannine Christology, and we shall find that they are the rubrics of Luther's Christology also.

Yet there is a further sense in which both the traditional description of Luther as a Paulinist, and also the corrective emphasis on the influence of St. John, may obscure a basic conviction of Luther's, a conviction which informs all his exegesis. It is the principle of Holy Scripture's consistency. All Scripture is not equally important; nevertheless, "even though Christ is named, preached, pictured in various ways, He is ever one and the same Christ." [14] It is typical of him that he should lump together the Fourth Gospel, St. Paul's letters, and I Peter as the outstanding teachers of justification by faith: together they constitute "the real kernel and marrow among all the books." [15] The Christ of St. John is the same as the Christ of the prophets and the psalms, of St. Paul, St. Peter, and the Synoptics. This conviction directly affects Luther's hermeneutic.

Luther's expository works perhaps give a first impression that he has paid little attention to careful word for word exegesis and is capricious in making cross-references. This first impression is entirely erroneous. Anyone who has examined the painstaking biblical labors of Luther's translating committees can retain no

14. 45, 507, 22.
15. DB, 6, 10, 10.

doubt of his devotion to the words; but a penetrating study of his exposition—including preached exposition—yields the same discovery. The notion is abroad that Luther blatantly stretches any text to fit his own view of justifying faith. This is a travesty of his prodigious expository genius. The possibility remains, however, that the exegetical grounding of all his exposition will be overlooked because of his method. Luther has developed a technique of expounding the whole of a verse in the context of the entire passage in which it occurs; the passage, in the setting of the book in which it occurs; and the book, within the unity of the whole Scripture's testimony to Christ. Furthermore, this testimony is then set in the context of the common experience of the people of God, and hence the immediate experience of his hearers. This method, combined with his phenomenal agility in locating and recalling parallels and allusions over all the face of Scripture, may obscure his arduously attained sensitivity to the finest points of biblical vocabulary—a sensitivity at which no critic has earned the right to sneer, for it is virtually without peer in the history of exegesis. The firmness of the exegetical base upon which Luther's exposition is built is revealed at all points by his consistent use of biblical words and phrases in the manner and intention in which Scripture itself uses them.

We shall see this exemplified repeatedly in the course of our study; and the materials will be arranged in the order of the history of Christ (which is normally also the order of our "learning Christ aright"). First, we shall hear Luther speak of the external Word; of Christ in all the Scriptures; then of the narrative history of Jesus of Nazareth. Next, we shall examine the mission of Christ, His proclamation of the kingdom, and His own unique identity as the final revelation of God. Then, we shall turn to His death and Resurrection, His "going to the Father," in which He attained and opened to men the kingdom of righteousness. Finally, we shall address the issues of dogmatic Christology, traditionally defined, and try to answer the question of how cogently Luther integrates these issues with his evangelical concerns and how successfully he carries out his attempt to revivify the static standards of Chalcedon.

# 1. The Word Made Flesh

St. John, Martin Luther says, is not a Platonist; he is an evangelist.[1] Luther is scornful of lofty interpretations of the Johannine Prologue borrowed from Neoplatonic philosophy: "St. Augustine says that this Word is an image of all creation, and like a bed chamber is full of such images, which are called 'Ideas,' according to which each creature was made, every one after its image . . . But this seems unintelligible, obscure, and farfetched to me, a forced interpretation of this passage; for John speaks quite simply and straight-forwardly, with no desire to lead us into such fine and subtle reflections."[2] To avoid such speculation is a thorough-going intention with Luther —to such an extent that he abandons the long-standing practice of making "the Logos" the subject of christological statements. Indeed, he rarely uses "the Word" as a christological title outside his expositions of the Prologue and Genesis I. Needless to say, the doctrine of the written and spoken Word of God is pivotal for Luther, but he does not systematically connect this doctrine with "Christ, the living Word of God."[3] There is a very great difference, he argues, between the Word incarnate, that "inner, eternal Word" Who is God substantially, and the external Word, which is God effectively, not substantially.[4] The theme "Christ the Word" is therefore infrequent, but where the biblical text does warrant it, Luther's exposition is fresh, imaginative, and vivid.

---

1. 10/I/1, 227, 18.
2. 10/I/1, 196, 6; cf. Augustine, *Tract. in ev. Ioh.* I; Walter von Loewenich, *Die Eigenart von Luthers Auslegung des Johannes-Prologes* (München, 1960).
3. 25, 62, 36.
4. *Tr*, 4, 695: 5177; cf. 23, 257, 20.

First, to set the stage, Luther gives one of his rare descriptions of the Holy Trinity in an exposition of John 16:13f.: "Christ describes a conversation that is held in the Godhead, apart from all creatures, and He sets up a pulpit for both a speaker and a listener. He makes the Father the preacher, the Holy Ghost the listener . . . Scripture calls our Lord Christ, in His divine essence, a word which the Father speaks with and in Himself, yet it does not fall away from the Father, but remains in Him eternally . . . Now, where there is a speaker and a word, there ought to be a listener, too; but all this speaking, being spoken, and listening happens entirely within the nature of God, and remains there where no creature is or can be." [5]

The opening statements of the Fourth Gospel, Luther says, are founded on Moses' words in Genesis 1:1–3.[6] Here the Scripture speaks in strong and lucid words: "God said." "What sort of speaker would he be who is himself the word he speaks? Either a mute, or else a word which sounds by itself without a speaker!" So Moses clearly and forcibly establishes that God and His Word must be two distinct things; yet since this Word preceded all creatures and all creatures came by the Word, it cannot be a creature itself,[7] for "beside God and His creatures there is nothing." [8] Thus the distinction between speaker and spoken is such that "a most single singleness of essence remains." [9] This is that omnipotent Word and wisdom of God through Whom God makes everything in the old creation and the new.[10] Luther offers "a rough illustration" of the might of this creating Word: "I think of the oral word that a man in a position of power and authority speaks before everyone. This word which comes from his lips is merely the word of one single man; yet it resounds in the ears of many men, and with such force that it achieves what it commands. So we can say, 'He said it, and it was done.' And yet,

5. 46, 59, 17ff.; cf. 21, 380, 1–8.
6. 10/I/1, 182, 6; 11, 226, 8; 24, 32, 3; 42, 13, 34; 46, 542, 31.
7. 10/I/1, 182, 15ff.; 46, 553, 37.
8. 10/I/1, 183, 9; cf. 27, 528, 2.
9. 42, 14, 10.
10. 42, 14, 18.

if you look at a mouth, it is scarcely a finger's breadth wide. Nevertheless, this voice can do so much that our life and possessions depend on it—a prince could do away with them if he were angry! How much more must you reflect, 'If God in heaven speaks a Word, heaven and earth depend on it; and if He is angry, all that is must be consumed!' " [11]

How are we to think of this conversation within the being of God, and this Word Which comes forth from Him, yet remains one with Him in very essence? Luther collects a series of proverbial and biblical epigrams that suggest a limited analogy: "The human heart is known by a man's word. So we often say, 'I understand his intention' when we have heard only his words; for words follow the heart's intention, and the heart is known *through* the words as if it were *in* the words. The heathen had proverbs to express this fact of experience: they said, *Qualis quisque est, talia loquitur* ('A man is as he speaks') or *Oratio est character animi* ('Speech is an express image of the heart'). A pure heart utters pure words; an impure heart utters impure words. That is what Christ said in Matt. 12:34: 'Out of the abundance of the heart the mouth speaketh,' and then, 'How can ye, being evil, speak good things?' And John the Baptist says in John 3:31, 'He that is of the earth is of the earth, and of the earth he speaketh.' So also the German proverb: *Wess das hertz voll ist, des geht der mund ubir.* Thus all the world knows that nothing reflects the heart so exactly and so surely as the speech of the mouth—just as if the heart were really in the mouth. The bird is known by its call; for 'as the singer, so the song.' Thus it is with God—His Word is so exactly like Him that the Godhead is wholly in it, and he who has the Word has the whole Godhead." [12]

How, then, are we to know the abundance of God's heart? John gives us the answer when his Prologue ascribes to this eternal, ineffable Word a series of names which describe His unique saving acts. He calls the Word "life," "light," and finally "flesh," not in order to speculate about naked deity but to direct us to the earthly history of the man Christ as the perfect expression of the

11. 27, 526, 5.
12. 10/I/1, 187, 9.

Father's will and heart.[13] "When a man has a word, a conversation, or a thought within himself, he speaks incessantly with himself, he is full of words and suggestions about what he should or should not do—without respite he converses and debates the issue within himself. And especially when it is something of such consequence to him that it makes him rage or rejoice, his heart is so full of anger or happiness that it spills over involuntarily into his mouth; for a word bespeaks not merely the utterance of the mouth, but much more, the thought of the heart, without which the external word would not be spoken—or if it is spoken, it means nothing unless the mouth and the heart speak as one! If so, the external word means something: otherwise it is worthless. Thus God, too, in eternity, in His majesty and divine essence, has a Word, a speech, a conversation or a thought within Himself, in His divine heart, unbeknown to all angels and men; and it is called His Word, Which was from eternity in His fatherly heart, through Which God willed to create heaven and earth. But no man had any inkling of this will of God until at last this self-same Word became flesh and proclaimed it to us, as St. John says: 'The Son, Who is in the bosom of the Father, has revealed it to us.'" [14]

## Lord of the Scriptures

Luther, in short, uses "the Word" not as a comprehensive christological title but specifically to present Christ as the perfect expression of the Father's will and heart—a subject we must later examine in detail.[15] The temptation to suppose that Luther applies this title more comprehensively is nowhere keener than in the relation between Christ and the Scriptures. Luther perhaps gives rise to potential confusion himself when he draws a striking analogy between the Incarnation and Scripture: "Holy Scripture is the Word of God written and (so to speak) lettered, composed in letters, just as Christ, the eternal Word of God, is clothed in

13. 10/I/1, 201, 14; 46, 624, 18.
14. 46, 543, 34.
15. See below, Chap. 3.

humanity." [16] But in practice, the fact that Christ is called "the Word" is never Luther's warrant for calling Scripture "the Word of God." Such a contrived connection between Christ and the Scriptures is quite unnecessary, since at all points Scripture bears the most intimate literary and historical relation to Him.

Because this literary relation is so close, Luther can insist that the correct sense of Scripture is at once the plain, literal sense [17] and the sense which "drives home Christ" (*Christum treibet*).[18] These are not two senses, but one sense. The Christocentric sense is not an extrabiblical norm of interpretation; rather, it is plainly stated by Scripture itself. However, all Scripture does not speak equally plainly about Christ. As a result, the Christocentric principle can be stated in two different ways.

Stated theoretically, everything that was later to be fulfilled in Christ was proclaimed in the Old Testament, and there is not a single word of the New Testament which does not look back to the Old: "The New Testament is not more than a revelation of the Old Testament . . . the Old Testament is a testament-letter of Christ." [19] Everything in both books is connected with Christ and points to Him.[20] One of the reasons for calling Christ "the light" is that all the prophets, from the beginning of the world, were illumined to testify of Him; [21] and the "single purpose of all the prophets" was to look to the future Christ.[22] Christ Himself has shown us "the right technique for interpreting Moses and all the prophets," whereby "all Moses' stories and pictures signify and pertain to Christ . . . All the stories in Holy Scripture, if rightly viewed, lead to Christ." [23] John 5:39 is Christ's own "wonderful gloss and interpretation" for the man who wants to be a true master of the Scripture: "Study it so that in it you discover Me, Me." [24] The only alternatives to reading Scripture in order to

16. *48*, 31: 36.
17. E.g. *42*, 568, 1.
18. *DB*, 7, 385, 27
19. *10/I/1*, 181, 20 to 182, 1.
20. *20*, 539, 22.
21. *46*, 562, 34ff.; 565, 29.
22. *13*, 68, 4; 88, 1.
23. *47*, 66, 18.
24. *51*, 2, 22.

find Christ are to read it so as not to find Him, or else not to read it at all.[25] But these are fatal alternatives, for the discovery of Christ and eternal life is the one thing needful: "the person who does not find that in Scripture has found nothing in it" ; and no other book teaches about eternal life—that is, about Christ the Son of God—as Holy Writ alone does.[26] When it is read with this aim, the Scriptures are open and can be seen to teach nothing but Christ.[27] But any interpretation which does not lead to Christ must be rejected as an unscriptural use of Scripture: in such a case we "urge Christ against Scripture." [28] For there is no lord over Scripture but the Lord Christ. He alone is its author and lord.[29]

In exegetical practice, however, this Christocentrism is both formulated and executed in a less sweeping fashion. It was the great weakness of allegorical exegesis that by imposing too uniform a christological sense upon the text it obliterated and ignored the historical particularity and diversity of Scripture's literal witness to Christ. But no one is more pointedly aware of this diversity than Luther, the meticulous translator and painstaking expositor. As a result, the ways in which Luther relates the literal sense to Christ are multifarious and extremely flexible.

In the first place, even if the Old Testament does proclaim everything that was later to be fulfilled in Christ, it does not do so with the pellucid directness of the apostolic gospel. "What was previously taught as it were in enigmas, Christ clarified and commanded to be preached in plain speech." [30] So it is not surprising if those who refuse to believe the plain gospel cannot make sense of the darker statements of the prophets. This is the affliction of the Jews, who "lack the Sun that sheds its light on these things and makes them plain—Christ, through Whom we have remission of sins and eternal life." [31] Christ must first be heard in the gos-

25. *48, 138: 182.*
26. *48, 145: 189; 20, 540, 21; 48, 136: 181.*
27. *44, 508, 3.*
28. *39/I, 47, 3 and 19; 40/I, 458, 32.*
29. *37, 576, 34; 40/I, 458, 33.*
30. *42, 44, 30.*
31. *42, 162, 33; 243, 36.*

pel, then the Old Testament—His "swaddling clothes"—must be read in harmony with Him.[32] God's clear message to men is stated in plain words in some parts of Scripture; in others it is concealed beneath obscurities: "but when something stands in the broad light of day, and the weight of evidence for it similarly stands in full daylight, what does it matter if there is also some evidence for it in the dark?"[33] In fact, even this obscurity redounds to the glory of Christ, since the Old Testament is sometimes obscure "in order that everything might be reserved for Christ and His Holy Spirit Who was to shed light abroad through the whole world like the noonday sun and open all Scripture's mysteries."[34] It was the especial honor of the future teacher to break the seals.[35] "For what solemn truth can the Scriptures still hide now that the seals are broken, the stone rolled away from the tomb, and daylight shed upon the greatest mystery of all, namely that Christ, the Son of God, became man, that God is three in one, that Christ died for us and reigns eternally?"[36]

Luther follows Augustine both in the saint's insistence that "all passages of Scripture speak of Christ" and in his advice to use "the plainer expressions to throw light upon the more obscure."[37] Where Luther departs from Augustine and the medieval tradition, however, is in abandoning a largely figurative christological sense (except as an explicit literary device: "Since the gospel points to Christ, it is fitting that figures should also point to Him").[38] The living voice of Christ in the gospel remains "the plainer expression" which illumines the dark passages of Moses and the prophets; but Luther's insistence that the historico-literal sense "drives home Christ" predicates a remarkably various series of relations, of which the least significant is the fig-

32. 10/I/1, 81, 20.
33. 18, 606, 33; cf. 8, 237, 4.
34. 42, 109, 28.
35. 42, 44, 34.
36. 18, 606, 24.
37. Augustine, *Contra Faustum* XXII, 94 (MPL XLII, 463); *De doctrina christiana* II, 9; III, 26 (MPL XXXIV, 42, 79).
38. 25, 465, 27; cf. 14, 561, 17; and see Gerhard Ebeling, *Evangelische Evangelienauslegung* (München, 1942), pp. 44ff.

urative sense. Each Testament must be read in the light of the
other, yet in such a way as not to destroy the other's autonomy.
Every passage must be read in the light of the whole Scripture,
but in such a way that its integrity is preserved: it must be read
in its own sense, and that sense be permitted to affect the whole.
In short, the ways in which Scripture testifies of Christ are as various as the components of Scripture themselves, but they all testify to the same Christ.

Luther's method has been the subject of several learned
monographs.[39] Here we need only sample the many ways in
which he finds Christ in the Old Testament. And first we must
note how Luther attempts scrupulously (though to the modern
reader not always successfully!) to avoid forced christological interpretations. He berates previous commentators for twisting the
text of the prophets to yield inappropriate or incorrect applications to Christ.[40] Even where this attitude forces him to the reluctant conclusion that one of the prophets, Nahum, has only general and not specific reference to Christ, he insists: "I do not wish
to intrude Christ where the prophet himself does not do so." [41]
As a result, page after page of Luther's Old Testament lectures
contains no reference to Christ, or else simply analogical references. In place of interpretations which distort the text, Luther
permits two sorts of explicit christological application: the first,
where the details of the grammar or subject matter inescapably
refer to Christ; the second, where the text is sufficiently general
to permit its valid application in various contexts, including the
Christian context.

The first group, specific predictions of Christ, are the texts which
Luther quotes most often in his preaching. They are a relatively
limited group of fairly obvious texts, most of which have apos-

39. In addition to Ebeling's work, see also Heinrich Bornkamm, *Luther und das
Alte Testament* (Tübingen, 1948); Willem Jan Kooiman, *Luther and the Bible*
(Philadelphia, 1961); Gerhard Krause, *Studien zu Luthers Auslegung der Kleinen
Propheten* (Tübingen, 1962); Walther von Loewenich, *Luther als Ausleger der
Synoptiker* (München, 1954); Jaroslav Pelikan, *Luther the Expositor* (St. Louis,
1959); James Samuel Preus, *From Shadow to Promise* (Harvard, 1968).

40. E.g. *13*, 46, 1; 324, 12; 441, 16; 621, 3.

41. *13*, 354, 22 and parallels.

tolic warrant for their direct application to the gospel narrative. They include the promise of the seed of the woman, the covenant with Abraham, the prediction of a prophet to supersede Moses, the expectation of a Davidic kingdom, and the prophetic visions of gospel incidents—notably the place and manner of Christ's birth, His entry into Jerusalem, His betrayal for thirty pieces of silver, His crucifixion, and His exaltation.

Among these one of the most frequently cited is the *protevangelion*—the promise of a seed of the woman who would crush the serpent's head (Gen. 3:15). This was God's earliest promise in His Word, the promise in which the Church had its foundation (*21*, 430, 23; *24*, 109, 1). Through this promise Christ the light shone on Adam and Eve after their fall, comforting and gladdening them (*42*, 141, 34; *46*, 562, 34). Soon Adam began to proclaim, in nine hundred years of abundant preaching, that God would send His Son to crush the serpent's head; and through this promise the light shone on the patriarchs before the Flood (*46*, 564, 25; 596, 16). Abel's faith in the future seed gained him gracious acceptance with God: it was the promise that did it; what Cain's sacrifice lacked was that his faith did not rely on the seed of the woman (*47*, *144*, 30). For the sake of this promise, a few righteous souls were preserved in the Flood (*42*, 59, 12). Throughout the old covenant it was reliance on the future seed for salvation which availed for the godly (*47*, 145, 28). Whatever diverse means of purification and sacrifice, ritual and worship, obtained up to the day of the Baptist, "the one theme of the woman's seed was in these various and novel methods" (*47*, 147, 19). This was a promise very clear as to its consolation, but rather obscure as to the manner of its fulfillment. For instance, Luther sees a veiled reference to the virgin birth in the phrase, "seed of the woman": other women's children are properly "the seed of a man," but Christ is "truly the seed of Mary" (*42*, *144*, 19; cf. *21*, 233, 6).

Equally direct is the institution of God's covenant with Abraham. The preaching of the promised seed had been obscured by idolatry but was renewed in Abraham, to whom the same promise was given in a more circumscribed way: "Abraham certainly preached diligently about the seed promised to him"—namely, Christ, Who was to descend from him according to the flesh (*46*, 565, 15). Abraham recognized Christ through the promise of Genesis 22:18 and rejoiced to see His day: he realized that Christ would be of his seed, through a pure virgin, so as to avoid the curse of Adam and remain blessed (*17*/II, 236, 7; 29, 130, 16). Thus Abraham's faith and ours is one faith, his in the Christ to be manifested, ours in the Christ already manifested (*42*, 567, 25). The "Abraham's bosom" of the parable is the common faith of the saints in God's promise of the blessed offspring (*10*/III, 191, 17). "These words are highly esteemed by St. Paul and all the prophets, and rightly so, for in them Abraham and all his descendents were preserved and saved, and in them we too must all be saved. For these words contain Christ, here promised to be the savior of the whole world" (*7*, 598, 4). Even though Christ was Abraham's descendent according to the flesh, the blessing was promised in Him to all nations (*40*/I, 546, 31ff.). Therefore mere descent according to the flesh is not enough to make men children of Abraham; this was the error of the Jews (*33*, 669, 14ff.; *46*, 615, 38ff.). Rather, the heirs of Abraham are those of all nations who receive the promise as it can only be received—by faith (*40*/I, 547, 20). For the promise to Abraham is before and apart from the law (*40*/I, 464, 27ff.), assigning all blessing exclusively to Christ, the select and blessed seed, through Whom alone comes salvation (*46*, 616, 8; *33*, 53, 1).

It is notable how Luther fits these Pentateuchal promises into a history of the preaching of the Word of promise. He views the various divisions of the Old Testament in this light. The Mosaic writings are central, because they record how the promise was plainly declared to the patriarchs. The historical books are full of examples of those who heeded and those who rejected God's Word. The prophets devoted themselves to expounding in ever greater detail the promises they discovered in Moses, recalling the people to faith in the covenant and pointing them forward in hope to the fulfillment in Christ.[42] Within this history the explicit prediction which Luther quotes most of all is Deuteronomy 18:15–18, the "prophet like Moses." This plays so central a role in his picture of Christ as the consummation of the salvation-history that I shall postpone its detailed consideration until a later chapter. Meanwhile, between Moses and Christ, the prophets

42. *12*, 275, 16.

were able to understand the mysteries of the patriarchal Scriptures because the Spirit of Christ was in them.[43] Thus David in his "prophetic psalms" [44] was able "to promise Christ's death and Resurrection so plainly, and so portray His kingdom, the state and character of all Christendom, that the psalter could well be called a little bible." [45]

To take just a few instances: we have the most primitive apostolic warrant for reading Psalm 2 as a prophecy about Christ. Knowing this, we discover in it the clearest possible distinction between Christ's kingdom and the kingdoms of this world (40/II, 195, 26). Psalm 8 is "a glorious prophecy about Christ," which declares Him to be both God and man by calling Him "Lord, our ruler," conjoining the exclusively divine name "Yahweh" with the human title "ruler"; and again by foretelling both His human humiliation and His divine exaltation (45, 244, 9). When David wrote in Psalm 110: "The Lord said to my Lord," he not only alluded to the promise that the Messiah would be his descendant (the possessive "my" expressed his faith in this promise), but also declared that his heir would occupy that throne where only God Himself could reign. Thus in this Psalm, "as nowhere else in the Old Testament," we find a plain and powerful description of Christ's person (41, 97, 29; 83, 18; 87, 16). Luther rejects the specifically Jewish interpretation of Psalm 117, and insists that it must be a prophecy of the preaching of the gospel, because it calls on *all* the heathen and *all* the peoples to praise the one true God. Similarly, even the Jews must admit that Psalm 72 cannot apply to Solomon, but applies to the universal epiphany of the Messiah, for not only is this king's realm from sea to sea to the earth's end, but God's own judgment and righteousness are committed to this king—that divine lordship over life and death and all flesh declared by the first commandment, a glory which God will not give to another (49, 11, 25; 14, 5ff.).

Several of the principles employed here recur in exposition of the prophets. Sometimes the grammar provides puzzles which are easily solved christologically. For instance, in Zechariah 2:8–9,

43. 42, 109, 30.
44. E.g. 31/I, 580, 2; 40/II, 196, 14.
45. DB, 10/I, 99, 22.

"even grammatical reason convinces us that Christ is true God and man, because here the Lord God of Hosts sends the Lord God of Hosts!" [46] Sometimes the correspondence with the gospel history is so exact that no other meaning need be sought. This is the case with Micah's praise of Bethlehem, his "magnificent prophetic gift that uniquely and infallibly states the place of Christ's birth." [47] This is also the case with Zechariah's prophecy of the thirty shekels of silver: "Because all these details square so excellently with the gospel narrative about Christ's being sold, we do not seek another, roundabout interpretation." [48] A similar warrant functions in a more general form, where it is not so much the narrative detail but the *Christus pro nobis* of the gospel, which is exactly captured by the prophet. This is obviously so in the servant songs of Isaiah, especially Chapter 53, which "even the Jews cannot deny speaks of Christ," and which proclaims Christ's kingdom "as plainly as if it had already arrived." [49] Another notable instance is Micah's prophecy of the latter days when the mountain of the Lord will be established. It applies "to the new and perpetual reign of Christ; nor can this passage be understood of a renewed outward kingdom (though the Jews think so), because the vastness of the promises is too great." [50]

This argument draws our attention to one of Luther's most interesting form-critical observations. Of all prophetic themes the most important is the theme of the kingdom. While the immediate office of the prophets was to address the Word of God to their own generation, their admonitions and promises concerning the kingdom had a constant tendency to break suddenly out of their immediate and particular setting and to refer as well to God's great future universal kingdom. Throughout his lectures on the prophets Luther repeatedly points to a literary device which he calls *transitio* or *transitus*.[51] He defines this "prophetic cus-

46. *13,* 572, 6.
47. *13,* 324, 29.
48. *13,* 649, 28.
49. 31/II, 428, 14; *DB, 11*/I, 19, 32.
50. *13,* 317, 13.
51. E.g. *13,* 27, 3 (Hos. 6:1); 63, zu 16 (Hos. 3:14); 108, 21 (Joel 2:28); 186, 17 (Amos 5:24); 216, 5 (Obad. 17); 312, 24 (Mic. 2:12).

tom" in this way: "When they have announced that prophecy to which they themselves were sent, they dismiss whatever happened in the interval after the prophecy was revealed, and go on immediately to prophesy of Christ." [52] If these transitions "seem absurd and rather difficult, it nevertheless behooves us to attune to prophetic conventions." [53] The *transitus* is not unlike the Hebrew practice, when treating particular acts of God, of drawing parallels with the Exodus.[54] These transitions had a double purpose: to reassure the people that God's promises to the patriarchs and to David would surely be fulfilled, and to declare that the present limited temporal kingdom would be utterly superseded by the coming universal and spiritual reign of God. Accordingly, in identifying the transition points, Luther relies on a premise which is sometimes stated, sometimes not—namely, that the prophecies in question cannot refer to the Jewish nation, either because they have not been fulfilled in Israel's history or because they could not possibly be fulfilled in any earthly kingdom. But they both can and do apply to Christ's kingdom: no other application is feasible.[55] The case is stated in its bluntest form in the elderly Luther's anti-Jewish arguments based on Jacob's blessing of Judah (Gen. 49:10). The scepter has departed from Judah; the kingdom has lain in ruins for 1500 years and its people dispersed; and so this prophecy has already been fulfilled. Shiloh has come.[56] A more elaborate form of the argument finds the priestly and kingly offices ("after the order of Melchizedek") reunited for the first time in Christ, in a way which was not permitted by the Mosaic law nor effected in Jewish history.[57] Thus Zechariah is using the *transitus* convention when he seems to apply to Zerubbabel prophecies which were not fulfilled in his own person but which were later fulfilled in Christ.[58]

It becomes clear that these transitions are not purely literary or

52. *13*, 108, 25.
53. *13*, 272, 11.
54. *13*, 440, 16ff.
55. E.g. *13*, 220, 23; 299, 9; 324, 32; *DB, 11*/I, 401, 25.
56. *44*, 754, 1; *53*, 450, 19; cf. *13*, 572, 30; *42*, 655, 12.
57. *13*, 609, 1; *41*, 182, 19ff.
58. *13*, 593, 15; cf. *23*, 586, 1ff.

arbitrary in character. Just as the recollection of the deliverance from Egypt played so systematic a role in Israel's view of her history, so for Luther the prophecies of the coming kingdom are systematically related to the historical experience of the Hebrews. When Zechariah sets side by side the time of the rebuilding of Jerusalem after the exile and the time of the founding of Christ's kingdom, he makes it clear that the first serves the second.[59] When Zephaniah foretells the destruction of the kingdom of Judah by the Chaldeans, he speaks of a spark of Judah to be preserved and revived for the sake of Christ, Who according to the promise was to be born from Judah.[60] This is the force, too, of Isaiah's phrase, "a shoot from the stump of Jesse" (Isa. 11:1).[61] And so with the other prophets: their common purpose in placing present and future in apposition is to show the paradoxical but unwavering relation between the historical vicissitudes of God's people and His culminating purpose in the kingdom of Christ.

As we move, then, from more or less direct Old Testament references to Christ to passages which may be applied to Christ permissibly but not necessarily, we find that Luther's use of typology falls now into the first group, now into the second. Moses, for example, is a type of Christ not simply because a fitting analogy may be drawn, but because the Mosaic ordinances were divinely given patterns of the true priesthood of Christ, provisional signs pointing to the "prophet like Moses" who would fulfill them and supersede them.[62] This connection may then give rise to spiritual interpretations of the Torah, but the connection itself is not merely analogical.[63] Similarly, Joshua the high priest (Zech. 3) is a type of Christ because his priestly role "is a sort of minimal preparation for the future great priesthood of Christ the priest, for Whose sake alone all these things happened." [64] In such cases the connection between type and antitype is essential and historical. In most cases, however, typology is based on similitude and

59. *13*, 615, 25.
60. *13*, 480, 4.
61. *31/II*, 83, 9; cf. *13*, 572, 20.
62. *43*, 263, 24.
63. *25*, 411, 12; 469, 1.
64. *13*, 581, 6.

is therefore not essential. Nevertheless, even where it is not essential, it is quite proper and has clear apostolic warrants. Paul, for instance, draws our attention to the parallel between Adam and Christ.[65] (This is a type of which Luther makes remarkably little systematic use.) We have Christ's own warrant for taking Jonah as a figure of the sin-bearing savior.[66] Isaac, Joseph, Samson, David, Solomon, and Aaron are all "appropriate and fitting types of Christ." The exemplary characteristics which make these men prefigurements of Christ are essential neither to their own salvation nor to ours, but as types, they greatly nourish and strengthen faith.[67]

Christ and the apostles not only give us warrants for this figurative use of Scripture, they also show us how to take general statements and give them a particular application to the gospel. For one general statement may have a variety of applications. For example, Hosea 10:8 is applied by the prophet himself to the Assyrian captivity, by Christ to the fall of Jerusalem (Luke 23:30), and we may aptly apply it to the Last Judgment.[68] What Habakkuk applies to devastation by the king of the Chaldeans (Hab. 1:5), Paul applies to disbelief in the Resurrection of Christ (Acts 13:41): the sentence applies equally well to all unbelievers.[69] Luther himself provides us a wonderfully illuminating instance in his double exposition of Psalm 111, first interpreting it as a faithful Jew would have used it in its Old Testament liturgical setting, then expounding it again as a Christian hymn in the eucharistic liturgy.[70] Words of great human import are perennially apt in a multitude of parallel settings. Scripture is full of statements about the wrath of God against sin, and His mercy and loving-kindness toward men, which Christians cannot but read in the light of the perfect revelation of God in Christ, in Whom wrath is swallowed up in mercy, and the mystery hidden from ages and generations is now made known.

65. 17/II, 137, 17; 22, 224, 17; 42, 163, 33; 46, 41, 35.
66. 13, 248, 2.
67. 10/I/1, 416, 24.
68. 13, 50, 1.
69. 13, 426, 29; cf. 31/II, 544, 29.
70. 31/I, 391 to 426.

*The Messiah*

The divinely ordained mission of Moses and all the prophets was to bear witness to the coming and birth of the Messiah.[71] At the end of the old covenant stood the Baptist, whose office was to announce the Messiah's presence, to be His "finger and hand." [72] This office was especially needful because of the deeply rooted delusions the Jews had developed about their Messiah, imagining Him to appear "encompassed by the world's glory, arms, silver, and gold," to take a spectacular earthly kingdom, to associate with "the bigwigs, the clever and educated people"; [73] John was sent to warn them and shatter these carnal dreams.[74] Furthermore, John's task was necessary, not only because the Jews entertained false hopes, but because Christ came as an "unknown Messiah," of lowly, humble, and unimposing demeanor.[75] But the fact that He was Messiah in spite of the appearances was at least no secret as a result of John's mission.[76] Moreover, Christ's own miracles and preaching revealed Him as the Messiah.[77] Thirdly, God Himself witnessed that Christ was the Messiah.[78] In spite of all this evidence, however, such a Messiah was not to the Jews' liking.[79] "To them it seemed ludicrous and offensive to acknowledge and receive a poor beggar from Nazareth as their nation's promised Messiah." [80]

No one was in a better position than they to recognize Him, for they worshiped the true God, the promiser of the Messiah; but this merely proves how insufficient is an intellectual knowledge of God! [81] Moreover, all the promises of Scripture pointed to Him: they either knew or could have known from Holy Scripture that

71. *46*, 571, 35; *47*, 194, 20.
72. *46*, 574, 25; *47*, 155, 15; 187, 30; *51*, 6, 7
73. *10/I/2*, 45 n.; *46*, 572, 32; *47*, 177, 5; *46*, 700, 36.
74. *22*, 393, 34; *46*, 699, 38; *47*, 187, 29.
75. *21*, 431, 35; *46*, 572, 40; 576, 30.
76. *46*, 675, 9; 755, 22; *47*, 187, 30.
77. *33*, 474, 1; *46*, 602, 13; 755, 23.
78. *46*, 688, 20; *47*, 216, 18.
79. *46*, 603, 31; *51*, 7, 27.
80. *46*, 647, 17.
81. *21*, 434, 32.

it was He.[82] As we have seen, the patriarch Jacob had foretold
the Messiah's birth in the fullness of time, and the weeks of His
birth were computed by Daniel.[83] Micah prophesied that He
would be born in Bethlehem, and the prophets declared that He
would come from Judah and the lineage of David.[84] Isaiah
foretold that the Messiah was to do miracles,[85] and moreover
that the scepter of His kingdom would be not a physical cudgel
but "the rod of His mouth." [86] From the beginning it was
promised that the Messiah was to be a teacher bearing a new
doctrine, to supersede Moses and the old law eternally;[87] and
it was faith in this coming Messiah which justified the patriarchs
and constituted the substance of the covenant ceremonies of cir-
cumcision and purification.[88]

Indeed, there were some who accepted these testimonies.
When the common people "saw His signs and believed in His
name" (John 2:23), this meant that they "regarded Him as the
Messiah of the world." [89] The disciples were able to acknowledge
this "poor beggar" as the Messiah because they knew God's practice was to exalt the poor and humble, and transform shepherds
into kings. So they accepted the Baptist's witness and were convinced they had received the prophesied Messiah.[90] (But even
they were rebuked for their humanly physical notion of the
kingdom.) [91] The woman at the well in Samaria and the guards
dispatched by the Pharisees confessed the fulfillment of the
prophecy that the Messiah would come preaching a new
doctrine.[92] But the Jews persisted in their delusions: they misap-
plied the prophecies of the kingdom to the earthly Jerusalem; they
mistook the bride of Psalm 45:10ff. as a "beautiful woman com-

82. *46, 755, 21; 51, 7, 3.*
83. *46, 603, 40f.; 47, 215, 33.*
84. *47, 215, 34.*
85. *46, 604, 4; 51, 8, 24.*
86. *31/II, 86, 38; 46, 730, 23.*
87. *33, 52, 32; 47, 12, 22.*
88. *46, 672, 2; 47, 144, 25.*
89. *46, 764, 1.*
90. *46, 699, 28; 700, 14.*
91. *47, 546, 27.*
92. *47, 215, 15; 33, 473, 40ff.*

panion"; they ignored the prediction that the Messiah must be rejected, suffer, and die, and that His coming would coincide with the extinction of the physical kingdom.[93] They could not harmonize His status as King of kings with suffering and death.[94] Their reason was unable to tolerate the scandal of a Messiah crucified between criminals.[95] They could not see that the promised kingdom was a universal kingdom of peace and righteousness, and that such a spiritual kingdom meant the end of their limited, carnal kingdom.[96]

Yet in fulfilling the messianic office in accordance with prophecy, Christ became "the only savior of the world, the Lamb of God . . . our Messiah." [97] Christ's titles in the apostolic gospel constitute a radical reinterpretation of messianic expectations in the light of the actual accomplishment of Jesus of Nazareth. The Messiah was to redeem not only the Jewish people but all the world: Christ speaks of Himself as the Messiah promised and sent by God to perform the office of mediator.[98] In the discharge of this office, "He is called Christ our Messiah because as a mighty lord He would rescue us from death's jaws, so that we need not fear sin, and we can overcome the devil, find grace with God, and be His dear brothers." [99]

Literally, Luther explains, "Messiah" means "the anointed one." [1] The Hebrew word means not any sort of anointing (as do the Greek, Latin, and German equivalents) but, specifically, the anointing of kings or priests at their consecration.[2] In His work of salvation Christ is called Messiah because He is both king and priest to us: [3] He does not only rule, but also blesses, and these two offices encompass "the foremost benefits of Christ." [4] He has

93. *46, 572*, 15ff.
94. *41, 231*, 24.
95. *31/II, 430*, 25.
96. *13, 299*, 9; *627*, 24. See below, pp. 172ff.
97. *46, 581*, 10.
98. *21, 545*, 11.
99. *33, 310*, 31.
1. *20, 676*, 12; *46, 700*, 9.
2. *20, 676*, 5; *31/II, 515*, 17.
3. *20, 253*, 7.
4. *43, 260*, 36,

transformed and consummated the expectation of Israel, for His kingdom is a spiritual realm ruled by His Word of forgiveness, and His priesthood confers an eternal blessing and holiness upon sinful men. (The name "Christ," Luther points out, translates the Hebrew "Messiah"—*Unctus* in Latin, *Gesalbter* in German—and similarly implies the twofold unction of royal priesthood; even so, it is a rare exception when Luther uses "Christ" as a title rather than as a proper name.) [5]

The reuniting of the kingly and priestly offices of Jesus of Nazareth signals the fulfillment of the messianic promises: now, therefore, "faith applies no longer to the future Christ, but to the Christ Who has come." Now that He has come, He is savior to all eternity. It is therefore wrong, and a denial of Jesus' Messiahship, to say henceforth: "He will come." [6] Jews, Turks, and papists all stand contradicted by the Christian creed—Jews, because they still expect Messiah to come; Turks, because they replace the one Who has come with another prophet; papists, because they presume to merit Christ by good works, although He came long ago to bring deliverance. [7] But thirsty souls accept His Word and cry out, "This is the true prophet and the true Christ." [8] For God's promised Messiah is "a king and ruler Who will be a teacher, different from Moses and his priests and law teachers who existed hitherto; and He will be a lord, ruler, and king, different from David and all kings in their worldly realms. He will subject them all—not that He will found a new earthly realm, or extend Jewish suzerainty over the Gentiles, but rather that they both, Jews and Gentiles together, should hear Him, believe in Him, and through Him receive fulfillment of the promise Isaiah calls 'the covenant of the sure mercies of David.' This covenant (God says) will I make and maintain with you as a divine, sure, inviolable covenant in this Christ: through Him shall be given all that God's grace grants and bestows—forgiveness and blotting-out of sins, redemption from death, and life eternal." [9]

5. 10/I/2, 152, 29; 32, 256, 13. E.g. 10/I/2, 188, 5; 33, 412, 38; 47, 47, 12.
6. 47, 145, 34ff.; cf. 40/I, 339, 18.
7. 47, 194, 4; 145, 41; 167, 11.
8. 33, 428, 17.
9. 22, 446, 12.

*Jesus of Nazareth*

The Jews were offended at the idea of believing in "a poor carpenter's apprentice";[10] they derided Him as "carpenter's apprentice, beggar, poor simpleton."[11] The rejection of their Messiah had been foreseen and lamented by the prophet Isaiah; but
without the convicting power of the Holy Spirit, reason is incapable of accepting as Messiah so shameful and ignominious a
figure.[12] Yet in Isaiah's words, "He was wounded for our transgressions," we have "a definition of Christ, perfectly and absolutely: Christ is a man, a minister of the Word, Who by suffering
bore our sins."[13] He is by definition the justifier, the redeemer
from sins.[14] The Hebrew name "Jesus" means "savior," one who
saves, redeems, brings salvation, and helps all men.[15] "God's own
beloved Son was not called Jesus without reason, but because He
was to save His people from their sins."[16] He became man and
died for us, rose again and ascended to heaven: because of this
office He is called Jesus Christ. To believe that this is the truth
about Him is "to abide in His name."[17]

The rejection of the lowly figure of Christ by Jews, Turks, and
papists using rational criteria is, Luther contends, an error shared
by Zwingli: "Thus our *Schwärmer* too, Zwingli and others, preach
that we should exclude the manhood in Christ, that the divinity
and not the manhood gives eternal life; and they divide the Lord
Christ."[18] Luther insists that it is precisely in the lowliness of the
man Christ that the power of God is operating.[19] Reason sees in
Christ "only a poor beggar who died."[20] But if reason is annoyed
at His claims when He appears just a poor, weak, despised, ordi-

10. *33*, 451, 11.
11. *33*, 667, 29.
12. *31/II*, 430, 21.
13. *31/II*, 432, 33.
14. *40/I*, 249, 16.
15. *10/I/1*, 518, 9.
16. *46*, 574, 1.
17. *17/I*, 255, 17.
18. *33*, 154, 4.
19. *33*, 346, 1ff.
20. *33*, 177, 29.

nary man, faith clings to its "dear Lord Christ" in spite of the appearances.[21] For where man despises, God attends. This poor Jesus preaches in the temple, and God esteems His words higher than all creation.[22] If God were not with Him, such a beggar would not dare direct all faith to Himself.[23] In the weak, beggarly things that reason despises, faith finds its resting place. Luther's refusal to divide Christ's manhood from His divinity means, among other things, a refusal to separate His human lowliness from His divine power in the narrative of Christ's earthly life. We shall see how the ineffable conjunction of the two is a constant feature of Luther's accounts of His birth, His ministry, and His death.

The discovery of the power of the Most High in utter lowliness begins with the story of the Nativity:

> Th' eternal Father's only Son
> Now is to the manger come:
> In our poor human flesh and blood
> Hath clothed Himself th' eternal good.
>    Kyrioleis.
>
> Whom all the world could not confine
> See on Mary's bosom lying;
> He Who doth the world sustain
> A tiny infant child became.
>    Kyrioleis.[24]

He came down from heaven into this lowliness in our own flesh, placing Himself in His mother's womb and in the manger, and He went to the cross. "He placed this ladder on earth so that we might ascend to God on it." [25]

> He came to earth a pauper thus
> So that He might pity us,
> And make us rich in heaven above,

21. 33, 173, 13.
22. 33, 634, 33.
23. 33, 637, 15.
24. 35, 434, 7.
25. 40/III, 656, 25.

To share with angels in His love.
Kyrioleis.[26]

Luther's Christmas sermons graphically and imaginatively paint the meanness and misery of Christ's birth but never fail to marvel at the sublimity of God's humbling Himself to take our sinful flesh.[27] For this was no imaginary birth, as the Manichaeans supposed; it was a birth just like any other birth. Mary's son was truly and naturally a child, receiving from His mother "flesh and blood, skin and bone, and all His members, a body which sweated, slept, became soiled, and everything else, except without sin."[28] This last qualification, in fact, makes Christ's birth different from other births in one practical respect: it was painless. Luther believes that since the curse of Eve was the result of sin, where a conception and birth are without sin, the curse does not apply. That the birth was painless, however, made it no less natural.[29] The conception was sinless not because (as some of the scholastics had speculated) some pure strain had been preserved in Chirst's lineage from the beginning of the world:[30] in fact, Christ's ancestry was replete with prostitutes and fornicators;[31] not because the Virgin herself was born without original sin:[32] on the contrary, "Mary was born of parents in sin just like other human beings."[33] No, Christ's conception was sinless because the Holy Spirit took Mary's flesh and blood and by His power and grace purified them, and because as a supernatural act of the Holy Spirit this conception escaped the lust and sin of ordinary human begetting.[34] "Certainly the Messiah was not born of the power of flesh and blood—as it is stated in John: 'not of blood nor of the will of man'—yet He wanted to be born

26. 35, 435, 6.
27. E.g. 9, 439ff.; 10/I/1, 58ff.; 17/II, 298ff.; 32, 251ff.; 41, 477ff.; 52, 36ff.
28. 41, 480, 29.
29. 41, 480, 25.
30. 44, 311, 13.
31. 10/III, 327, 1.
32. On the status of the late medieval disputes on this issue, see Heiko Oberman, The Harvest of Medieval Theology (Harvard, 1963), pp. 283ff.
33. 49, 173, 9.
34. 7, 573, 4; 39/II, 107, 10; 45, 51, 11; 46, 136, 9; 7, 599, 15.

from the mass of the flesh and from that corrupt blood. But in the moment of conception by the Virgin, the Holy Spirit cleansed and sanctified the sinful mass and wiped away that poison of the devil and death, that is, sin." [35]

"Behold this child in His ignorance—all things belong to Him!" [36] Luther does nothing to attenuate the transcendent mystery of the incarnation; he drives it home with all the rhetorical skill at his disposal. He does not hesitate to affirm the ignorance of the child (nor, as we shall see, the weakness of the man). He rejects as hairsplitting the age-old christological problem about how Jesus could grow in wisdom. It is no more a problem than His growth in stature, he suggests; the hairsplitters have created perplexity "by inventing for themselves an article of faith which has Christ utterly filled with wisdom and the Spirit from the moment of conception—as if the soul were a wineskin which could be filled up to the brim!" Luther does not attempt to explain how it could be true, but he affirms: "Though from the moment of conception the Holy Spirit was in Him, yet as His body and reason developed naturally as in other men, so He was increasingly filled and moved by the Holy Spirit. Luke's words are no mere appearance." [37] In fact, His childhood was like any other boy's. [38] Luther is scathing with those who, not content with Scripture, compile books of silly legends about the boy Jesus—"inane and blasphemous drivel!" [39] But he takes Luke's words to mean that Christ was an unusually clever child, even though He never went to school (for there were no schools to go to).[40] Elsewhere, Luther expresses in passing his opinion that Christ was also physically well-built and finely proportioned—an opinion probably based on the absence of disfigurement by sin.[41]

This juxtaposing of pitiful lowliness with startling power is also characteristic of Luther's descriptions of the adult life of Jesus.

35. *44,* 311, 23.
36. *9,* 441, 12.
37. *10/I/1,* 446, 7.
38. *46,* 599, 5.
39. *10/I/1,* 443, 17ff.
40. *10/I/1,* 445, 18.
41. *40/II,* 484, 25.

His accounts of Christ's weakness and insignificance are not especially original or startling; nor are they by any means a leading
theme of his preaching. (They do seem to have a place of special
importance in Luther's exposition during and immediately after
the climax of the sacramental dispute—most of all in the 1530 series of sermons on John 6, a passage central to the debates with
Zwingli. Earlier in the 1520s Luther's accounts are largely con-
ventional; later, Christ's weakness is more evenly balanced with
startling, heroic elements in His biography; but in the early '30s
the weakness and poverty of the man Jesus are stressed more
than at any other period, along with a generally greater emphasis
on Christ's humanity.)

Christ was a lowly and common man. "He came as someone
humble and plebeian, one of the hoi polloi." [42] No one noticed
Him: He went thirty years unknown on earth. [43] Luther describes
Christ's literal poverty. He was a pauper, and no one in Wittenberg owned less than He. "The Lord must have gone about in a
gray coat, and had not even a morsel of bread to feed Himself,
for He was a poor man." [44] And yet He described Himself as the
bread of life! He claimed to be able to give everlasting food—a
claim made "by a poor person, yes, a beggar, for Christ had not a
foot of ground to His name." [45] Peasants interested in food for
their bellies were (and are) not interested in this sort of offer
from a beggar. [46] On the other hand, as Luther is quick to indicate, Christ's poverty was not the assumed poverty of Francis-
cans: after teaching the five thousand, for instance, He and His
disciples at least had five loaves and two hundred pence, and the
moneybox which Judas managed may well have had thirty
gulden in reserve. Christ's real poverty was poverty of spirit. [47]

Humility was not only an external setting but a personal characteristic of the man Christ. When He emptied Himself of all His
divine glory, His "taking the form of a servant" meant being not

42. 10/I/2, 150, 7; 13, 626, 21.
43. 10/I/1, 212, 15; 27, 531, 8; 28, 138, 2.
44. 33, 57, 31; 56, 26; cf. 33, 451, 6.
45. 33, 14, 31.
46. 33, 11, 13.
47. 10/III, 404, 6–19.

only less than the Father but also lowlier than all men.[48] His bearing before men was kind, friendly, sympathetic, that of a servant who wanted to help everybody. None was so bad that He did or wished him harm.[49] Rather, "the gospel everywhere shows Christ to be a merciful, gracious man, ready to help everyone by word and action in body and soul."[50] His humility revealed itself in obedience to His parents, in the way He tended the infirm and lepers like a slave—"love made a slave of Christ"[51]—and proved Himself everyone's servant (as He often described Himself, in terms which scarcely the lowliest man on earth should use).[52] Most striking of all, Christ's humility was physically demonstrated when He washed the disciples' feet—a lowly service that fills us with awe when we see the high majesty acting thus. For Luther this action not only has a deep sacramental significance but it evokes both faith in His will, and love by His example.[53] The one Who did this was lord of all angels; and it is a staggering example of humility that He Who is lord and God should have done all these servile, and not lordly, deeds.[54] It is an example that His disciples should not forget but keep ever before them.[55] For since Christ was lord over all, yet did nothing but a servant's work, so too the Christian man, emptying himself like Christ, is properly a lord, king, priest, brother, and coheir of Christ, when he knows and feels in his heart that he ought to act as if he were not.[56]

Matthew applies to Jesus' works of healing love the words of Isaiah: "He took our infirmities and bore our diseases" (Isa. 53:4; Matt. 8:17). At first sight, Luther says, this seems mistaken, since Isaiah was speaking of the Passion. But on reflection, Matthew is right to apply the prophet's sentence to Christ's whole life, which

48. *45, 633, 22.*
49. *10/I/1, 97, 10; I/2, 392, 15; 45, 516, 2; 10/I/2, 35, 11.*
50. *37, 507, 17.*
51. *17/II, 74, 21.*
52. *17/I, 276, 11; 45, 556, 39.*
53. *15, 507, 1; 497–506; 21, 159, 7.*
54. *20, 307, 13 and 21; 52, 219, 8.*
55. *52, 216, 34; 218, 11.*
56. *20, 308, 2.*

consisted always in taking and removing our evils from us: "for it was for our sakes that He was born, circumcised, traveled, ate, drank, and slept and (as Paul says in Phil. 2) 'was found in fashion as a man.' " [57] For our sakes Christ freely and willingly subjected Himself to the ordinances of the law and finally to the curse of the law, even though, as the only man in all human history Who was holy, innocent, and free from sin, the law had no claim upon Him.[58] When Christ came in utter obedience to do the Father's will, that obedience revealed the downfall of the devil's reign, "because He is here Who obeys the Father." [59] So everything that He did, said, and thought was good, beneficial, and salutary.[60]

When Luther describes Christ's self-emptying for our sakes, he follows the traditional emphasis of medieval preaching in stressing those aspects of Christ's human existence which He shares with the less fortunate side of human kind—weakness, poverty, wretchedness, misery, and impotence. "In our flesh, the Son of God Himself was weak and weary, He was afraid, and He fled from danger." [61] But does not perfect love cast out fear? Yes, but in the midst of battle against the devil and tribulation, the time of joy alternates with the time of fear, and "not even Christ rejoiced when He was thrust into the fray and was overcoming the common trial of Christians." [62] Is not joy a fruit of the Spirit? Is not gentleness? Yes, but we must acknowledge that Christ, Who was full of the Spirit, was not always serene, nor was He always gentle and calm, but was vexed and indignant, grieved and angry.[63] Indeed, Luther wonders whether Christ's greatest suffering was not His agony of spirit in Gethsemane rather than on the cross.[64]

Sometimes, however, the theme of Christ's historical lowliness recedes, and Christ is seen as a startling, frightening, wonder-

57. 38, 468, 12.
58. 10/III, 221, 11; 25, 469, 24; 46, 630, 27.
59. 29, 372, 11ff.
60. 46, 640, 33.
61. 43, 131, 1.
62. 20, 760, 4ff.
63. 10/I/1, 447, 5; cf. 22, 191, 1ff.
64. 44, 524, 10.

working figure, Who submitted to weakness and wretchedness only in His Passion.[65] Even His weakness is of a different sort: "I am weak while I sojourn on earth in the flesh, and do only small and slight deeds like raising a few dead people"![66] If it is a shame that He was a beggar, He need not have been, but He did it to direct men from the human to the divine. He went destitute and thirsty on the earth in order to demonstrate that His kingdom was not by might but by His Word.[67] The contrast between what reason and faith sees in the fact of Christ's weakness is replaced by a contrast between present weakness and future glory. Christ was lowly because He emptied Himself for His earthly office but has openly resumed the might of His eternal kingdom.[68] In His temporary sojourn here on earth, He was regarded as "poor, wretched, and powerless," but His "real office and reign" was accomplished by the Ascension, for then men could accept Him as their comfort and reliance.[69] So on earth the Christian is a beggar, like Christ was, but his treasure is in heaven.[70]

Sometimes, indeed, Luther seems to place Christ in one of his more romantic categories, the hero-idea. Luther believed that the historical process was decisively affected at crucial points by specially gifted and courageous "salutary heroes or phenomenal men," God's extraordinary and rare gifts to the world—an idea he set out at length in his commentary on Psalm 101.[71] Christ's stance as an impressive human figure during His ministry seems to evoke the heroic epithets in Luther's descriptions. Faith confesses Him not only as Lamb of God and Son of the divine majesty but also as "the great man."[72] Nicodemus recognized that Jesus must be "an extraordinary man."[73] The Lord acted master-

65. *45, 469*, 6.
66. *45, 538*, 28.
67. *47, 230*, 29; *177*, 38.
68. *45, 633*, 12ff.
69. *45, 480*, 4.
70. *45, 537*, 25.
71. *51, 215*, 1: "gesunden Helden oder Wunderman" (cf. *43, 62, 36*). For a case study of the hero-idea, see Rudolf Hermann, *Die Gestalt Simsons bei Luther* (Berlin, 1952).
72. *46, 680*, 35: "der grosse Man."
73. *21, 526*, 25: "ein sonderlicher Man."

fully, as always, when He met the Pharisees' challenge to His authority in the temple. When they tried to subject Him to the tyranny of the law, He withstood them fiercely "like the unicorn which, it is said, allows itself to be pierced, shot, and killed, but never to be taken." [74] In speaking out so boldly against all men, especially the wise and holy, He proved Himself a "daring, fearless man." [75] And in His preaching, He was such an "astonishing" person that, to reason, His words sounded like dreams or drunken ravings.[76]

The Jews were the more amazed at Jesus' masterful preaching because of His humble and untutored background. This brings to our attention an amusing curiosity of Luther's narrative. The Gospels state, he says, that Christ took up residence in Capernaum (doubtless because the seaside offered His family and disciples prospects of a better livelihood). So He became a burgher of Capernaum. But He was not merely citizen here: "this became the city where He had His parish, preached, and performed miracles." [77] Here He taught, not privately, but in His capacity as bishop and pastor He occupied the Capernaum pulpit publicly. For He was preacher there "just as I am preacher here and someone else teaches elsewhere" ; "He preached in Capernaum in His church, where He was chief superintendent in His pulpit, where He was doctor and preacher, and His disciples heard many fine sermons from Him." [78] Not that He was tied down by this parochial responsibility: He chose it as the place to dwell as bishop and pastor, just as the local pastor dwelt in Wittenberg. But in the same way Dr. Pomer (Johann Bugenhagen, for whom Luther was preaching as *locum tenens*) made occasional visits to Denmark and other places in the course of duty, so Christ too went on circuit all over the country, but based His activity on Capernaum.[79]

Having been assured that Christ was pastor and bishop of Capernaum, it comes as somewhat of a surprise, when we arrive at Je-

74. *46*, 751, 11; *36*, 274, 22.
75. *21*, 364, 24: "ein ebentheurlicher Man."
76. *45*, 551, 6: "ein wunderbarlicher Man."
77. *46*, 723, 9; 10/I/1, 243, 9.
78. *33*, 158, 32; 244, 35; 245, 2.
79. *46*, 724, 1ff.

rusalem, to discover that Christ was, after all, a layman. He was brought up as a layman without clerical instruction.[80] The administrators of the temple were apparently in the right when they challenged His authorization, seeing He was not a Levite but a carpenter's son.[81] For "Christ is from the laity, from the stem of Judah and not the priestly stem; He stands up to preach even though the priests alone were commanded to study Holy Writ," and the scribes were the more amazed that a layman should know their profession better than they.[82]

Clearly enough, the paradox arises out of Luther's attempt to deal at once with a variety of issues. He was concerned during the 1530s to insist on the urgent centrality of the preaching ministry, at the same time as he fulminated against infiltration by unauthorized preachers—*Winkelpredigern*.[83] His text sometimes gave him opportunity to predicate a normal, external authorization for Christ's ministry (for example, John 6:59). At other times, it forced him to admit that such authorization was lacking (John 7:14): "He takes no notice of the spiritual or worldly office or regime, whether they would permit Him or no, but quite blandly assumes the spiritual function and regime, and preaches." [84] At the beginning of the Reformation, Luther had used Christ's example and the practice of the primitive Church in urging Melanchthon to preach publicly, even though he was a layman; [85] later, however, the exigencies of church administration led him to a far more inflexible stance. In Christ's case, perhaps the hero-role, His acting "under a special star," [86] may provide a way of escape.

Always associated with Christ's preaching, and marking Him out as an extraordinary man, were His miracles. They were great miracles and startling deeds, unparalleled, unprecedented.[87] Yet in Luther's thinking they play an incidental role: miracles them-

80. *33,* 352, 3.
81. *46,* 749, 28.
82. *33,* 350, 25.
83. *30*/III, 518ff.
84. *33,* 343, 35.
85. *Br, 2,* 388, 48; cf. *12,* 188, 20ff.
86. *51,* 207, 22.
87. *45,* 469, 8; 720, 28; *46,* 604, 29; 646, 25.

selves are the least significant of Christian works, for the devil
was defeated by weakness, not magnificent miracles; the earthly
effect of Christ's miracles cannot compare with the heavenly effect of faith in Him; and it is one of St. John's superiorities over
the Synoptics that he stresses faith where they stress miracles.[88]
This is at least one reason why discrepancies in the evangelists'
record of the miracles are unimportant;[89] and perhaps it also explains the minor discrepancies in Luther's own use of the miracle
stories. To them he attaches various meanings.

In some earlier sermons he tends to give miracle accounts a tro-
pological application. Thus the feeding of the five thousand is "a
lesson in faith" about our temporal existence; the wedding feast
at Cana is recorded for an "example of love in Christ" and an assurance that "those that believe in Him shall not suffer want
. . . rather water must become wine, and every creature be
changed into whatever the believer needs."[90]

Though the exemplary character of the miracles is never forgotten,[91] Luther is more concerned later to treat them in their historical setting; but he cannot decide precisely how they signify in
that setting. A characteristic remark is that no one accepted these
public proofs of Christ's identity.[92] It was astounding that the
Jews could reject them; but reject them they did, so that His miracles were offensive, wasted, ignored, mocked, and forgotten.[93]
The people were offended by His insignificance rather than im-
proved by His works, nor could they tolerate the teachings He
joined to these signs.[94] They were, nonetheless, proofs of His
calling, evidence of His identity, and the fruits of His commission
from the Father.

First, miracles were proofs of Christ's calling. Here Luther has
little difficulty. These signs were the Father's witness, corroborating both the testimony of the Baptist and Christ's own claim.

88. *45*, 532, 32; 635, 33; 33, 175, 9ff.; 167, 21.
89. *46*, 727, 12.
90. *17/II*, 223, 25; 64, 30ff.
91. *37*, 539, 11.
92. *46*, 577, 18; 630, 38; 47, 187, 12.
93. *46*, 576, 18; 33, 252, 40; 557, 1ff.
94. *33*, 40, 8; 46, 645, 14.

They were testimonies by which Christ should have been known.[95] Matthew, in particular, constantly tried to demonstrate how Jesus' miracles showed Him to be the Christ of the prophets.[96] It is when Luther turns to the role of miracle in establishing Christ's identity that inconsistencies appear. On the one hand, Luther says Christ performed His miracles "according to His humanity." He was revealed as a "true and natural man" in His preaching and miracles (and the disciples—even renegade disciples—also performed such works).[97] On the other hand, Luther says the miracles were divine works, wrought by divine power.[98] As proofs of His Sonship, they should have led to His acknowledgment as lord in divine majesty, the God of Sinai.[99] Even reason could say nothing but that they were God's miracles: Christ's works were the sort that God alone could perform.[1] Luther goes to quite extraordinary lengths to assert that the devil is incapable of copying them except in illusion, pseudomiracle, or artifice.[2]

Do the miracles then give us ground to identify Christ in His Godhead or simply in His divinely attested manhood? Very occasionally, Luther tries to resolve the dilemma by one or another christological rubric. Miracles are listed amongst the *larvae Dei*: the masks in which God is certainly present and active, but concealed.[3] Again, as the man Christ is the essence of God's will and heart toward us, so the attitude of mercy and consolation shown us in His miracles is surely the revelation of the Father.[4] Or, since the disciples knew Christ through His preaching and miracles, in knowing this person they knew the way to the Father.[5] However, it is clear that any great concern about the Christology of the miracles is foreign to Luther.

95. 33, 556, 23ff.; 47, 187, 12ff.; 45, 719, 6.
96. 38, 468, 17.
97. 33, 116, 33; 251, 40ff.; 295, 31; 300, 36; 40/I, 172, 12.
98. 33, 330, 10; 45, 527, 14; 531, 20.
99. 47, 210, 39ff.
1. 45, 723, 11; 46, 759, 7.
2. 32, 525, 26; 45, 528, 15ff.; 626, 3; 46, 63, 16ff.
3. 45, 522, 11.
4. 46, 101, 14.
5. 45, 489, 18.

Instead, in the great majority of his references to miracles, he subsumes them under the category of preaching, to which they are merely ancillary, and by which they must be judged.[6] As we shall see later, Christ's preaching is a central category in Luther's whole doctrine. Here we may note, in anticipation, that Christ's miracles (like the preaching they accompany) formed part of the ministry for which the Father sent Christ.[7] They began at His baptism, they proclaimed the institution of the new covenant until it was consummated in His "going to the Father," and their purpose was to evoke and confirm faith in the person of Christ.[8]

Finally, the ineffable mystery of the Word made flesh, the utterly unexpected Messiah, culminates in that most impenetrable mystery of all, the cross. "On the cross Christ was powerless; yet there He performed His mightiest work, conquering sin, death, world, hell, devil, and all evil."[9] As He enters the glory of His Father, all glory disappears. He says to His disciples, "I go to the Father," and He goes to the grave.[10] He Who alone is holy and blameless becomes a sinner for us in His cross and Passion; He Who alone is innocent and free of the law becomes a curse for us.[11]

Luther's usual practice during Passion Week was to relate the story of Christ's betrayal and arrest, judgment and death, as a harmony of the four accounts. He preferred to give a continuous *Passions-* or *Leidensgeschichte,* rather than single out any one gospel account. (There are three recorded exceptions—expositions of the Passion according to St. John in 1524 and 1533, and an undated St. Matthew Passion series.) In his Passion sermons there is considerably more narrative concern than in all his other New Testament preaching. But this assertion must be qualified in two ways. First, in the case of the Passion, Luther's narrative concern is itself a theological concern: he lays great stress on Christ's submission to suffering as a major part of His saving obedience to

6. 33, 178, 38; 32, 531, 13; 33, 359, 30.
7. 33, 556, 25; 46, 93, 30.
8. 46, 603, 21; 15, 557, 16; 10/III, 426, 16; 45, 489, 18.
9. 7, 586, 15.
10. 43, 393, 24.
11. 21, 337, 21; 40/I, 433, 15.

the Father, and he is firmly convinced of the essential role of Christ's physical humanity in the accomplishment of salvation. Secondly, for all his narrative concern, Luther never tires of saying that a knowledge of the Passion history is worthless without a knowledge of its use; and to that end one might well devote the whole year to the Passion story.[12]

In the case of Christ's ministry Luther treasured His teaching far above the record of His deeds (hence his preference for the Johannine discourses over Synoptic narratives). In the case of the Passion, on the other hand, the events themselves constituted Christ's "going to the Father." Luther therefore felt impelled to present a factual, topical account, while avoiding the resulting pitfall of that maudlin sentimentality about the sufferings and wounds of Christ he had experienced under the papacy.[13] He took seriously Christ's injunction, "Weep not for Me, but for yourselves." The mere *fides historica* which resulted from the medieval vogue of diligent meditation on His sufferings "really perverted the Passion of Christ and degraded it." [14] Nevertheless, it is Christ's body and blood, His sufferings and death, to which true faith clings.[15]

The ignominy of Christ's Passion remains a consistent burden of Luther's exposition.[16] God "offered up His beloved child for me in ignominy, shame, and death." [17] He was so shamefully condemned that He was cast outside the gates. "Men let others die in their homes with honor; He was not held worthy to die with men, but was damned as a malefactor, was made a curse to the whole world." [18] We see Him in death "not beautiful or honorable" but masked in disgrace on the cross, "like a murderer and evildoer": What is more wretched than He? [19] It was "the most

12. E.g. *47*, 712, 12; *52*, 226, 8ff.

13. *52*, 228, 30.

14. *33*, 225, 12.

15. *33*, 288, 18.

16. E.g. *10/I/2*, 304, 11; III, 149, 3; *12*, 511, 10; *15*, 505, 6; *40/I*, 361, 24; *41*, 573, 17; *45*, 511, 16; *46*, 93, 6; etc.

17. *10/III*, 155, 6.

18. *25*, 470, 4.

19. *10/I/2*, 305, 25; *21*, 337, 21; *28*, 85, 6; *31/II*, 430, 25; *43*, 140, 1.

ignominious death, lifted on a cross and suspended in mid-air." [20] As He laments in Psalm 22, He hung like a serpent, a noxious worm, an object of scorn and contempt in the greatest weakness and infirmity.[21] He was crucified as a rebel, the vilest malefactor, deceiver and blasphemer,[22] so that the holy people sought to honor God by killing the accursed one, and the devil exulted that Christ was cursed by God and man.[23] He was subjected to torture, scourging, reviling, mockery, and indescribable sorrow.[24] The devil and his cohorts set about to seize Him, get Him between the spurs, vanquish, and crush Him; death assailed Him and pressed Him in.[25] Christ became a stumbling block to all and the ruin of many.[26]

So it is that a wretched figure is presented to us for faith.[27] But to look to the crucified is faith: we must love the shameful Christ fully bound to the cross, picture Him to ourselves as He hangs suspended, despised and spat upon, love Him in His humanity obedient to the sacred cross.[28] It is, indeed, hard to see God's grace at work in this most shameful death. Yet to the eyes of faith the very love of God is here poured out for us.[29] Faith must ask whether, after all, this death is as ignominious as it must appear. Christ's painful death is also the hour of His glorification; His Passion is the way to His lordship.[30] "This shameful death, cursed by God, is an offense to behold, yet to us it is a blessed death, for it takes the curse away from us and brings God's blessing in its stead. The tree which itself is accursed is a blessed tree to us, for it is the precious altar whereon God's Son offers Himself to God for our sins, the glorious altar where He now appears as our true and eternal priest." [31]

20. *21*, 484, 7.
21. *17/II*, 244, 21; *21*, 550, 28; *47*, 67, 19.
22. *21*, 336, 21; *431*, 36; *33*, 608, 33.
23. *46*, 15, 14; *72*, 30.
24. *19*, 610, 30; *45*, 637, 40; *46*, 74, 31; *52*, 802, 24.
25. *21*, 476, 34 and 37; *33*, 608, 31.
26. *Br*, 2, 242, 15.
27. *47*, 71, 16.
28. *21*, 550, 4; *12*, 578, 5; *29*, 359, 5; *47*, 180, 24 and 35.
29. *10/III*, 149, 8; 155, 2ff.; *17/II*, 173, 34; *29*, 359, 3ff.
30. *52*, 807, 39; *28*, 79, 12; *10/III*, 129, 35; *45*, 491, 18ff.
31. *52*, 808, 31.

So Christ hangs on the cross with arms outstretched as if to call us to Him with gentle words, "Come unto Me all ye who travail." [32] In the last analysis, it cannot but be impressive how often Luther abandons descriptive or explanatory discourse about the Passion and instead says simply, "He died for us." For this is the use of the Passion: this sentence conveys joy and gladness to poor sinners that no amount of embellishment or theory need augment.

32. *48*, 169; 219.

# 2. The Office and Mission of Christ

The earthly activities of the man Christ have their place in the way of salvation because they are the fulfillment of an office and calling committed to Christ by the Father. The nature of this office is a concern central to all Luther's thinking. Without an understanding of the way he uses this concept, it is impossible to grasp the direction—or the centrality—of his doctrine of Christ.

Accordingly, we shall be much concerned with this theme in all that follows. But first, we have to remove a potential confusion. Luther's use of the term "office" has little to do with the practice of describing Christ's mediating work by means of "the threefold office." While the threefold pattern appeared occasionally before the Reformation,[1] and in the writings of both Bucer and Osiander,[2] it was Calvin who first elaborated this specific use of "office." In order that faith may be firmly based, he said, "the principle must be laid down: the office enjoined upon Christ by the Father consists of three parts. For He was given to be prophet, king, and priest."[3] After Calvin this concept became widespread as a systematic principle, in Luther study as in dogmatics.[4]

1. For a short catena of pre-Reformation occurrences (from Eusebius, Chrysostum, Chrysologus, Aquinas), see John F. Jansen, *Calvin's Doctrine of the Work of Christ* (London, 1956), pp. 30f.

2. Martin Bucer, *In sacra qvatvor evangelia, Enarrationes perpetvae* (Basel, 1536), p. 607; Andreas Osiander, *Schirmschrift zum Augsburger Reichstag* (1530), quoted in Jansen, p. 37.

3. *Inst.* 2.15.1.

4. See, e.g., Joh. Gerhard, *Loci theologici* (Jena, 1610–22), Loc. Quartus, cap. XV, Thesis 2, pars. 321ff. (Cotta III, 577); Joh. Andr. Quenstedt, *Theologia didactico-polemica sive systema theologicum* (Wittenberg, 1685–91), III, 3.2;

Luther's use of the term "office," however, has little to do with the traditional practice. Theodosius Harnack is imposing a pattern on Luther when he expounds Luther's doctrine of the work of Christ under the rubric of the threefold office (the *stamina* of which he claims to find in Luther).[5] And while other commentators are not as explicit as Harnack, it is quite normal to use the heading "Luther's Doctrine of the Office of Christ" for his soteriology.[6] Now, there can be no prima facie objection to the use of acceptable and widespread formulas for classifying Luther's teaching; but in this case it may be objected that a number of distortions have resulted.

First, it implies a way of doing soteriology which is foreign to Luther; and it may well be that he would have shared the impatience of Jo. Aug. Ernesti's eighteenth-century "disputatiuncula" with the result. Ernesti objected to the distortion of biblical materials resulting, he argued, from the application of this schema—especially the scholar's tendency to treat Christ's work not as three aspects of one saving office but as three successive stages.[7]

Secondly, it has distorted Luther's real relationship to this very tradition. For, as we have seen, Luther was not ignorant of the ancient practice, stemming from the typology of Melchizedek in Hebrews 7, of applying the twin titles priest and king to Christ. The practice was readily accessible to him not only in Scripture but in the Fathers, including Augustine,[8] and verbal parallels indicate that he knew it directly from Peter Lombard.[9] Moreover,

---

David Hollaz, *Examen theologicum acroamaticum* (Rostock and Leipzig, 1707), III. 1 cp. 3, 71; Friedrich Schleiermacher, *The Christian Faith* (2d ed.; E.T. reprinted Edinburgh, 1960), sec. 102, esp. Pt. III; and see Heinrich Heppe, *Reformed Dogmatics* (London, 1950), pp. 452ff.; Heinrich Schmid, *Doctrinal Theology of the Evangelical Lutheran Church* (Philadelphia, 1876), pp. 361ff.

5. Theodosius Harnack, *Luthers Theologie, mit besonderer Beziehung auf seine Versöhnungs- und Erlösungslehre*, 2 (neue Ausg., München, 1927), sec. 50, p. 214 (erste Ausg., pp. 269f.).

6. E.g. Emanuel Hirsch, *Hilfsbuch zum Studium der Dogmatik* (Berlin and Leipzig, 1951), pp. 50ff.

7. Jo. Aug. Ernesti, "De Officio Christi triplici," in *Opuscula theologica* (Leipzig, 1773), pp. v, 412ff.

8. E.g. *Enarratio in Ps. 26:2* (MPL XXXVI, 199); *Civ. Dei.* XVII, 4, 9.

9. Cf. Peter Lombard, *Collect ad Rom.*, 1 (MPL CXCI, 1304), and 10/I/2, 152, 29.

Jansen rightly suggests that Luther's use of this tradition (for instance, in *The Freedom of the Christian Man*) [10] was an immediate source of the schema in Calvin.[11] It is certainly true that Luther does employ the priest-king theme and actually applies the word "office" to it.[12]

> He speaks of Christ's "priestly office" as "priest over against God and king over against death" (28, 174, 5; 33, 310, 19, 17), of His completing the office of mediator by becoming man, dying for us, rising again, and ascending into heaven, and it is "because of this office He is called Jesus Christ" (17/I, 255, 16); of the messianic office of redemption (21, 545, 11; 46, 98, 22; 47, 178, 18); of Christ's office to found a spiritual kingdom (21, 295, 1; 40/II, 518, 18) and of His ordination as king (46, 602, 29–32); of the overthrow of death and awakening of the dead as "His true office" (47, 713, 3). "Christ's office," he says, "is to save, to free from sins, and to give eternal life" (40/II, 273, 10).

But Luther's use of the twofold "priest and king" form is relatively infrequent (despite Jansen's unfulfilled offer of "any number of illustrations"); [13] and the application of "office" in this sense is the exception, not the rule.

Thirdly, and most importantly, to force Luther's doctrine into the procrustean bed of traditional usage is to obscure what Luther himself means by "office." Certainly Luther abounds in the soteriological materials that others have classified under the threefold heading; and it is easy to see how his stress on Christ's office as preacher, superimposed on a priest-king pattern already in currency, led directly to the evolution of the threefold prophet, priest, and king schema. Nevertheless, to use "office" as a general classifier for speaking of Luther's soteriology, when the word has

10. 7, 56, 15ff.

11. Jansen, *Calvin's Doctrine*, pp. 32ff.

12. E.g. *41*, 168, 17. The influence of the tradition is aptly illustrated by Vol. 22 of *Luther's Works, American Edition* (St. Louis, 1957), when on p. 200 it translates "aber zur zeit Christi da ists wider ein ding worden, denn Christus war beides, Priester und König" as follows: "In the time of Christ the two offices were again united in one person, for Christ was both, a Prophet as well as a King" (*46*, 710, 8ff.).

13. Jansen, p. 33.

another specific connotation for him, is, to say the least, confusing
—and in the light of later developments, tragic. For the emascu-
lation of the prophetic role before the Enlightenment, and therefore of the priestly and kingly roles after it (the process Barth so
deplores),[14] could scarcely have happened if Luther's concept of
the office of Christ had been remembered.

The office of Christ, then, for Luther almost always means His
role as preacher or teacher. We have just noted that there are
some exceptions, but they are very few in number. By contrast,
there are more references to Christ as preacher and teacher than
under any titles except savior and lord. "The office of Christ is
very clearly described: He will not bear the sword or found a
new state, but He will be a teacher, to instruct men about an un-
heard of but eternal decree of God." [15] To have seen Christ and
His office is to have heard His preaching and seen His miracles.[16]
Luther's normal word for Christ's ministry is *Predigtampt*—
"preaching office." Christ's mission and ministry was "to preach
truth and to apply it to us"; proclaiming the gospel was "the highest function of His office." [17]

This is the context in which Luther develops his vital concept
of office. By vital I do not imply complicated. This is an idea of
great simplicity. "Office" means simply a God-given task—that is,
a task based explicitly on God's Word, and thus deriving its
efficacy and authority from God. In its nature Christ's office differs not at all from the offices of prophets, apostles, magistrates,
ministers, parents, and all Christians in their daily callings. "Tell
me, why did Christ not take a wife, or become a cobbler or tai-
lor? If any calling or office were not worthy because Christ did
not pursue it, then what would become of all the callings and
offices apart from the preaching office, the only one He did practice? Christ followed His own office and calling, but He has not
thereby rejected everyone else's!" [18] For Luther, as in all his

14. Karl Barth, *Church Dogmatics*, IV/I (4 vols. in 12, Edinburgh, 1936ff.),
sec. 58:4, 137–8.
15. 40/II, 242, 29.
16. 10/I/2, 357, 29.
17. 12, 191, 12; 12, 285, 29.
18. 11, 258, 13.

teaching about office and vocation, to possess such an office is not
merely a theoretical construct or an individual attitude; rather, it
involves the fact of external relationships and life in the world.[19]
And so it was for Christ. His preaching office meant practical application to three and a half years of ministry.[20] Christ entered
upon His office at His baptism in Jordan—His "real advent" at
the age of thirty, when He received ordination from God—and
by exercise of His preaching office began the new convenant and
the time of grace (as only He was qualified to do).[21] His preaching office was according to the counsel of God, and He fulfilled it
faithfully; it was according to prophecy, and He performed it
incomparably.[22] It meant withstanding the Pharisees, for to attack their presumption was incumbent on His office.[23] Because
this task required such boldness, Christ could comfort Himself
with the knowledge that His office was from the Father and was
true; [24] and He could rub His calling under their noses.[25] Indeed, He was emboldened by a certainty and confidence of His
calling and office that distinguished all the words and acts of His
ministry from the world's: He gloried in His office, knowing that
since He Who sent Him entrusted this office to Him, He could
not err or fail in His destiny.[26] (So, too, every Christian in his
office and calling must take refuge in this "strong and mighty
fortress.") [27]

Christ became man to undertake His ministry of preaching and
to open heaven to us.[28] But this required that He empty Himself
and take a humble servant's office in order to preach to us: He assumed a most lowly and menial office, and it led Him to His
death.[29] For the office of the true shepherd (which for Luther

19. On this, see Gustaf Wingren, *Luther on Vocation* (Philadelphia, 1957).
20. 46, 727, 3ff.
21. 12, 285, 27; 46, 723, 4; 602, 30; 10/I/2, 202, 22ff.; I/1, 214, 14.
22. 46, 94, 10; 33, 445, 4.
23. 33, 402, 28.
24. 33, 396, 3; 33, 596, 29; 40/II, 150, 27.
25. 33, 357, 41.
26. 33, 533, 35.
27. 33, 534, 29 to 535, 2.
28. 46, 712, 1.
29. 21, 475, 4; 45, 633, 24.

meant the preaching office) was a lowly service, without pomp and glory, but like a menial servant.[30] But the time of His humility, when He was "only a preacher," stands in contrast to the time when, relieved of this human office, He declares His might from heaven and gives the Holy Spirit.[31] Sometimes, in fact, the "kingly office" is identified as "nothing other than the office of the Word."[32] When Christ said, "My Father is greater than I," it was as if He had said to His disciples, "I have two offices: now I am here on earth, performing My office of preaching for which I was sent by the Father; but when I go to the Father, I shall execute My other office—I shall send the Holy Spirit into your hearts."[33] The exalted but human office of preaching He committed to His disciples,[34] and the self-same office is continued in the Church's ministry of preaching and teaching.[35]

What, then, was He commissioned to say in fulfillment of His office? Here we must be careful to distinguish between the offices of Moses and Christ. This shepherd and His office are different from all others.[36] For the work and office for which He was sent was only to bring comfort and remove fear. It is true that the first office of His kingdom was to make all men sinners; but His primary office and mission was not to judge but to help. This was His proper office, and we must keep it in our hearts.[37] "His title and office is to bless, help and advise . . . He is to be a comforting preacher, a friendly man and helper, Who with all His might will do nothing but teach and work, assist and bless—there is sheer aid and consolation with Him."[38] Christ glorified His office by contrasting Himself with those who are quick to carnal judgment: "That is not My mission on earth—no, I abolish judgment in order to attract people to Me and enlighten them."[39]

30. 10/I/2, 243, 1; 21, 502, 20.
31. 33, 609, 6; 611, 24.
32. 5, 63, 22; 31/II, 515, 30.
33. 10/I/2, 283, 29.
34. 21, 502, 32; 28, 466, 11ff.
35. 8, 24, 13; 45, 521, 4ff.; 581, 22ff.
36. 14, 676, 29ff.; 46, 663, 25; 21, 320, 37.
37. 33, 508, 17; 47, 102, 14; 33, 544, 35; 545, 4.
38. 33, 545, 25.
39. 33, 539, 5.

"My office dispenses pure grace and forgiveness." [40] For the express purpose of Christ's presence was to communicate the gracious will of the Father—that His attitude toward us was no longer wrath but love.[41]

This He could do, not only because He was sent in the capacity of preacher, had the Father's testimony for His office, and preached another's words—namely, the Father's divine words [42] —but especially because it was in Himself that the Father's gracious purpose was fulfilled. And here we may anticipate in outline one of the most striking motifs of Luther's exposition. Luther says that it is the office of Christ to be a witness to the fact that Christ came to make satisfaction for our sins.[43] We shall find the curious circularity of this statement paralleled by assertions that Christ was sent to proclaim that He was the one sent from God. By the preaching of the Word, our hearts are drawn to the man Christ, Who is Himself the Son of God and both by nature and by His "going to the Father" has life in Himself. "Office" means the office of preaching this gospel. It is a human office (Luther several times makes distinction between Christ's nature as God and His office as preacher),[44] and it is an office whose continuation in the Church still draws men to the man Christ: "our office is not ours, but Christ's." [45] But the accomplishment of the salvation which is ours through this office is Christ's own sole, unique, and exclusive work, on which nothing in heaven or earth may encroach.

### The One Sent by God

Christ came in the capacity of preacher, because to this the Father sent Him. The constant but neglected New Testament

40. 33, 541, 36.
41. 45, 522, 38; 28, 191, 11.
42. 33, 598, 11; 552, 2ff.; 358, 18; 40/II, 255, 20.
43. 47, 180, 1.
44. 33, 357, 41 to 358, 17; 550, 33ff.
45. 5, 61, 1; 45, 706, 19.

theme of the "sending" of Christ receives its due weight in Luther's impressive treatment; [46] and the way he expounds "sending" both as an aspect of Christ's office and of His whole work of salvation is another mark of his extraordinary sensitivity to scriptural vocabulary. For, like the New Testament, Luther understands Christ's commission as a purpose of salvation (Matt. 15:24, Luke 4:18, John 3:17, Rom. 8:3, I John 4:9, 10, 14), as an obedient accomplishment of God's purpose (John 4:34, 5:30, 6:38f., 9:4), as an issue of authority (Matt. 21:33ff. and parallels, John 17:18, 20:21), as an office of preaching (Luke 4:43, John 3:34, 5:24, 7:16, 8:26, 12:49, 14:24; cf. Rom. 10:15), and as the crux of the lively knowledge of God in Christ (Matt. 10:40, Mark 9:37, Luke 9:48, 10:16, John 5:37f., 6:29, 7:28f., 8:42, 12:44f., 13:20, 15:21, 17:3, 8, 21, 23, 25). Yet these are not many commissions, but one commission. We shall find all these strands in Luther's rich and complex exposition of Christ as the one sent by God.

First, Christ was sent as savior,[47] explicitly to save sinners and help a lost and condemned world.[48]

> God sent Christ into the flesh to bring us forgiveness, redemption, eternal righteousness, and life (*41*, 149, 9). Christ was commissioned to give Himself for us (e.g. *12*, 544, 22; 571, 16; *21*, 353, 24; 358, 37; *33*, 369, 38). This mission in the flesh required that He should suffer for us, shed His blood and die on the cross (*46*, 19, 16; 93, 26). For He was sent into our filth, misery, and sin (*10/III*, 157, 14) as a ransom and sacrifice (*21*, 358, 37; 435, 2), to bear our sins and make satisfaction for them by His death (*21*, 358, 37), to atone (*21*, 363, 15), propitiate (*21*, 359, 1), redeem (*10/I/2*, 238, 3; *12*, 545, 15; 571, 16; *46*, 24, 26), rescue (*20*, 744, 15), reconcile (*46*, 10, 10; 40, 22), overthrow death, and bring grace, justification, and forgiveness (*28*, 113, 3; *32*, 510, 25)—in short, He was

---

46. For a recent parallel, perhaps influenced by Luther's treatment, see Rudolf Bultmann, *Theology of the New Testament*, 2 (2 vols. New York, 1951–1955), par. 45 ("The Sending of the Son," pp. 33ff.) and par. 48 ("The Revelation as the Word," pp. 59ff.).

47. *33*, 631, 32; *45*, 589, 41.

48. *10/I/2*, 235, 27; *33*, 547, 7; *47*, 97, 39.

sent to the whole work of redemption and salvation (21, 363, 10; 25, 64, 32).

While such references abound in Luther until the end of his life, it is only in his sermons before 1528 that Christ's redemptive mission is the virtually exclusive connotation of "sent by God." In that year Luther gave a running exposition in Wittenberg of Christ's prayer in John 17, with its repeated references to the Father's sending Christ. It seems to have been Luther's meditation on this passage that led him to the far greater richness of his later doctrine of Christ's mission. He here discovered "the treasure that lies wholly in this little word 'sent.' "[49]

Now there is a new awareness of the connection between Christ's sacrifice as redeemer and His obedient accomplishment of all the Father's will in His earthly words and actions. For one who is sent fulfills whatever he is commanded: to be sent involves a task.[50] That was what Christ meant when He said, "As Thou hast sent Me"; now He could say, "All that Thou hast commanded Me I have accomplished."[51] Eternal life consists in the knowledge that Jesus Christ was sent by God the Father, and that this "sending" includes everything He did, His life and His death.[52] "His being sent means nothing else but that He, the true Son of God from eternity, became true man and revealed Himself on earth in human nature, being, and form; let Himself be seen, heard, and touched; ate, drank, slept, labored, suffered, and died like any other man."[53]

Central to the task committed to Christ was the office of preacher.[54] He was sent to preach, sent to proclaim the Word of God.[55] Because God sent Him to preach, what He said carried the authority of God: His words must be accepted.[56] Christ's own testimony to this mission was validated by the testimony of

49. 28, 98, 4.
50. 28, 98, 3.
51. 28, 172, 9.
52. 28, 103, 12.
53. 46, 69, 25.
54. 12, 285, 27; 31/II, 515, 23; 33, 413, 36.
55. 25, 13, 30; 40/II, 249, 22; 47, 180, 37; 185, 39.
56. 33, 34, 5.

His Father, Who sent Him to be the light of the world.[57] It is the Father's will that we should give ear to Christ as the one sent.[58] And we can draw the precious conclusion that when Christ says this or that, we hear not Christ but God: Christ's mouth is the mouth of God.[59]

But other messengers have also come with the Word and authority of God: special emissaries—the prophets and apostles like Moses or Paul—or regularly called priests and preachers in the Church's ministry. All these are sent and possess the authority of their office. Indeed, God's Word must not be understood except as having been sent.[60] Do we then have any special knowledge when we know that Christ was sent? Moses' law was given and the prophets sent, but they pointed forward to Christ. The Church's preaching is sent by Christ, and its message cannot deviate from Christ.[61] Thus in one sense many are sent; in another sense, now that He is here "Whom God wanted to send and now has sent," only He is to be known as "the one sent." The ears of all the world are glued to His mouth: He is the one truly sent. No other has been sent in this way, and His Word alone is accounted valid.[62]

What, then, is it that Christ was sent to preach? His original hearers, Luther says, were "dull and foolish": they heard that He was truly the Son of God, sent by the Father as man in order to preach to them. "But what He preaches and proclaims they do not understand, namely that the Son was sent by the Father." [63] Here is the circular motif: Christ was sent to preach that He was sent.

One thing this could mean is that one phase of Christ's mission was to preach about another phase of His mission; but this is to oversimplify. It seems that the motif is more properly spiral: at each turn we are borne one step further toward the knowledge of

57. 33, 518, 1; 534, 1. See below, p. 93.
58. 33, 362, 10.
59. 28, 118, 5; 123, 10; 47, 191, 27ff.
60. 47, 193, 10; cf. 30/III, 519, 12.
61. 47, 193, 41; 194, 22.
62. 47, 194, 21; 33, 557, 31; 47, 194, 37ff.
63. 33, 602, 38; 603, 4.

God. If we start at the level of historical narrative, Jesus of Nazareth was in fact a preacher. He said about His own preaching
that He did not speak of His own accord, but because the Father
sent Him.[64] His opponents rejected this claim: [65] this was precisely the point where He was assailed (for God must be judged
not in His majesty but in His words).[66] If the learned had only
believed that He was sent by God, they would have listened and
taken note of what He said. But this part of His mission succeeded with the disciples, who accepted Him as their preacher
sent by God.[67]

Those who received Christ as preacher from God found that
He then directed them to Himself. This teacher taught men to
come to the knowledge of Himself. "Listen to Me, believe in Me,
I point you to Myself: I am sent by My Father. Thus I preach to
you: I come as a preacher to you and bring a word from the
Father—do not doubt it, and you will discover Who I am and
whence I am." [68] He said not only, "I am sent," but also "I am
He." [69] This meant, on one level, that He was not merely another
emissary but uniquely the one sent, the one Who says everything
needful. On a still higher level it meant that to know Christ as
sent was to know God as sender. Here Luther's reflections on John
17:3 are illuminating.[70] In this verse, he says, Christ affirms that
there is only one true God—namely, the One Who sent Jesus
Christ. The word "only" excludes all other possibilities. There is
no other God.[71] Then He says that eternal life consists in the
knowledge of this sender, Who is God, and of Jesus Christ,
Whom He sent. But in conjoining sender and sent in this way as
the object of life-giving knowledge, Christ identifies Himself as
true God with the Father.[72]

64. 33, 390, 8ff.; 40/II, 255, 20.
65. 33, 413, 36; and 45, 716, 5 and 23; 717, 9.
66. 47, 180, 19 and 25.
67. 28, 102, 1; 45, 530, 27.
68. 10/I/2, 434, 24; 33, 394, 22.
69. 33, 592, 35.
70. 33, 36, 30; 28, 90–107.
71. 28, 94, 10; 20, 727, 6; 30/III, 132, 23; 35, 456, 14; 40/II, 256, 20.
72. 28, 94, 14.

Thus there is an essential and organic connection between the knowledge of Christ as sent and God as sender. We can have no inkling where Christ comes from unless He tells us of the One Who sent Him; we can have no knowledge of the One Who sent Him unless we give ear to Christ as sent.[73] For God will no longer be known as creator, nor as the one Who spoke through Moses.[74] It is disaster to flutter up to heaven or clamber up to peek at the Father and not seek Him in the one He has sent.[75] Hereafter He will be known only as the one Who sent Christ, Who speaks exclusively through Christ.[76] And what does God say through Him? He also points us to Christ: He says, "I have sent Him to you."[77] Why would God send His Son if He were angry with us? Now that the Son has been sent into the world, if the world were still to be condemned, the Son would be condemned with it! But this is impossible; all our thoughts of wrath can be put to death.[78] The sending of the Son into the world is the immense, poured-out mercy of God and His inestimable love, and by it we are made acceptable.[79] That Christ was sent to die for us is the outpouring of the love of God's fatherly heart, His counsel, will, and pleasure.[80] God is called Father because He sent His Son to forgive, to loose the bonds of death, and to bring us mercy; this name of Father is the name that Christ glorifies on earth.[81]

In summary, then: to know that Jesus Christ was sent means first that we acknowledge His authority as a preacher sent from God, and heed His words. If we receive Him in this way, we discover that He is sent not simply as a preacher but as *the* preacher. We then hang upon His every word, knowing that exclusively His words are God's words, conveying finally all that we

73. *33*, 389, 12ff.; *395*, 5; *45*, 481, 33.
74. *45*, 17, 6; *28*, 94, 9.
75. *33*, 141, 18.
76. *25*, 503, 18–22; *28*, 94, 11.
77. *28*, 94, 13; *33*, 141, 34.
78. *47*, 98, 37; *99*, 15 and 30.
79. *20*, 741, 1ff.
80. *28*, 199, 5; *33*, 131, 11.
81. *28*, 113, 6 to 114, 3.

need to know. This decisive emissary, unlike any other messenger of God, tells us that all we need to know (in order to know God) is to cling to Him—the one sent. He alone, of all God's messengers, can point to Himself, because He is the Son, sent for our salvation. " 'God brings you to Me by sending Me into the world, and speaking to you through My mouth'; by thus drawing your heart, when you receive the Word which Christ speaks to you as the Father's own Word; and by allowing that Word to lead you nowhere else but to this person, and thence to the Father." [82] Thus to know Christ as sent is to know Him as the Son, true God with the Father. "The highest article of our faith is to know that the Son of Mary is the eternal Son of God, sent by the Father to preach . . . And He sums up all His teaching when He declares: 'The eternal Father has begotten Me in eternity.' " [83]

God will not be known in any other way: knowledge of the one sent is the only possibility of knowledge of the Sender. But what we know of the one sent is that He comes to take away sin, wrath, condemnation, and death, and instead to bring us grace, mercy, and forgiveness—in short, to show us that we have a gracious God, Who will not be known by any other name.

Therefore that man is blessed who knows in his heart that Christ was sent into the world. This is the only blessedness, this is the true Christian learning. Whoever does not know that Jesus was sent does not glory only in Christ and has shut himself off from the only way to eternal life.[84] For eternal life is not won by any work but this, that Jesus Christ was sent into the world.[85] "Thus He draws us and holds us to Himself, for to this He was sent, that He should draw those who would believe in Him up to the Father, as He is in the Father. These bonds has He forged between Himself and us and the Father and enclosed us within them. Through such a union and fellowship our sin and death are abolished, and we have instead sheer life and blessedness." [86]

82. 33, 134, 28: ". . . und lesst das wort dich nicht weiter treiben denn auff die Person, auff den Vater."

83. 40/II, 249, 22.

84. 28, 96, 2 to 97, 8; 96, 3; 102, 5; 33, 103, 34; 141, 37.

85. 28, 103, 2.

86. 45, 587, 37 to 588, 5.

## Messenger, Witness

Here we may notice in passing two ancillary titles which Luther applies to Christ in His office and mission. He was God's messenger: "Believe in the Son, accept His mandate, listen to Him, for He is My messenger—He will tell you everything you should do; and what He does not say, leave alone, because it is worthless." [87] Everything is to be compared with the message heard from Him. If it differs, it is "darkness by which a lie is superimposed on God." [88] Christ spoke in His official capacity as public messenger and preacher, not merely as a private individual. And as Christ was the Father's messenger, so His disciples are sent as His messengers. [89] "The message is simply this: Christ alone is the way to heaven." [90]

Joined with the title "messenger" as Christ's public capacity is His role as witness. In taking office His own testimony was supported by His Father's testimony, and He could therefore be a powerful witness to His own public capacity. "I am a witness and bear testimony to Myself." [91] Luther's use of this title is echoed by Rudolf Bultmann when he says of Christ, "Not once does he communicate matters or events to which he had been a witness by either eye or ear . . . his theme is always just this one thing: that the Father sent him, that he came as the light, the bread of life, witness for the truth." [92] The decisiveness of Jesus' word is for Luther, as for Bultmann, the central connotation of Christ's witness. To deviate from this testimony, either to the left (by despising it) or to the right (by trying to improve on it), is fatal. [93] Luther, of course, could not have agreed with Bultmann's conclusion that therefore "Jesus is not presented in literal seriousness as a pre-existent divine being who came in human form to earth to

87. 33, 36, 29: "Bot[h]e.
88. 20, 613, 34; 615, 26.
89. 33, 550, 38; 28, 172, 10.
90. 20, 615, 24.
91. 33, 550, 39; 552, 28; 553, 13.
92. Bultmann, *Theology*, 2, 62.
93. 47, 35, 1; 44, 7.

reveal unprecedented secrets." [94] Rather, "Whoever will be justified before God must heed the witness, that is, the preacher. His is a preaching which witnesses only of things you will not see or hear, in the textbooks or anywhere else in the world: it testifies of invisible things." [95] Christ is the Father's witness par excellence from heaven, and the content of His testimony is how the Father is disposed to us and how He wants to make us blessed and free from sin, death, and the devil's might.[96]

The titles "messenger" and "witness" occur very infrequently and have little importance in themselves. But they have significance as pointers to a persistent theme in Luther—one we have already remarked upon—namely, that Christ's words are the Father's words. Whoever hears Christ, hears the Father. His word is the word of the divine majesty.[97] "The personal voice of God is now the discourse of Christ: if you have heard Him speak, you have heard God in person." [98] He has come in the Father's name and forgiven our sins.[99] This is a central element of Luther's doctrine, to which we shall shortly devote more detailed attention.[1] The constant refrain of the 1528 exposition of John 17 will again serve as an example of its importance to Luther: Christ speaks the Word of God, God speaks only through Him, He says everything God wants us to know—that is, necessary or salutary to know—and we can therefore have utter confidence that His words of forgiveness and gracious invitation are the perfect expression of God's loving will toward us.[2]

## Prophet

One of Ernesti's most cogent barbs against the traditional threefold-office formula was directed against the general dog-

94. *Theology*, 2, 62.
95. *47*, 178, 3.
96. *47*, 178, 8 and 10.
97. *28*, 118, 5; 124, 14.
98. *47*, 637, 35.
99. *29*, 586, 7.
1. See below, p. 88.
2. *28*, 94, 12; 123, 5–127, 15; 156, 1–5; 166, 2.

matic use of the *munus propheticum*. Scriptural usage, he argued, did not apply "prophet" as a general title to Christ.[3] Rather, he argued, the christological use of "prophet" was confined to the specific promise of "the prophet like Moses."

Ernesti here faithfully reflected Luther's usage: Luther almost always connects Christ's title as prophet with Deuteronomy 18:15ff. So far, then, from being a general heading for Christ's role as revealer, it is usually a specifically messianic term, as we have seen above.[4] Of course, the function of a prophet is to proclaim God's Word, so that Luther may call Christ's prophetic activity an "office," in his specific sense of "a preaching office."[5] It was, in fact, by His unprecedented preaching and miracles that Christ fulfilled Moses' prediction of the great prophet. So He could be recognized (as, for instance, Nicodemus recognized Him), and so he can still be acknowledged by thirsty souls as "the prophet, yes, the Christ Himself."[6]

The promise of a prophet like Moses is for Luther "the leading passage in the whole book" of Deuteronomy.[7] It provides him with very fruitful material for distinguishing the law from the gospel. There would have been no call for a prophet to supersede Moses if this prophet were merely to repeat what Moses had already transmitted most amply.[8] But the promise makes abundantly clear that the new prophet will bring another word, a new teaching: "it is therefore necessary that He be a teacher of life, grace, and righteousness, just as Moses is a teacher of sin, wrath, and death."[9] Moses yields his ministry to the future prophet.[10] This prophet, then, is the end of the law: with Him the teaching of Moses terminates.[11] It is the character of the law to place demands upon us; but "this prophet demands nothing—He grants

3. Ernesti, *Opuscula theologica*, pp. 420ff.
4. E.g. *33*, 425, 1; *47*, 162, 30; *51*, 5, 40; and see above, p. 31.
5. *46*, 602, 40.
6. *46*, 648, 9; *47*, 3, 20; *33*, 433, 33.
7. *14*, 675, 11.
8. *10/I/1*, 386, 3.
9. *14*, 676, 36; cf. *18*, 679, 30.
10. *14*, 679, 10; *31/II*, 1, 16.
11. *42*, 612, 27; *10/I/1*, 385, 22; *14*, 677, 12.

what Moses demands." For "it is two different things, to give a command and to be the truth." [12]

The point of God's promise of a prophet was dramatically illustrated by the experience of the children of Israel at Mt. Sinai, who cried out in terror when God spoke in the voice of His majesty, "with trumpetings and thunderclaps, and the whole mountain blazing, smoking, with a mighty rumbling of thunder." [13] For we could not endure if God were to confront us in His majesty and power: [14] nature cannot bear even a small glimmer of God's speaking. So God has acceded to our weakness, and utterly submerged His power, and spoken to us gently, plainly, humanly, in the person of His prophet. [15] But we will have Him in neither guise: [16] "the one we cannot endure, the other we will not accept." Yet it remains true that now God will be found only through the preaching of Christ, the prophet according to God's promise. [17] We have God's express command to listen to Him. [18] "'HIM you shall heed'—as if to say, 'Him alone and no one else!'" [19]

### Strange Work, Proper Office

It is true that the first office of Christ's kingdom—first in sequence, that is—is to make all men sinners. [20] But this is immediately contrasted with the real purpose of Christ's coming, which is the very opposite. This contrast brings to mind the significant distinction Luther drew, very early in his teaching career, between the "strange work" and the "proper work" of God—a distinction he based on Isaiah 28:21. [21] Corresponding to it was a

12. *14*, 677, 3; 22, 224, 1.
13. *47*, 37, 23.
14. *47*, 37, 21; *Br*, 2, 425, 32.
15. *47*, 210, 1 and 12; cf. *14*, 678, 21ff.
16. *47*, 38, 4; 210, 26.
17. *47*, 194, 18.
18. *30/III*, 340, 23; 42, 612, 25.
19. *40/I*, 456, 27.
20. *33*, 508, 17.
21. *1*, 112, 24; 5, 63, 5; 57 (III), 79, 15; 128, 7; cf. later *31/II*, 168, 31ff.

parallel distinction between Christ's "strange work" and "proper office" in the gospel. Because of its great importance in Luther's emerging *theologia crucis,* this distinction is widely held to be a persisting element of the dialectic of law and gospel in Luther's later writings.[22]

While the distinction does not entirely disappear from his later work,[23] it is a theme of so little importance to the older Luther that its appearances are very few and far between. Furthermore, insofar as remnants of the distinction do persist, it has undergone a decisive change. It has, in fact, been swallowed up by the law/gospel dialectic. Luther can no longer conceive of the gospel operating first and necessarily as a *cacangelium.*[24] Only the law, not the gospel, operates as a schoolmaster to drive us to Christ. This is precisely one of the points at which Luther's distinction between law and gospel is a decisive movement away from Augustine (and from mysticism). The movement consists in this: the site of the gospel's efficacy is no longer the transaction in my soul, by which, *per humilitatem,* the Word of God works upon me to make me conformable to Christ. Rather, its efficacy lies solely in what Christ accomplished. In other words, the gospel's efficacy is construed no longer as achieved within me, psychologically, but as achieved outside me historically. The gospel itself, therefore, has no other purpose than to tell me what Christ has done for me.[25]

In these terms, the dialectic of law and gospel is not primarily a dialectic of the existential impact of the Word of God. If it were, a given passage of Scripture could function as either law or gospel depending on the soul's response; the gospel could be either bad news or good news. But if this is the case in Luther's early lectures, he has later replaced it with a quite different dialectic. Now the distinction is between Moses and Christ, between demand and promise, and is located in the character of

22. *1*, 113, 5. On the distinction, see, e.g., Walther von Loewenich, *Luthers Theologia crucis* (4. Aufl., München, 1954), passim; Philip S. Watson, *Let God be God!* (London, 1958), pp. 156ff.

23. E.g. *25*, 190, 2ff.; *42*, 356, 23.

24. *1*, 113, 20.

25. *10/I/1*, 9, 11ff.

law and gospel themselves. In purely semantic terms the appropriate response to a demand is compliance, and the appropriate response to a promise is belief. The two must not be confused, however much our conscience tends to confuse them.[26] "To demand and to grant, to receive and to give, are exact and mutually exclusive opposites."[27] The law places demands upon us; the gospel makes no demand but is a promise, a gift, a declaration of God by which He offers us something.[28] Even though law and gospel are both addressed to us by God, the gospel has an eternal priority over the law: only the gospel has eternal validity. How does it gain this priority? With the demand of the law God makes us answerable, but with the promise of the gospel He makes Himself answerable. When God makes a promise, "He alone wants to be the agent and worker, and demands nothing from us but faith."[29] In the case of the law we are committed; in the case of the gospel God commits Himself. "When God makes a promise, He Himself undertakes the transaction with us—He gives and offers something to us. But when He issues a command through the law, He is requiring something from us and wants us to do something." As we have just heard, "it is two different things, to give a command and to be the truth."[30]

Christ is the subject of the gospel; He is the content of the promise. "We must therefore learn to distinguish all laws (even God's laws) and all works from faith and Christ, if we are to delineate Christ rightly. Christ is not the law. He is therefore not a taskmaster for the law and for works; but He is the Lamb of God Who takes away the sin of the world."[31]

Accordingly, Luther's descriptions of Christ as a preacher of reproof are introduced on a rather pragmatic level and are clearly not intended (as the earlier distinction was certainly intended) to carry much doctrinal weight. Christ is depicted ironically en-

26. *42, 567, 8; 637, 29.*
27. *40/I, 337, 17.*
28. *40/I, 337, 20; 42, 565, 12.*
29. *42, 660, 6; cf. 7, 588, 10; 13, 551, 18.*
30. *42, 566, 10 (cf. 30/II, 468, 29); 22, 224, 1.*
31. *40/I, 241, 17.*

couraging those who think they can keep the law to try! He threatens the obdurate, preaches repentance to the self-righteous, and makes explicit what reason could never admit—that all the world is subject to God's wrath, death, sin, hell, and everlasting damnation.[32] This is because the world is determined to go unreproved; but Christ (and His preachers) intend the reproof to continue, come what may.[33] This reproof is set in the context of God's worldly regime, in which the government and the hangman bring to light and punish blatant darkness and coarse vices, but Christ and the Church reveal the subtle darkness of false doctrine and religion.[34] Yet if threats must be directed without hesitation to the wicked, hypocritical, smug, proud, and insolent [35]—if it is pious people like Nicodemus who need "a good, sharp sermon of repentence" [36]—such threats are not directed to Christ's own little flock. The worldly realm must be distinguished from the spiritual realm. Christ does not stop at reducing all men to sinners, but He absolves them.[37] Unlike the devil, even if Christ begins by terrifying, He is sure to bring comfort: He does not want us to remain terrified.[38] Those who feel the weight of their sins know that to them Christ addresses not His rebukes but His consolation.[39] "You fear God and believe in God; so it is not the law but the gospel that applies to you." [40] Everyone should hear the words intended for him—the obstinate words of wrath; the fearful, sweet words of consolation.[41] "Therefore even though Christ Himself sometimes threatens and frightens, I should not apply it to myself. For it is directed to the puffed up, impenitent, hardened, and reckless despisers of His Word and grace." [42] It must be applied at the right time and place: to burden a Chris-

32. *47,* 143, 9; *45,* 473, 22; *21,* 529, 26; 530, 6; *33,* 508, 23.
33. *47,* 129, 23; 130, 5.
34. *47,* 129, 31–36.
35. *40/I,* 534, 19; *43,* 65, 6; *45,* 473, 26.
36. *21,* 529, 35.
37. *33,* 505, 31.
38. *21,* 245, 4.
39. *33,* 507, 38ff.; 509, 6ff.
40. *43,* 65, 4.
41. *43, 47,* 21.
42. *45,* 474, 32.

tian man with threats of judgment is a devilish perversion of God's truth.[43]

## Preacher

The "proper office" of Christ upon earth was as preacher of the gospel [44]—a "blessed, comforting preacher" Who spoke "only sweet words," Whose "every utterance spoke of consolation," Who would "still the conscience, not alarm it." [45] For this preacher preaches something higher than Moses. He brings not rules but life.[46] "Make a distinction between Me and Moses. You are thirsty because of Moses, who has performed his task and fulfilled his office of frightening you and making you thirsty—but now, this time, come to Me; believe in Me, hear My teaching. I am a different kind of preacher. I will give you drink and refresh you." [47] Luther comments, "He who masters the art of making the essential distinction between law and gospel really deserves to be called a theologian" and illustrates the law's office and ability to terrify consciences by his own anguish and that of Staupitz, his Augustinian superior and confessor.[48] At last, weary of despair, one abandons piety, Moses, and the law, and clings instead to Christ's words, "Come to Me." "For this preacher does not teach you that you can love God, or how you should act and live, but says how you can be innocent and blessed despite your inability—a different preaching from Moses and the law!" [49]

It is easy to see why "preacher" and "teacher" occur so frequently among the titles Luther applies to Christ. They appear in his preaching at every period of his career, but reach a peak in his sermons around the year 1530. For example, in the running exposition of John 6–8 in 1530–32, there is scarcely a sermon where one or both of these titles does not appear.

43. *45*, 474, 37 to 475, 3.
44. *28*, 62, 11; 31/II, 515, 30.
45. *46*, 650, 7; 33, 393, 25; *21*, 456, 30; 29, 362, 18.
46. *29*, 355, 17; 17/I, 277, 31.
47. *33*, 431, 10.
48. *33*, 431, 27.
49. *33*, 431, 40 to 432, 13.

As we have seen, preaching is at the center of Christ's office and His mission. Here we must recall that for Luther "preacher" was not (like the *munus propheticum* of the orthodox) a theological category but a matter of fact. The historical Jesus was a preacher. The fact that Luther so often employs the present tense when speaking of the work of Christ must not be allowed to obscure his strictly historical approach: the usage is a genuine historic present. So far from implying any sort of transcendent activity symbolized by theological words, his very use of the present tense is for Luther a function of the historical continuity between the words of the man Christ and the contemporary preacher's words. He no more intends to depart from the historical events than our use of the present tense about Luther (in this sentence, for instance) implies that we have some access to Luther's thought other than Luther's recorded utterances.

On the contrary, Luther makes much of the historical setting of Christ's preaching. Christ began His preaching after His baptism in Jordan.[50]

He came in obscurity as a preacher to the Jewish people (33, 231, 8; 387, 37). He preached in only a small corner (49, 149, 12), over a period of three and a half years (47, 131, 31; 133, 38), much of it in His Capernaum parish and Jerusalem (33, 244, 35; 571, 24). It was in His preaching that He was assailed and rejected (33, 463, 4ff.; 37, 591, 33; 47, 180, 25), and in His preaching, too, that He was confessed (33, 467, 33; 469, 24; 473, 38ff.). Even Luther's superlatives are applied not only devotionally to the content of Christ's preaching but historically to their original delivery: "the Lord Christ was the very best preacher, better than the other apostles" (47, 60, 17); He was "a faithful preacher" (21, 529, 36), "an excellent preacher," equipped with testimony from heaven (47, 185, 26), a preacher altogether more excellent than Moses and the prophets, since He possessed the Spirit without measure (47, 196, 13); His "greatest work" was preaching the gospel to the poor (10/I/2, 159, 22; 31/II, 516, 4); if He, the best of preachers, provoked trouble, little wonder that the gospel is still opposed (33, 463, 4ff.). So, too, the words, "He came unto

50. 10/I/2, 202, 22ff.

His own and His own received Him not," apply not to His Incarnation but to "His coming as preacher, for His coming is His
preaching and illumining" (10/I/1, 225, 15; cf. 12, 285, 27).

A vital concomitant of the historicity of Christ's preaching is
the essential role of the external word—a favorite theme of Luther's, which may not be facilely explained by his need for a stick
to beat the *Schwärmer*. Certainly he belabored them with it; but
his initial opposition to them was the effect, not the cause, of his
devotion to the external word, a devotion resting not on expe-
diency but on a sound intuition of the role of "the words" in unit-
ing the soul to Christ. "Christ penetrates your heart through the
medium of the gospel, by way of your hearing, and dwells there
by your faith." [51] (Ernst Bizer is undoubtedly correct in assigning an all-important place to this intuition in Luther's
evolution.) [52] Christ "came with the external word," and He ini-
tiated the ministry of that external word.[53] When He said, "The
word which ye hear is not Mine but the Father's Who sent Me,"
He spoke "of the oral word which they heard from Him, and
magnifies it so greatly that whoever scorns and rejects it, scorns
not the speaker, but the divine majesty." [54] Such an insistence on
the external word implies, first, the normative character of
Christ's preaching as the yardstick of true Christian discourse.
Even the Holy Spirit is bound by the limit and standard of
Christ's word [55] (just as Christ bound His own preaching by the
limit and standard of the Father's word).[56] Secondly, the external word of Christ's preaching is not only normative but efficacious. The reason why this preacher must not be supplanted is
that His is the Word of God: He has divine power in His
words.[57] Unlike some modern writers (such as Wingren and

51. 10/I/1, 48, 16; cf. 19, 490, 4.

52. Ernst Bizer, *Fides ex auditu: Eine Untersuchung über die Entdeckung der
Gerechtigkeit Gottes durch Martin Luther* (2., erweiterte Aufl., Neukirchen, 1961).

53. 12, 521, 23; 50, 629, 17.

54. 21, 466, 36; cf. 40/II, 254, 23; 43, 71, 1.

55. 12, 576, 1ff.; 18, 137, 13; 21, 445, 13ff.; 468, 35.

56. 21, 471, 7.

57. 47, 195, 11 and 16ff.; 45, 186, 13.

Bultmann),[58] who are dependent on Luther's doctrine of the Word, Luther himself does not attribute this character to Christ's words on the ground that He is the Word. Luther does not draw systematic lines between "the cosmic Word" and "the historical Word." On the contrary, according to Luther, Christ's calling as preacher is the function of His human office, not of His divine nature.[59] Christ could have coerced men by His power but chose to win them by His preaching.[60] His human words are efficacious not because He is the Word but precisely because "the words which I speak are not Mine, but the Father's Who sent Me." [61] The divine power in the words of Christ's preaching is to be sought in three factors—their source, their content, and their application.

I have already spoken at length of the source of Christ's words in His commission by the Father as messenger, prophet, witness, and especially preacher. Because of this office, we take what Christ preaches to be the Word of God the Father.

> When Luther uses the expression "the Word of God" (as he does constantly), he may refer to one of several objects. Very often "God's Word" is simply identified with Scripture (e.g. 8, 484, 11ff.; 30/II, 472, 23; 45, 494, 12; 510, 7; 48, 31, 4: 36). Just as often, it means the gospel—either the whole doctrine of the gospel (e.g. 32, 540, 16; 33, 237, 4 and 9; 45, 653, 19 to 654, 28; DB, 11/I, 7, 2), in which case even the Creed can be "God's Word," (45, 732, 6), or the gospel presented in a given sermon or sacrament (e.g. 30/II, 483, 8; 45, 521, 34). Sometimes it means the law (14, 547, 20); sometimes, both law and gospel (46, 12, 15); sometimes, particular statements attributed to God within the Scriptures, especially those that set God's seal upon earthly callings (12, 235, 24; 42, 80, 2). In each case "the Word of God" is not something different from the external words, nor is it a symbol of God manifest, but has its almighty power simply because it is God Who says it (e.g. 30/II, 483, 12; 45, 544, 35ff.; 664, 9). The truth and power of the

---

58. Gustaf Wingren, *The Living Word* (Philadelphia, 1960), pp. 65f. and passim; Bultman, *Theology*, 2, 63ff.

59. *33, 358, 1.*

60. *10/III, 175, 17.*

61. *40/II, 255, 29; 45, 521, 21.*

Word are guaranteed by the person of the speaker. So it is with the Word of God as we receive it now exclusively in the words of Christ the preacher, Who speaks nothing but grace, love, consolation, help, and bliss (45, 612, 26–34).

We have also spoken at length about the second aspect of the power of this preaching—namely, its content. We have seen that Christ preached of His commission as the preacher from God. Luther can say, almost in the same breath, that this preacher "does not point away from Himself to another" and that His preaching "constantly points to Another." [62] In obedience to His commission He preached to propose faith in Himself, to direct men to Himself as the only way to the Father.[63] For what the Father commanded this preacher to offer was "everlasting life, forgiveness of sins, and redemption from death and eternal damnation," treasures to be found only in Christ, the "blessed, comforting preacher Who not only proclaims but brings and gives" light, mercy, fullness, and the power and privilege of being God's child.[64] "He alone brings us the Word which contains everything . . . We possess a preacher Who has all . . . a preacher from Whose inexhaustible fullness we can draw, and drinking at this fountain assuage our thirst of body and soul." [65]

This brings us, thirdly, to the application of Christ's preaching to His hearers. It is to thirsty souls that His gospel is offered. He preaches not to the smug and self-satisfied but to the afflicted, to men buffeted by the flesh, the devil, and the world. To those who thirst, His preaching is a refreshing stream of life, exerting such torrential force "that it can wash a myriad of devils from the heart." [66] But the operation of this mighty power is deceptive in its simplicity. "It is a simple process," Luther says. "All you have to do is hear it, read it, and preach it." [67] The weak sound of a voice or the puny symbols of a printed page or the mere thoughts

62. 33, 394, 20–37.
63. 33, 153, 19; 394, 22.
64. 33, 572, 7; 46, 650, 7 (cf. 20, 391, 5).
65. 47, 196, 21, 29, and 36.
66. 33, 433, 29; 10/I/2, 160, 2; 45, 567, 23; 33, 436, 26 and 37.
67. 33, 436, 29.

of the heart certainly do not appear so potent, but "Oh! the spoken Word can achieve more than you can see and understand." [68] (The gospel is more appropriately spoken than written.) [69] "The oral Word is a living Word . . . I know it well, for I have experienced it in tribulations and afflictions." [70] The context for the significance of the gospel does not need to be supplied from without: it is supplied by the need of the heart in bondage to sin and death.

This is the proper context for the appropriation of the gospel even though it remains true that no one comes to Christ unless the Father draw him and the Holy Spirit write the Word upon his heart. For in the light of Luther's frequent use of such expressions it must be observed that he does not teach a secret *testimonium internum*. The Spirit's testimony is not secret, in the sense that the Spirit makes entrance into our hearts and brings conviction, peace, and joy by no other means than the public, oral Word. Certainly the Spirit may be described as present "in a twofold way, manifestly and secretly in the heart"; [71] but the means by which He effects His presence in the secrecy of the heart are not themselves secret. The Spirit bears witness "not as He is in heaven, invisible in His divine essence, but publicly manifests Himself by His external office and allows Himself to be heard through His Word." [72] God has ordained that no one shall receive the knowledge of Christ, or forgiveness, or the Spirit apart from the external Word and public ministry: the oral Word must be grasped with the ears if the Spirit is to enter the heart.[73] It is not flesh and blood that reveal to us the truth, but the Holy Spirit reveals it. Nevertheless, it is only flesh and blood that the Holy Spirit employs to teach us the truth. By the same token, it is the Father's revelation, through Christ's preaching, of His abundant mercy and paternal love that draws us to Christ. "You hear that God is not angry with you, but is your gracious and merciful

68. 33, 438, 6.
69. 10/I/1, 17, 7; 12, 259, 5.
70. 33, 438, 12.
71. 20, 750, 6; cf. 18, 136, 9; 31/II, 674, 10.
72. 21, 286, 33; cf. 25, 412, 27; 29, 578, 38ff.; 579, 9ff.
73. 29, 579, 25ff.; 43, 187, 7.

Father Who gave His Son for you, let Him die for you, and raised Him from the dead—He points you to the Son and has Him preached to you. If this is rightly taught, then we come to Him: that is what this 'drawing' means." [74]

So the words of Christ's preaching (and every word that conforms to that preaching) is the living Word of God. The Word is living and powerful not because it is the means of redemption; for Luther it is not the means of redemption but the account given so that we may use the means (not the means of redemption, we could say, but the means of grace); [75] not because it ever becomes a living Word in a mysterious act of God: this would have seemed to Luther a docetic (suprahistorical) disparagement of the external Word, which was the living Word in the historic act of Christ's preaching; not because it makes Christ contemporaneous: a proposition which, of the presence of the historical Christ, is untrue, of the presence of the ascended Christ by His Word and Holy Spirit, is tautologous. No, the liveliness of Christ's preached Word in its application to us is none of these things. Rather, it is the means by which the Father draws our hearts to Christ, so that clinging in faith to His achievement alone, we are one with Him as His words become one with our hearts. [76] That is to say, it is the means by which we are taught the use of Christ's life, death, and Resurrection—namely, that it is for us. This is the sense in which Luther can say that Christ's birth would have been useless unless it had been preached to us; that He could have been crucified a thousand times without our reaping the benefits of His Passion, had we never learnt the use of His Passion. [77] But if we locate the context of the Word's application in the need of the sinner, and the effect of the Word's action in the discovery of the *pro me*, we must be doubly cautious not to ascribe to Luther a subjective principle of individual interpretation. The *pro me* is not a hermeneutical principle for Luther but is explicitly declared in the gospel itself. (Luther's principle

74. 33, 131, 20.
75. 26, 40, 9.
76. 45, 679, 6.
77. 10/I/1, 79, 14; I/2, 203, 5; 17/II, 234, 13; 26, 40, 10; 34/I, 318, 12; etc.

of correct interpretation was not, we recall, justification by faith but *"Christum treiben,"* which he correctly believed to be the early catholic principle of apostolicity and canonicity.[78] It was not a norm or canon which he applied *to* the Scripture, but a principle he found insistently applied *by* the Scripture.)

Without question, Luther would have reacted to the utter complexity of modern theologizing about the appropriation of the gospel with the same dismay he felt toward the turgidities of late scholastic logic-chopping. For to Luther the glory of Christ's preaching was the limpid simplicity of it. We have no need to search desperately for ways to appropriate His gospel: He Himself, in His preaching, has told us how we may. Those who seek according to this preacher's directions will find.[79] And the directions are simplicity itself. First, in order to understand, we must accept Christ as our preacher from God.[80] Next, we must learn to understand Christ's language; but this is no occasion of difficulty, for His speech is "so simple and childlike . . . His words and actions accommodated to His hearers." That He will "chat and whisper" with us in order that we may be gently drawn to faith "is great and abounding humility, that the highest majesty would humble Himself utterly to the level of poor, weak disciples without understanding." [81] Luther implies that because of our blindness or hardness of heart, learning Christ's language may take a long time—indeed, will occupy us all our days; yet by persistence in clinging to the words of Christ's preaching we will find ourselves drawn by this preacher, first to Himself, and thus to God, as we allow His words and our hearts to become one.[82]

## Teacher, Master, Doctor

To make graphic the identity of faith with learning Christ's language and how to use it, Luther very often employs "teacher,"

78. *DB,* 7, 384–85, 27.
79. 33, 158, 15.
80. 33, 366, 11.
81. 49, 267, 13; 46, 99, 33; 100, 19 and 33.
82. 45, 612, 8; 679, 6.

"master," or "doctor" to express the same activities he has ascribed to Christ as "preacher." Because much emphasis has been
placed on Luther's occasional remark to the effect that Christ is
*not* a teacher, it is interesting to discover that his positive use of
the title far outweighs this special negative use.

Since "Christ the teacher" means much the same to Luther as
"Christ the preacher" (the titles are sometimes joined), our summary need only be brief. Christ was instituted teacher at His baptism: the sign of the dove was His doctor's biretta! [83] He was an
unrivaled, wonderful, and surpassing teacher, confident of His
teaching commission and faithful to it.[84] He was both recognized
as a teacher from God and slandered, mocked, and ignored in
this capacity: it is appalling that this teacher, shepherd, and
bishop was not received.[85]

> It is an inexpressibly precious gift that God has given us in this
> doctor and teacher (46, 603, 13; 718, 40). For God is known as
> Father insofar as Christ is acknowledged to be our teacher (47,
> 229, 6 and 10ff.). The teaching of Christ is exclusively the light
> of the world (33, 512, 9; 47, 108, 15). What He taught is the yard-
> stick and touchstone of true doctrine. He is the only teacher Who
> can teach us correctly (40/II, 278, 29). He is the master commenta-
> tor on Scripture, the best dialectician in theology (37, 588, 23; 45,
> 638, 20; 47, 777, 16), for He taught how we might know God, how
> to live and how to die—not too much and not too little (10/III,
> 171, 15; 46, 768, 28 to 769, 16; 770, 24 to 771, 3; 780, 15–20). In
> this He must be distinguished from Moses and all other teachers;
> indeed, all other teachers must be dismissed (21, 317, 28; 320, 37;
> 330, 27ff.; 25, 432, 24–29; 46, 770, 26). His teaching comes with a
> divine power that defies human reason (17/II, 234, 3). It is differ-
> ent and imperishable, for no other teacher but He graciously re-
> veals God's loving heart (45, 695, 37ff.). This teacher instructs us
> how we may come to the knowledge of Himself (10/I/2, 434, 24).
> For the content of His instruction is God's eternal decree, "Thou
> art My Son" (40/II, 242, 30). Therefore He teaches that man be-
> comes blessed only through faith in Him (34/I, 435, 11).

83. 10/I/1, 214, 13; 13, 647, 38; 34/I, 25, 13; 46, 602, 32.
84. 33, 331, 3; 533, 35; 46, 649, 7; 47, 196, 13.
85. 17/II, 231, 35ff.; 46, 603, 13; 47, 3, 20.

We learn that He is both gift and teacher when He says that not only is the Word of everlasting life His, but that He is also the way to that life.[86] (In this connection, Luther does occasionally say that Christ is not a teacher—that is, He is not a teacher of works, but master and teacher in that He both declares and is the way.[87] The error of the scholastics is that they call Christ only a teacher Who proclaims good works.[88] In this sense Christ is to be known as offering and gift rather than teacher, since He cuts across the world's pious talk with His new doctrine, not of works, but of rebirth.)[89]

Rather infrequently, Luther uses "doctor," the formal academic title, in place of "teacher" as a title of Christ. Reflecting Luther's own reliance on his doctor's degree as the source of his official prerogative to expound Scripture and combat heresy, "doctor" applied to Christ seems also to underline Christ's right and commission to teach.

> We must away with unsealed doctors, and hold fast to the doctor Whom God has sealed—hence the sign of the dove as His biretta (33, 19, 34; 46, 602, 32). Not only at His baptism but also at the transfiguration, God designated Him our doctor and teacher (14, 27, 15). "In questions of doctrine we must hang on the lips of none but this man and disregard the *Fladdergeister*—there is only one doctor, and His name is Christ" (33, 563, 15). Christ is the light of the world and set apart from all other teachers, doctors, and preachers (33, 512, 1ff.). As preacher and doctor He has an indisputable commission to propose faith in Himself (33, 153, 20). There is no other doctor, teacher, or preacher who resides in the Godhead and bosom of the Father but the one doctor, Christ (46, 672, 17).

More frequently, Christ is called "master." In some of these instances "master" is used to describe the relation of lord to servants. Christ corrects as a friendly and kind lord and master; the Christian's life is service to this master, Who though He was our

86. *47*, 230, 35ff.
87. *45*, 497, 24ff.
88. *33*, 172, 6.
89. *17*/I, 277, 22; *21*, 364, 5ff.; *528*, 34; *47*, 8, 6.

master freely became our servant.[90] Usually, however, the relation is rather of teacher to pupils. (Luther often links "master
and teacher," [91] and sometimes for clarity uses *Magister* instead
of *Meister* whilst preaching in German.) [92] Christ is the master,
we are His pupils.[93] Of course, it is not enough to begin as this
master's disciple and then forsake Him when He speaks against
our liking.[94] This was precisely the Pharisees' reaction when
Christ discomforted them with His masterful dialectics.[95] We,
however, must occupy ourselves with the learning process, devot-
ing ourselves to reading, hearing, and delighting in the Word
until we exclaim, " 'This is truly God's Word.' Thus faith is
educed, and if you confess it and feel in your heart that you confess it truly, then you may count yourself one of the Lord Christ's
pupils, will let Him be your master and submit to Him. In this
way you will be saved, for everything rests on not forsaking or
leaving the Word of His mouth." [96] For we must deal with God
at the point where He directs—namely, this master and teacher
called Christ.[97] The world will not have Him thus: the self-righteous despise Him as master and teacher.[98] But though He lets
Himself be mastered, He remains the supreme master, to Whom
God subordinates the holy and the wise. He is the one and only
master.[99]

90. *45*, 490, 21; *22*, 293, 24; *12*, 339, 15.
91. E.g. *33*, 24, 35; 119, 31; 521, 30; *45*, 497, 24; 514, 6.
92. E.g. *33*, 521, 33; 648, 10.
93. *28*, 146, 5; *33*, 369, 17; *45*, 683, 14.
94. *33*, 648, 9.
95. *37*, 588, 27.
96. *33*, 147, 23 to 148, 9.
97. *45*, 514, 5.
98. *33*, 24, 32.
99. *33*, 119, 27; 17, 33; 29, 12, 6; 13, 4; *31*/II, 117, 17.

# 3.   The Knowledge of God in Christ

The office of the preacher Christ is to direct us to Himself as both the source and content of the faithful knowledge of God. Three traits of Luther's doctrine of Christ have emerged persistently in our study of this theme: its historical realism, its soteriological orientation, and its insistence on the uniqueness, necessity, and all-sufficiency of Christ. This last characteristic becomes so predominant that in it consists not only the thrust of his doctrine of Christ but the focus and pivot of all his theology, to which even the doctrine of justification is ancillary.

The epitome of this concentration is Luther's famous dictum, "There is no other God." [1] This is not some form of Monarchianism or Christomonism. In fact, on the level of dogma it is actually an affirmation of the undivided Godhead of the Holy Trinity. Because Christ is one essence with the Father, there is no God but the one Who in Christ became man, suffered, and died. [2] However, this is not the primary usefulness of the expression for Luther: here, as usual, he is speaking soteriologically. Luther allows that there is a feeble natural knowledge of God attainable through reason or the law. [3] But now that He has revealed Himself decisively and exclusively in Christ, God will be known no longer as creator or lawgiver. [4] Now God wants to be known only by faith; that is, God wants to be known only in Christ (these

1. E.g. 20, 727, 6; 30/III, 132, 23; 35, 456, 14; 40/II, 256, 20; 45, 550, 13; 589, 1; 46, 763, 2; etc.
2. 45, 550, 22 to 551, 4; Tr, 2, 16: 1265.
3. 8, 629, 23ff.; 19, 206, 7; 21, 509, 18; 46, 667, 10ff.
4. 28, 94, 9; 40/I, 602, 18; 607, 28; 45, 717, 6.

statements are identical). In this sense especially, "there is no other God" beyond Christ.

We may take this further. The knowledge of God by reason or the law is a *cognitio legalis,* a "left-handed knowledge," partial, corrupted, and ultimately invalid.[5] It is a knowledge of God with His back turned. "So walk round God and look at His face!" Luther exclaims.[6] In the only-begotten Son we look directly into God's face. In Him we see the glorious God; we see this glory face to face. This is the true and proper "right-handed knowledge," the knowledge of the God of grace and truth.[7] "It is sure knowledge, a true and divine certainty which does not deceive us but portrays God's very self in a specific form, apart from which there is no God."[8]

In Luther's earlier thinking he had been much exercised by the concept of the *deus absconditus.* Because the Luther who found the mystics congenial has in turn been found congenial by modern scholars, especially of the Ritschlian school, his early reflections on this theme have received very close attention.[9] So much emphasis has been placed upon them, however, that the extent to which Luther later modified his *theologia crucis,* and in particular his concept of *deus absconditus,* generally has been misrepresented. In his early works Luther conceives of the hiddenness of God on two levels—the abysmal incomprehensibility of the divine essence and majesty, and the hiding of divine grace *sub contraria* even in His self-revelation. In this latter sense the cross is both the revelation of God's love and yet perhaps the ultimate expression of His hiddenness: the paradox of the *deus crucifixus* epitomizes the tension of faith which finds God's "yes" hidden in His "no," His revelation hidden in the very means of revelation.[10] For such a faith the highest expression of confidence in God's

---

5. *19,* 206, 7ff.; *46,* 668, 11ff.

6. *46,* 672, 26.

7. *40/III,* 587, 30; *42,* 514, 31; *46,* 669, 1ff.

8. *40/I,* 602, 24.

9. See John Dillenberger, *God Hidden and Revealed* (Philadelphia, 1953), and the extensive literature reviewed by Dillenberger's essay; von Loewenich, *Luthers Theologia Crucis,* 21ff.; and cf. Luther's comment in *46,* 667, 7: "Diese frage wird einmal noch unglück anrichten"!

10. E.g. *1,* 362, 23; 613, 23; *3,* 301, 34 to 302, 7.

goodness is *resignatio ad infernum*. At this juncture the "visible things"—that is, the vehicles of revelation—mean the same thing for Luther as "the back parts of God" and are identified with cross and suffering (Christ's and ours).[11]

Now we have just seen that, later, Luther contrasts "the back parts of God" with the revelation we have received in Christ, in Whom we look directly into God's face. The "back parts" are now the rational knowledge of God from creation and law.[12] This contrast strikingly demonstrates the way in which Luther has changed his mind. It remains true that God is utterly incomprehensible in His essence and majesty; but in Christ, God is not hidden but revealed—revealed not *sub contraria* but as He truly is. Of course, to reason this revelation is still hidden *sub contraria*, but strictly speaking, the revelation is not offered or available to reason.[13] Whereas earlier, however, the revelation was hidden *sub contraria* even (perhaps especially) for faith, now Luther insists that faith in Christ is the right, proper, open, enlightening, and unobscured knowledge of God's true mind and heart.

Much of the confusion over this issue arises from two circumstances. First, in his academic discussions of the knowledge of God (that is, in polemics, lectures, and disputations) Luther continued throughout his life to use the technical scholastic terms familiar to his readers and students even as he modified their use; and while much of the development we have described is complete by the time of *De servo arbitrio* (1525), remnants of his earlier view still appear. This is especially true of the curious argument that hiddenness is essential to make possible a faith in things not seen (a shallow notion not even consonant with later sections of the same treatise, but persisting into even later works).[14]

Secondly, because Luther's use of the language of hiddenness is largely confined to the polemic against inordinate reason, to read it as an epistemology of faith is to misrepresent him. It is addressed not to the capacity of faith but to the capacity of reason.

11. *1*, 354, 17–20; cf. Augustine, *De Trin.* II, xvii, 28 (MPL XLII, 864).
12. *46*, 672, 24.
13. *21*, 516, 5.
14. *18*, 633, 7–24 (n.b. "Qui nostra legerunt, habent haec sibi vulgatissima"); cf. *37*, 73, 28. For technical terminology, see, e.g., *18*, 684, 35ff.; *42*, 294–96; etc.

Luther came to apply a simple but neglected rubric to all his mature treatment of the knowledge of God—namely, that reason,
faith, and the unveiled vision of God are related to each other as
areas of distinct competence.[15]

Reason (if only human presumption could keep within
bounds) is in fact competent to attain a genuine rational knowledge of God—genuine in the sense that if it discloses the awe of
the creator God and the wrath against sin of the holy God of the
law, it concludes rightly within its area of competence.[16] But
precisely because this is as far as its competence extends, it yields
only a left-handed knowledge of God with His back turned. Luther does more than refer to Exodus 33:17ff. with this image: that
God turns His back on us implies that our minds can properly divine only the disfavor of God, and raises the central question,
"How can I get a gracious God?" Here, human reason is out of its
depth; but God takes pity on our estate and preaches the gospel
of Christ to us, declaring His true will and heart of love and favor
toward us in spite of our bondage. This goes against all human
reason: only faith is competent here. The knowledge of God
yielded in faith is genuine and true—"right-handed"—in a way in
which rational knowledge can never be. It is really the vision of
God's countenance because God has indeed swallowed up judgment in mercy, wrath in grace, terror in gentleness, and death in
life. This is the way God is disposed to us, and it is declared to us
without any contrariety in Christ.

Is it not true, nevertheless, that the majesty of God is hidden in
the humanity of Christ and the weakness of the external Word
and sign? Certainly (even though Luther says so far less often
than he is reputed to do).[17] This in no way qualifies the assertion
that Christ and His Word are the light for faith or that in Him
we see God as He really is. Luther very carefully guards against
the danger attendant upon any *deus absconditus* concept, that in

15. Cf. the "three lights"—of nature, grace, and glory—in *18, 785, 26*: "vulgata
et bona distinctio."

16. E.g. *46, 667, 10* (cf. *666, 14*). See Brian Gerrish, *Grace and Reason* (Oxford, 1962); Watson, *Let God Be God!*, pp. 73ff.

17. *10/I/1, 223, 23; 47, 210, 17.*

Christ faith is left with an announcement or anticipation of revelation, but no real fact of revelation. This is the very point of the
affirmation, "There is no other God." The distinction between the
*deus nudus* and the *deus incarnatus* is not an ontological distinction between God and His revelation but a statement about the
capacity of human nature to endure the presence of God. It is
parallel, we may recall, to the contrast between the terror of Sinai
and the gentleness of Christ. "I know what I am talking about
from experience!" Luther exclaims.[18] In other words, his purpose
is not the axiomatic logical distinction between God as incomprehensible and God as apprehended by men, but an empirical distinction between two ways in which men do apprehend God.[19]
If it were not so, we could not say, "There is no other God," for
we should have no way of knowing whether God as revealed in
Christ was the same as God hidden in Himself. But Christ is indeed God's very self, and therefore God can and will be known
only by faith in Christ; to seek Him apart from the Word is devilish and the sure road to disaster.[20] The revelation in Christ is not
a makeshift, interim revelation, one day to be superseded by the
real revelation. We see through a glass darkly not because the
glory of God in Christ is not visible to faith, but because our faith
is so weak. We possess, but do not see, our eternal felicity.[21]
Christ as the light shining in darkness will one day yield up the
kingdom to His Father, and then we shall no longer see through a
glass darkly, but the unveiled majesty of God will be seen by the
light of glory.[22] Until that day the man Christ is the light of men,
and because Christ and faith belong together, the external, visible things are not to be regarded as hiddenness, for they are the
true revelation of God as He is for us.

We must assiduously bear in mind Luther's soteriological purpose if we are to avoid the complexities modern theology has im-
posed upon this theme. The faithful man must simply cling to the

18. 40/I, 78, 18.
19. Cf. also 42, 294, 36ff.; 43, 403, 8.
20. 28, 135, 15; 45, 481, 9ff.; 47, 58, 1ff.; 90, 38ff.
21. 28, 194, 11 to 196, 13; 31/II, 655, 6ff.
22. 10/I/1, 223, 7ff.; 14, 27, 22ff.; 45, 232, 16.

person of Christ, and Christ alone, if he is to discover a gracious God—that is, to discover God as He is, for God is gracious. Thus Christ is solely sufficient for our salvation. This is the point at which God has designated we shall deal with Him. Here we meet God in Christ, Who is the image and quintessence of God for us. Here God pours Himself out for us, so that there can be no inconsistency between the veiling of His majesty and His presence fully as He is.

### The Essence and Fullness of God

Christ alone is the truth and the embodiment of the Father's will.[23] Everything—eternal majesty, life, and power—is concentrated in the Son.[24] To seek God outside Him is not only vain but leads to damnation.[25] Everything has been placed upon Him: we dare take no other way. Outside Him is sheer blindness, idolatry, and ignorance.[26] Therefore the man who ignores the person of Christ has not encountered the right God.[27] Obversely, to trust in Christ is to encounter God.[28] He who wants to encounter God must encounter Him where He may be grasped as He cannot be grasped in His majesty: in the incarnate God, Who lies in His mother's lap, and in the crucified God.[29] To cling solely to Christ as He goes through death to the Father is the only way to find God.[30]

Therefore faith is centered completely in Christ. It does not want to know anything else; there is no God except Him.[31] Even though we know that the Father and the Son are to be distinguished in person, yet for our faith we hold them as one. When

23. 40/II, 256, 20; 46, 772, 25.
24. 28, 135, 10; 47, 59, 22.
25. 20, 605, 9; 32, 348, 7; 40/I, 602, 18; 46, 762, 24; 47, 90, 38.
26. 47, 197, 10; 198, 39 to 199, 9.
27. 45, 482, 1.
28. 45, 483, 16 and 25; see the summary of such passages in Eduard Ellwein, *Summus Evangelistica: Die Botschaft des Johannesevangeliums in der Auslegung Luthers* (München, 1960), pp. 113f.
29. 28, 486, 23 to 487, 10; 43, 73, 4.
30. 45, 511, 24.
31. 20, 605, 11; 40/II, 305, 36; 45, 549, 29–32.

we see Christ with the eyes of faith, we see the Father too. Because there is no God apart from Him, His words and works are the words and works of God.[32] What He says, the Father says;[33] what He does, the Father does;[34] what He gives, the Father gives;[35] what He accepts is accepted by the Father,[36] and as He is disposed, the Father also is disposed.[37] As Christ spoke, acted, and died, so did God Himself.[38] So also, whoever adores Him adores God; whoever despises Him despises God.[39] That "Christ is in the Father" (with the identity of will, word, and work this implies) is for Luther "the chiefest article and cardinal point" of Christian faith.[40]

Luther's favorite passage for expressing this oneness is Colossians 2:3 and 9, which he uses occasionally as a formal christological affirmation, but constantly to point to Christ as the only and all-sufficient essence of the knowledge of God.[41] If in other things there are, so to speak, only tiny particles of deity, in Christ we have the entire inheritance. The entire Godhead dwells in Christ "in such a way that whoever does not find or receive God in Christ shall nevermore and nowhere have or find God outside Christ, even if he goes above heaven, below hell, or clear out of the cosmos!"[42] God is to be found only in the Son born of Mary. In Him alone is grace, salvation, and life: apart from Him all notions of God are vain speculation and empty idolatry.[43] "In this crucified God dwells all the fullness of the Godhead bodily."[44] John 14, too, we should frame in gold of Araby, Luther says. For

32. 45, 549, 33; 515, 8; 521, 2.
33. 28, 123, 5 to 127, 15; 33, 392, 1.
34. 15, 506, 10; 28, 117, 2.
35. 48, 178: 233.
36. 28, 127, 1; 135, 6.
37. 20, 393, 16; 28, 126, 8f.; 45, 515, 28; 522, 26.
38. 28, 117, 2; 125, 1.
39. 40/II, 594, 30.
40. 45, 589, 25.
41. E.g. 20, 605, 11; 23, 131, 20; 28, 486, 24; 40/II, 305, 19; 43, 73, 3; 45, 481, 20; 515, 10; 520, 38; 549, 31; 46, 555, 35; 759, 7; 762, 23; 47, 196, 15; 202, 13 and 38; etc.
42. 40/II, 584, 29; 50, 267, 7.
43. 40/II, 305, 17.
44. 28, 486, 24.

in His Son, God has given us a gift as great as Himself, Christ, the fountain of all grace and goodness, the very essence of the treasures of God.[45] He is not Son of God as other sons, but He is the quintessence, kernel, and only-begotten, Who alone has God's seal and testimony, that all should look to Him Who was given and offered to be our sole help.[46]

It is necessary here to distinguish Luther's position from Erich Seeberg's representation of it.[47] Seeberg accurately makes this sort of language about the centrality of Christ the dominant theme of Luther's doctrine. But because Seeberg maintains that the revelation of God in Christ is a disclosure of God's working paradoxically in opposites, the cross and Resurrection of Christ can be made to answer an a priori religious question about "the secret of God's work" in relation to human destiny.[48] The answer is that God works life through death, glory through humiliation, destiny through senselessness; and Christ is thus the archetype (*Urbild*) of human life in relation to God. But what Luther himself says is that Christ is the quintessence (*Ausbund*) of God's life in relation to man.[49] *Ausbund* was a mercantile term for a faultless sample bound to the outside of a package to indicate the quality of the goods within—such as a flawless swatch protruding from a roll of cloth. Luther presents Christ not as the archetype of human destiny but as the perfect and visible manifestation of the nature of the invisible God. That Christ has revealed the Father, that He is the very image of God, "the abyss of His nature and godly will," and that faith in God and in Christ is one

45. *28*, 486, 23; *21*, 483, 25.

46. *33*, 19, 20ff.; *46*, 637, 30.

47. Erich Seeberg, *Luthers Theologie*, Vol. 1: *Die Gottesanschauung bei Luther* (Göttingen, 1929); see esp. Vol. 2: *Christus Wirklichkeit und Urbild* (Stuttgart, 1937).

48. Seeberg, ibid., *1*, 144; cf. his *Luthers Theologie in Ihren Grundzügen* (Stuttgart, 1950), p. 81.

49. "Quintessence" seems a better translation of this rare word than "exemplar," as rendered by *Luther's Works: American Edition* (*22*, 117: cf. n.90; and *23*, 16); I have avoided "exemplar" as suggesting the sense of Erich Seeberg's term "Urbild." For Luther's use of "Ausbund" in other contexts (especially in the phrase "Kern und Ausbund"), see the article "Ausbund," in Philipp Dietz, *Wörterbuch zu Dr. Martin Luthers Deutschen Schriften*, *1* (Hildesheim, 1961), 162.

faith [50]—this is the *Kern und Ausbund* of Luther's gospel. God will be our God only through Christ.[51] Now for faith it is Christ Who is the subject of the first commandment, which is itself the gospel and is all: [52] "I am the Lord thy God: thou shalt have no other gods but Me."

## The Image of God

*Ausbund* is clearly a very apt term for christological use: here is a visible, tangible instance of what is hidden from sight, but an instance which is itself the very stuff exemplified. In this respect it has one advantage over the description of Christ as the image of God. In everyday use "image" normally means a likeness or portrait which, however lifelike, is made from a substance other than that pictured.[53] "When a painter or carver or sculptor pictures a king or prince in canvas, wood, or stone with every bit of exact likeness he can muster, so that everyone who sees the work of art exclaims, 'Look, it is King or Prince So-and-so, or such-and such a person!' it certainly is an image or replica, but it is not the substance or nature of the king, prince, or person—it is only a facsimile, or image, a copy of its original in a different substance." [54] When Christ, however, is described as "the image of the invisible God" or "the express image of His person," we are dealing with an image which is not only a resemblance, but fully contains the whole substance and nature of God.[55] "Here the Son is an image of the Father's substance such that the Father's substance is the image itself." [56] A crucifix is a wooden image of Christ, but Christ, so to speak, is a "god-den" image of God.[57]

Other beings, men and angels, are made in the image of God;

---

50. *28*, 112, 10ff.; *487*, 12; *46*, 671, 32 ("abgrund seiner natur und Göttlicher wille"); *28*, 93, 2; *486*, 31.
51. *40/I*, 99, 26.
52. *40/II*, 304, 34; *Tr, 1*, 160: 369; 358: 751.
53. *10/I/1*, 155, 7ff.; *20*, 375, 20.
54. *50*, 277, 1.
55. *10/I/1*, 155, 21; *20*, 375, 18; *50*, 277, 27.
56. *10/I/1*, 155, 17.
57. *50*, 277, 21.

but they are not the image of His substance, nor made out of His divine nature.[58] By the same token, the saints are created and exist for the glory of God; but only Christ is "the brightness of the Father's glory" in the sense that this brightness itself constitutes God's glory. "Christ is the whole light, the total brightness of God's honor." [59] If Christ were not the brilliance of the whole divine majesty, but only a part of it, He would not be the brilliance of God's glory at all, for God's glory is one and indivisible. If Christ did not possess the whole of the Father's Godhead in every respect, He could not be the image of His substance in any respect, for the divine substance is unique and indivisible: "wherever it is, it must be whole and complete, or not at all." [60]

### The Father's Will and Heart

"God is fully in Christ, where He sets and places Himself for us," and here only can we deal with Him.[61] Whatever else the discovery of Christ as the image, essence, and fullness of the Father may imply for the form of sound words and the life of discipleship, centrally it means this: as Christ is disposed to us, so God is disposed.

The evangelist St. John, Luther says, distinguishes the persons of the Father and the Son but constantly identifies their work. Christ's teaching, too, was intended to prevent our thinking of Himself and His Father separately.[62] Rather, Christ is the one in Whom the entire Godhead dwells, and therefore we must heed Him.[63] For it is impossible for men to know the mind and intention of God; but the Son, Who is in the Father's very heart, descends and reveals it to us. This is what St. John means by "Christ in the bosom of the Father" (1:18)—a strange expression for Germans, Luther declares, who use *Schos* ("bosom") for mothers, not fathers! But what St. John means is that "we have received it from the only-begotten Son Who clings to the Father's

58. 50, 277, 23; cf. 40/II, 251, 33.
59. 10/I/1, 154, 15 and 10.
60. 50, 276, 22; 277, 30.
61. 45, 482, 2.
62. 47, 89, 32; 80, 30.
63. 33, 183, 14.

neck and lies in His arms. Thus John wants us to know and be sure in our hearts that the Word revealed by the Son is in no way dubious. For the Son lies in the Father's bosom and arms, and is so close to Him that He knows surely what the Father has determined in His heart." [64] In Christ we are enabled to gaze into the depths and see what the purposes and thoughts of the divine heart are.[65]

We see here how Luther moves directly from asserting the coinherence of the Father and the Son to declaring its meaning for personal faith. He does not intend, he says, to use it as a technical argument against the Arians, as the Fathers did. "Rather, we speak here only about the use or necessity of this article— what our attitude should be in relation to God and Christ if we are to find the Father and know His will." [66] (The intimacy of this relation between dogma and faith is nowhere more eloquently expressed than in Luther's exposition of John 14 in 1537.) Because the Father is in Christ and Christ in the Father, one united and indivisible divine being, we are sure that the Word of Christ and the Father is altogether the same Word, heart, mind, and will.[67] For Christ reveals all the purpose and will of God, declares to us everything the Father has at heart.[68] "I can recognize the mind of God in Christ, for that is His will." Indeed, Christ Himself may be called the Father's will and heart.[69]

What, then, is the content of that "true and living faith" which in accordance with the words of the gospel "knows Christ and the Father's will and heart?" [70] It knows that Christ loves sinners at His Father's command.[71] It knows that Christ's words, "God so loved the world that He sent His only Son," are the means by which He leads us directly into the Father's heart, declaring that His love and the Father's are one love, and revealing that God's

64. *46*, 665, 36 to 666, 10.
65. *21*, 515, 36.
66. *45*, 588, 35; cf. Augustine, *Tract. in ev. Ioh.*, LXXI, 2.
67. *21*, 467, 12; *45*, 515, 19.
68. *20*, 229, 34; *28*, 199, 5; *45*, 515, 11; 696, 3ff.
69. *10*/III, 221, 8. E.g. *Tr, 1*, 298: 630; *45*, 589, 31.
70. *46*, 19, 15ff.
71. *45*, 696, 18.

great, wonderful, and eternal plan is not to cast us out but to bring us aid through His Son.[72] It knows that Christ's works, of healing, forgiving, raising to life, are the assurance and demonstration of the Father's merciful will, offering true and blessed consolation to distressed consciences. For if God were angry, He would not forgive us; if He intended to leave us in bondage to the devil, He would not remove the torments of evil; if He delighted in our death, He would not quicken the dead. "But this is precisely what He did in Christ," assuring us of His fatherly love and grace. "Christ is the Father's gracious manifestation whereby our hearts are drawn to Himself." Now we know on what terms we stand with God: the terms are only grace and comfort.[73] Therefore, if God is for us, what can stand against us? [74] When we experience Christ, we experience through Him the Father's compassion [75]—the "sheer passion and ardor of inexpressible fatherly love." [76] There is an infinitely rich depth of mercy given in Christ, Who is the pledge, token, and testimony of God's grace.[77]

So it is that I may climb upon the Son to the Father and see that Christ is God, Who placed Himself in my sin, death, and wretchedness; and then "I know also the highest love of the Father (which no heart unaided can discover or feel), lay hold of God where He is most tender, and think, 'Yes, that is God; that is God's will and heart, that Christ did this for me.'" "For where Christ is, there for a certainty come also the Father and the Holy Spirit, and then there must be sheer grace, no law; sheer compassion, no sin; sheer life, no death; sheer heaven, no hell." [78]

### God's Designated Place

We see Christ as a faithful savior, shedding His blood richly on the cross, breaking the bonds of death and hell, and offering the

72. 17/I, 263, 30; 21, 482, 1; 47, 80, 31.
73. 45, 527, 23ff.; 10/I/2, 84, 16; 45, 550, 15.
74. 45, 589, 31.
75. 10/I/2, 277, 31; 29, 361, 16; 40/I, 602, 20.
76. 45, 516, 21.
77. 10/I/2, 207, 16.
78. 10/I/2, 277, 24–31; 236, 12.

benefits of His Passion to us abundantly. He declares that He holds no anger or disfavor against us, but only help and comfort.[79]

" 'Yes' (you say) 'I see and hear that clearly—but who knows if God is similarly disposed toward me?' Answer: beware of the thought! For that is to wrench Christ and God apart" the way Philip did when he asked, "Show us the Father." It is really a form of unbelief and secret denial of God, a shameful delusion. For this is to flutter up into the clouds, clamber into heaven, speculate about sublime matters, peek and gape at the Father, while ignoring as superfluous the one place where God has commanded us to seek Him—namely, His Son. "Everyone who desires Me, and would be freed from sin and be saved, must seek Me there, and nowhere else." [80] Human presumption is always prone to distort and violate the proper knowledge of God; but so that we may not go astray, God has ordained that He will not communicate with men except through Christ.[81] "He has designated and identified a specific locus and a specific person where He will be found and encountered: none other than Christ Himself." As a result, to place one's faith anywhere but in Christ is idolatry; but "if you would believe in God, then believe in Me." [82]

Luther is fond of declaring that the analogous designations under the old covenant, Jerusalem, the temple, and the mercy seat, have been fulfilled and superseded by Christ.[83] "Just as the godly Jews knew no other God but Him Who commanded them to worship at the mercy seat, just as they knew no other service than that celebrated in the temple designated to this end by God, so we cling to the Son alone. In Him we find the Father; in Him receive life and salvation. Our Christian wisdom is to reject the vacillating notions of our hearts and cling to the Son alone—we do not know God apart from the Son." [84] Under the old covenant God would not be known in any place or manner except as the One Who dwelt upon the cherubim, and accordingly, the people

79. *45*, 519, 29ff.
80. *45*, 520, 2ff. and 16–35.
81. *33*, 562, 10.
82. *45*, 481, 17–26.
83. *8*, *32*, 33; *23*, 554, 18; *31*/II, 662, 8.
84. *40*/II, 305, 32.

acknowledged no other God. This was a figure of Christ. Was He so small that He might be found only there? No, but because they knew Him there, they were able to confess Him as God over all. "They could have expressed this conviction in the form, 'Let us not divide the mercy seat from the divinity' . . . So with us the person of God must not be separated from the humanity of Christ." [85] Now in the new covenant Christ is our Jerusalem, our temple, and our mercy seat. "God has established another temple for His dwelling place: the precious manhood of our Lord Jesus Christ. Here and nowhere else God wants to be found." At this proper mercy seat sheer mercy, love, and kindness are found; elsewhere God is a devouring fire. [86]

### Seal, Standard, Ensign, Pledge

Luther uses a cluster of minor titles to express this designation. Chief of these, provided by John 6:27, is "seal." [87] "It is Jesus Christ on Whom God has set His seal, and to Whom He has given His letter of authorization . . . God has a ring, a signet, and a seal on His thumb, with which He seals and notarizes the letters He writes: this seal is Christ and no other." [88] The significance for us of God's seal and bulla is this: "if any other doctrine claims that it will feed you eternally, yet lacks this seal and notarization, which is Christ, beware of it!" [89] Christ, then, may be called God's "standard," since His person is the touchstone of godly doctrine. [90] Again, since God will not and cannot be found except in and through the humanity of Christ, that humanity is the "ensign for the nations" of Isaiah's prophecy (Isa. 11:12). [91]

Simply because God's testimony to Christ is exclusive of all other saviors, doctrines, and ways to Himself, it is thereby His guarantee that He is mercifully inclined to us. The Father's testimony is a testimony to grace: Christ is a "pledge and veritable

85. 20, 605, 14ff.
86. 46, 760, 23ff.; cf. 51, 128, 22.
87. See 15, 467, 24; 33, 17, 9.
88. 33, 17, 7ff.; cf. 33, 19, 16; 54, 13.
89. 33, 21, 28–38; cf. 33, 390, 25.
90. 46, 768, 24.
91. 10/I/1, 209, 1; cf. 31/II, 88, 29ff.

testimony" of God's intention to bestow eternal life and bliss, for He would never have given His Son if He had not loved us.[92] Therefore Christ can say, "I am the pledge and earnest, gift and present, to show you that God is not angry with you." [93]

## *"This Is My Beloved Son"*

How has God designated this special site of encounter with Himself? We have already heard Christ speak of His commission by the Father and proclaim that He is the only way to God. To this witness of Christ, the Father has added His own public testimony. One avenue of this testimony (as we have seen) is miracle. However, the testimony to which Luther constantly recurs is God's declaration, "This is My beloved Son"—a key passage, in Luther's opinion. His citation is usually of the voice on Mt. Tabor, at the transfiguration of Christ (Matt. 17:5). Less often, it is the voice at Christ's baptism (Matt. 3:17) or a combination or conflation of the two accounts. Sometimes Luther connects the voice from heaven with Isaiah 42:1 and also with Psalm 2:7 (passages which have captured the attention of more recent form-critics).[94]

On the simplest level this voice of the Father "calling down from heaven in public testimony" [95] was necessary to provide external confirmation of the Baptist's witness. In one place, it is true, Luther questions whether the voice was indeed public; [96] but usually he regards it as "a visible manifestation and revelation" corroborating the Baptist's ministry.[97] The Father's voice was an additional witness to support Christ's own testimony, in accordance with the law, but a testimony which demands far greater acceptance than man's witness.[98] However, even the bare external fact of this manifestation has a much deeper significance,

92. *21, 487,* 20; cf. *20, 786,* 3.

93. *47,* 98, 31.

94. E.g. *33,* 447, 30; *46,* 639, 19; cf. Oscar Cullmann, *The Christology of the New Testament* (Philadelphia, 1959), p. 66.

95. *46,* 639, 22.

96. *16,* 365, 3 and parallels.

97. *46,* 685, 14; cf. *10/I/1,* 214, 12.

98. *20,* 783, 8; *33,* 552, 28ff.

Luther suggests. First, that Christ should claim and receive the Father's witness, in the face of the Jews' demand that they be shown His Father, indicates the correct order in the knowledge of God. Christ does not show us the Father; rather, the Father shows us Christ. The purpose of the manifestation was not that man should touch and handle the Father but that they should be led to Christ's words.[99] "Be directed by this, and let others dispute and vainly investigate what God is doing up there in heaven: for you would get nowhere, even if you speculate yourself to death! But here you have a certainty that leaves no shred of doubt, since for this very purpose He Himself has come down from heaven and declared: 'This is My beloved Son: listen to Him.'"[1] Secondly, this testimony was to inaugurate "a huge and extraordinary transformation" of the old order of nation, priesthood, and law, into the new and eternal kingdom of Christ by the gospel. The holy humanity of Christ, set apart by the unusual testimony of the dove and the voice, was ordained as king and priest, and the dove was His biretta and His crown.[2]

Above all, Luther's interest is in the content, rather than the fact, of the Father's testimony. The Father said, "Listen to Him." Christ alone is thus vested with authority: this is God's clear and insistent command and His only message.[3] It is as if God had said of this teacher, "When you have heard Him, you have heard Me."[4] God did not designate Gabriel or some other angel; "He did not say, 'Listen to Bernard or Gregory or someone else,' but He said, 'Listen to Him, Him, Him,—My beloved Son.'"[5] In obedience to this declaration we must judge all things in the light of Christ's words. It designates Him the truth and the embodiment of God's will, the quintessence of God's purpose and all His mercy.[6] It is an exhortation to those who yearn for God to "mark

99. 33, 557, 14; 566, 20ff.; 556, 39ff.

1. 45, 525, 12.

2. 46, 570, 7; 602, 30.

3. 32, 531, 37; 45, 520, 32; 30/III, 340, 21; 42, 457, 29; 45, 518, 21; 47, 160, 22.

4. 14, 27, 16.

5. 51, 129, 23; 10/II, 75, 15.

6. 46, 774, 10; 51, 131, 25; 33, 19, 20ff.; 46, 772. 25.

where He resides and wants to be found" ;[7] a direction to those who seek Him to let fanatics, hair shirts, rosaries, even the Fathers go, to seek no comfort or salvation in works (even those that are pleasing to God), but to shelter under the wings of this brood hen, Christ, and give ear to Him alone.[8] Because of this testimony we know that Christ is not any son, but the only Son, the head, the firstborn among many brethren. "This makes it unnecessary to seek for many mediators or saviors, for we gain this sonship not through the holiness of the patriarchs or prophets or the innocence of the angels, but only through the one and only-begotten Son from the Father."[9] Indeed, apart from the Son we are enemies of God, for by this designation every claim to the Father's love is consigned to Christ the savior. "Even if piety and holiness shine ever so brightly, they must begone—they count for nothing before the Father. For it is only the beloved Son Who is pleasing to Him. Now the man who would be beloved and dear to the Father must go to the Son in the Father's bosom, and thus come to the Father. As Paul says in Eph. 1:5, we have been accepted into sonship through Christ."[10]

### The Beloved

We know that we are thus accepted in the beloved because the Father's voice testifies not only that Christ is the Son but also that He is beloved and well-pleasing to God. With these words God "endues all creation with sheer sweetness and comfort."[11] Christ is called God's dear child, His beloved,[12] the only one Whom God loves.[13] It is He alone Whom the Father has in mind, to Whom the Father looks, without Whom He accepts nothing, and in Whom all the love of God reposes.[14] The ground of our ac-

7. 33, 187, 19; cf. 45, 514, 1.
8. 33, 192, 12ff.; 46, 770, 20; 45, 513, 28; 46, 770, 21.
9. 46, 637, 27 to 638, 3.
10. 20, 227, 20.
11. 20, 228, 29.
12. "Das liebe kind" (20, 227, 15; 46, 639, 28); "seinem gelibten" (47, 198, 14f.).
13. 40/II, 111, 16; 47, 206, 42.
14. 33, 27, 35; 20, 227, 25 to 228, 5; 266, 8; 47, 198, 24.

ceptance, then, is the Father's delight and good pleasure in Christ. "The Father is delighted in whatever the Son says and does, not simply from grace, but because what He says and does is perfect in itself: God finds nothing to condone in it." [15]

If Christ's favor with God is the ground of our acceptance by the Father, is Christ depicted here as the "representative man"? Should we suggest parallels between Luther and a number of other theologians working with more or less the same materials—perhaps Irenaeus' *recapitulatio* or Schleiermacher's "ideality" or Barth's "homecoming of man"? [16] Not at all: any such parallel would be misleading. Luther has no intention whatever of depicting Christ, in His favor with God, as "representative man"; rather, the stress is on the personal uniqueness of the relationship. Luther remains very close to Augustine, who stresses "the distinction with which it is said 'the Father loves the Son' . . . as a father loves (not as a master loves a servant); as the only Son (not as an adopted son); and therefore He 'has placed all things into His hand'—and the 'all' means that the Son should be such as the Father is. . . . So God having deigned to send us the Son, we must not imagine that something less than the Father has been sent to us: the Father, in sending the Son, sent His other self." [17] Luther is in complete accord with Augustine's judgment. In markedly similar terms he avers that "He loved Him so much that He placed everything into His hands, that is, made Him almighty . . . He is the almighty God." "This surely is great love, and it is recorded for our sake, so that we may know and believe it . . . We have a definite lord, Whom we can touch as He lies in His mother's lap and hangs on the cross, Who as eternal God became temporal and finite man: and right here we can be sure in our hearts that we possess one Who is really and truly lord, to Whom everything in heaven and earth is subject, angels and devils under His feet, for the Father loves Him as His only-begotten Son." [18]

15. *46*, 640, 5.
16. Irenaeus, *Adv. haer.*, Bk. V; Schleiermacher, *Christian Faith*, sec. 93 ("Urbildlichkeit"—the source of Seeberg's term: cf. above, p. 86, n. 49); Barth, *Church Dogmatics*, IV/2, par. 64.
17. Augustine, *Tract. in ev. Ioh.*, XIV, 11.
18. *47*, 198, 40; 203, 36 to 204, 5.

Since God, in His love for Christ, has placed everything in His hands, then anything we are to receive can come only from Him. To seek it elsewhere is to seek where nothing can be found and "to head for the devil's behind." "God's highest wisdom, righteousness, and truth have been reposed in the Son, and everything has been given to Him: everyone who desires to be a Christian dare seek no other God nor take another path, nor follow any will-o'-the-wisp . . . To this lord Christ all has been given without reservation—as much as God has, Christ has too." Faith declares "If I possess such a lord, I will also possess all things with Him." [19]

This lord Who alone possesses God's good pleasure has nothing but love for us, since He died for us.[20] It is He Himself Who invites us, "Come to Me, we shall become one entity, and God will be pleased with us." [21] There is no love and friendship, but only wrath, outside the Son; but united to Him by faith, we too are accepted in the beloved.[22] "You see how with these words God places Christ in Himself and Himself in Christ, indicating by them that His good pleasure is in everything that Christ does. Moreover with these self-same words He showers upon us both Himself and His beloved Son Christ—He pours Himself into us and draws us into Himself, so that He is utterly and completely made human and we are utterly and completely made divine.[23] How so? Because God says that what Christ is and does is well-pleasing to Him. Be instructed by this Word so that you discern God's good pleasure and His whole heart in Christ, in all His words and works; and conversely see Christ in the heart and good pleasure of God. These two are in one another to the very deepest and highest extent. You can make no mistake in this, because God cannot lie. Moreover, because Christ, the beloved and pleasing child in God's good pleasure and heart, is yours, complete with all His saying and doing, and because He serves you with them (as He Himself says), you also surely enjoy the very

19. *47*, 206, 37; 199, 1 and 15; 206, 26.
20. *47*, 206, 42f.
21. *33*, 35, 27.
22. *47*, 198, 14.
23. "Das er gantz und gar vermenschet wird und wyr gantz und gar vergottet werden" (cf. Athanasius, *De incarn.* 54: MGP XXV, 192).

same good pleasure and are as deeply in God's heart as Christ, and in turn God's good pleasure and heart are as deep in you as in Christ. So now God together with His beloved Son is utterly and completely in you, and you are utterly and completely in Him, and all together is one entity—God, Christ and you." [24]

### "I Am"

" 'For the Father loves the Son': the evangelist speaks about this subject as if he can see nothing else worth preaching about. He pushes out of sight every other way and looks only at God's Son; we should do this, too—and properly so, if we keep the great miracle before our gaze and hold all else as mere chaff compared with the Son of God." [25] The sole sufficiency of Christ is such a pervading theme in Luther's preaching that it can readily assume some highly abbreviated forms. Luther makes eloquent use of Christ's statement (in John 8:24), "You will die in your sins unless you believe that it is I." This means, according to Luther's exposition, "I am the man, everything depends totally on Me—where I am not, there is nothing . . . Do you want to know Who I am? I am God and absolutely so in every respect." [26] And when the Jews remonstrated that no one but God could deliver man from sin, death, and hell, and reviled His claim to be this God, Luther has Christ reply, "I am Who I am." [27] Such words are too sublime for any creature, from the highest archangel to the lowliest preacher, who must declare only that they are sent at God's behest. But Christ says, "I am not only sent, but it is I." [28] This is a claim that all things exist in Him, that life and death, sin and righteousness, God and devil, heaven and hell are all in His hands; and it is by the same stroke an instantaneous and categorical abolition of all the world's wisdom, sanctity, strength, and power: "these high words call for faith." That Christ should say

24. 20, 229, 28 to 230, 10.
25. 47, 203, 1.
26. 33, 591, 18 and 26.
27. 33, 592, 2–9: "der ich bin, der bin ich."
28. 33, 592, 28ff.; 610, 7ff.

of Himself, "I am," is not said on the basis of His manhood, but proves Him to be truly God.[29]

Here, two curious features of Luther's exposition are noteworthy. Unlike so many other commentators, Luther makes no special point of the ἐγώ εἰμι refrain in those Johannine discourses where the phrase is supplied with a complement: he places weight upon it only where it stands alone ("pronounced absolutely," in Bultmann's phrase).[30] Secondly, by what is probably a historical accident, we have almost nothing from Luther about the most striking of these "absolute" ἐγώ εἰμι passages—namely, John 8:58. In most of the dozen extant sermons on John 8:46ff. Luther's time seems to have elapsed before he even reached verse 58; and in the few cases where he did complete the chapter, his transcribers have recorded the very briefest of comments: "Christ says that He was predestined to the task of redemption before the world began, and speaks of His divinity" (17/I, 170, 3f.), or "He was from eternity and is Son of God, possessing equal power, glory, and wisdom with God" (29, 130, 28).

Yet however swift Luther is to underscore the claim to divinity in Christ's "I am," the naked doctrinal assertion is not its usefulness to him. Instead, its purpose is this: "God wants men to believe only in Me, Christ, so stop your defiance—it will achieve nothing." Against the apparent "arrogance, pride, and conceit" of Christ's claim, Luther sets man's proud despite of God's truth. God is not swayed by our boasts—He will break all such defiance —but concerns Himself only with this, "that men hear the Son and believe in Him." The man who possesses this faith can defy death, devil, pope, emperor, and world in the strength of this "I am."[31]

Luther even applies his passion for the theme of Christ's sole sufficiency to the very mechanics of preaching. It appears in those very many passages of purported direct discourse where

29. 33, 593, 3–29; 610, 22.
30. See Rudolf Bultmann, *Das Evangelium des Johannes* (*Meyers Kommentar über das Neue Testament*), (2. Aufl., Göttingen, 1950), pp. 142, 167; Eduard Schweizer, *Ego Eimi* (Göttingen, 1939).
31. 33, 616, 30 and 25; 617, 11ff.; 46, 106, 24 and 27.

Luther breaks without warning into first-person speech as if
Christ Himself were speaking. In such passages occurs an even
more abbreviated device, the repetition of the pronoun "I".

> Luther often has Christ repeat, "I, I . . ." as He directs men to
> Himself. When he says "I have said this to you" and "I have over-
> come the world," it is as if He was saying, "Beloved, write that 'I'
> with a great big capital letter." "You" is a tiny word, as small as
> "a speck of dust in the sun," but Christ created everything out of
> something smaller than a speck of dust—"out of nothing, so even
> if you were punier still, I can and will make you great enough. For
> it is I Who speak thus"—not emperors, not angels, but "I, I say
> it." Therefore we must think only of Christ's statements. We must
> consider the person who says it, not ourselves the hearers, and
> "cling to Him Who says, 'I, I have overcome the world'" (46, 105,
> 15–30; 106, 5). Our weakness is not only the occasion of His
> strength but the context for the reception, no longer of fearful
> threats but of the tender mercies of Christ. For He says, "I, I have
> founded a kingdom of grace" (49, 148, 38). Who is this "I?" Who
> is it Who says "I, I have yet much to say to you?" It is not the
> pope (46, 52, 15f.). The pope tries to devise and decree foolish
> additions to Christ's teaching in brazen blasphemy of the Holy
> Spirit—but "does God's Word also command this? I cannot see
> where! But I do know full well that God's Word declares, 'I,
> Christ, go to the Father, and he who believes in Me will be saved.
> For I, I have suffered for him and give him the Holy Spirit from
> above'" (47, 777, 14).

## The Man

In Luther's idiom Christ's "I am" is paraphrased, "I am the
man." [32] This idiomatic use of "the man" is a constant feature of
Luther's preaching—a usage parallel to the English idiom, "the
man for the job" (or perhaps even more to the American idiom,
"the Man," in military and political currency, for "the key figure,"
"the highest authority"). Like English, too, Luther sometimes
modifies the noun in this sense when he calls Christ "the right

32. 33, 591, 18.

man." [33] Occasionally it is difficult to tell whether Luther is using the phrase idiomatically or is asserting the humanity of Christ doctrinally; but in most cases the distinction is easy to make. And in those cases where he does speak idiomatically, he has no formal intention of stressing Christ's humanity. Rather the opposite: "the man" occurs not infrequently in passages which stress His divinity. (Luther, of course, sometimes speaks of God Himself as "the man," not as an anthropomorphism but simply as a synonym for "person.") When Luther calls Christ "the man Who is God" or "the man through Whom the whole world was created," or asserts that this man's ability to pierce hearts is divine, not human,[34] he takes as self-evident that the historical figure confronting us is a man: he will underline the uniquely divine functions performed by this human being and thus establish that "this man is God." To this we shall return later; [35] our present concern is the nontechnical use of "the man" to mean simply "person" or "key person."

Here, as ever, the axis of Luther's language is the uniqueness of the person of Christ. This man is uniquely sealed, authorized, and designated by God.[36] We are instructed according to God's ordinance not to conclude or recognize anything about God without hearing this man and His message. For God has His eyes fixed on this man's lips, and the history of the world must be ordered for the sake of His words.[37]

Christ is unique not only according to the ordination of God but in Himself and in His history. He is "the man from God," "the man from heaven." [38] According to John 3:13, "No man has ascended into heaven but He Who descended from heaven"—no one, that is, but "the one man only Who came down . . . for the pronoun 'no one' banishes everyone and leaves no remnant, it sweeps away all but Christ." [39] There is no one else who was

33. E.g. 33, 310, 3; 448, 9.
34. 46, 108, 25; 598, 40; 765, 3.
35. See below, chap. 6.
36. 10/I/2, 430, 1; 33, 20, 25; 45, 523, 29.
37. 33, 558, 19ff.; 563, 15ff.; 596, 15ff.; 635, 6.
38. 33, 471, 38; 47, 172, 34.
39. 47, 48, 28; 49, 26.

born of the Virgin, died, was buried, rose again, and ascended into heaven but this one man, Christ.[40] So far from portraying Christ prototypically, Luther insists that Christ's history is His own and no one else's. Correspondingly, Luther's view of any other man's salvation cannot be kenotic—that is, by conformance to a reenactment of Christ's experience. Rather, "I cling to the heavenly one and to His works, words, and suffering, all of which are heavenly . . . Then by faith I am incorporated into the heavenly man, and He says, 'You are Mine, and I am yours, for I have done these heavenly works for you.' " [41]

What are these unique heavenly works He has done for us? He is the man Who is to preserve life and salvation for every man (and He alone must be the man who can do it). In the face of our inability to keep the law, God has given us a man Who guarantees that He will not lose us: in His keeping we cannot perish or die.[42] It is true that the law must be fulfilled to the smallest jot, but only through this one man Who has fulfilled it purely and perfectly, and Who gives Himself to us with His fulfillment.[43] Accordingly, the law is no longer in force, since the man for Whose sake it was previously observed has come. No, only He can accomplish true spiritual purification: man is helpless, but the true purification calls for "another and unique man." [44] The Son of God was given to us as "the man Who will forgive sin." [45] More: He is "the man Who abolishes sin" and "crushes the devil." [46] Therefore (the Christian may say) despite my sin I cling to the life of the man Who died for me. He is the man Who can help men from death to life and give them abundance even after this life.[47] In short, Christ is to be known as the man Who is all in all, for whatever He says and does is worthy and good and must stand.[48] All else merely obscures "the heavenly right-

40. 33, 666, 15.
41. 47, 172, 32.
42. 33, 103, 26; 104, 10; 110, 1.
43. 32, 359, 22.
44. 46, 676, 4; 47, 154, 28.
45. 47, 118, 6.
46. 7, 808, 19; 47, 105, 30.
47. 45, 731, 20; 528, 7; 33, 462, 8.
48. 45, 589, 26; 46, 101, 13.

eousness of the heavenly man": there is no other way, the heavenly man alone must come to our aid.[49]

For we must learn what this uniqueness excludes, as well as what it accomplishes. The noblest works of piety upon earth do not compare with the man Who came from heaven. "The one man, my dear lord and savior Jesus Christ, must be worth far more to me than all the holiest people on earth, yes, more than all the angels in heaven." [50] The Father has withheld His will from all holy works. He will pay no regard to any work, for works can achieve nothing. God intends His will to rest on the one man, Christ, Who is to be acknowledged as the only man Who can carry it out.[51] The Father directs us away from all universities, laws of the worldly wise, sublime thoughts, saintly lives, all religions, faiths, and doctrines, monastic vows and practices—even from humility. Luther's strictures on humility as the condition of salvation—"Humility accomplishes nothing"; "it sounds too vague and equivocal to have been spoken by God" [52]—are immensely impressive when compared with the central role he had assigned to *humilitas* in his early lectures,[53] and constitute another striking instance of his radical development. "Forget about your humility and cling in faith to this one man, Christ—that is the sufficient and necessary condition." [54]

No, our entire salvation and bliss depend on the one man, Christ. He is the only man through Whom justification comes.[55] Only knowledge of this man makes a Christian,[56] and apart from Him there is no light, life, help, or salvation.[57] Therefore whoever does not possess this man possesses nothing: "everything depends on coming to this man"; "everything depends on whether you feel and find that you love this man." [58] This is the

49. *47, 173,* 23.
50. *47, 63,* 1; *46, 769,* 29.
51. *33, 104,* 13.
52. *33, 527,* 2; *565,* 28.
53. E.g. *3, 575,* 25; *56, 159,* 12; *246,* 21ff.; *408,* 23ff.; and passim.
54. *33, 566,* 15.
55. *47, 49,* 46; *10/I/1, 221,* 24.
56. *21, 333,* 36ff.
57. *10/I/1, 202,* 15; *33, 102,* 28.
58. *45, 594,* 29; *33, 78,* 25; *46, 650,* 1.

true confession: I will cling to this man, remain with Him even though the old Adam suffer shipwreck, and by God's grace persevere in this faith.[59] "Here is another man," I may say to the devil's insidious assaults. "Despite you I am determined to preach and praise the man all the more, and place my heart's comfort and confidence in His blood and death, even if you and all hell should erupt." [60]

The purpose of Christ's preaching and of the entire gospel is to induce us to place our reliance on the man, seek salvation nowhere else, and be secure against any other preaching, whether it be the pope's, the emperor's, or the law of God itself.[61] Christ alone—this is the sum of Christian doctrine.

### The Only One

By this point, to say that Luther constantly and in every connection applies "only" to Christ, is perchance to state the obvious. The further our study has progressed, the longer has grown the catena of such exclusive qualifications: "only" has been applied to every single facet of the person and work of our Lord. The number of such affirmations is too great for adequate illustration: compared with the total, those quoted here are (like the nations before God) "as a drop of a bucket and the dust of the balance." Luther never completely leaves this theme. "I know absolutely nothing but Christ alone," he declares. "Oh, if only we could stake it all on Christ." [62]

Hence our claim that the uniqueness, necessity, and all-sufficiency of Christ is "the focus and pivot of all his theology, to which even the doctrine of justification is ancillary." [63] To call *sola fide* the material norm of his theology [64] would be unequivo-

59. *45*, 501, 36; 671, 18; 687, 22.
60. *45*, 725, 5.
61. *47*, 197, 11.
62. *47*, 154, 36; 777, 23.
63. See above, p. 79.
64. E.g. Paul Tillich, *Systematic Theology* (3 vols. Chicago, 1951ff.), *1*, chap. 1; Werner Schwarz, *Principles and Problems of Biblical Interpretation* (Cambridge, 1955), p. 169; etc.

cally correct, if only Luther's disciples (old and new) had remembered his injunction, "Christ and faith belong together." For
Luther *sola fide* is simply another way of saying *a solo Christo*.
Faith is an empty vessel and justifies because of Christ alone.[65]
Unfortunately, in the hands of others justification—the doctrine
of justification—has been allowed to usurp the pivotal position
which belongs to Christ alone in Luther's doctrine (as in Paul's).
Justification is only one aspect—even if a most important aspect
—of that clinging to Christ which is faith: for Christ is our righteousness. But to elevate the formal content of justification (imputation of righteousness) to the level of dominant importance as a
normative principle is inevitably to distort Luther's passionate
concern. This is not to deny that Luther himself regarded the article of justification as *articulus stantis et cadentis ecclesiae,* and
contended repeatedly that this was the issue between himself
and the papacy.[66] So it was: for Luther, as for Paul writing to
the Galatians, justification by faith apart from works became the
decisive issue simply because the error they had to combat was
the error of works-righteousness, the system of merit.[67] And the
article of justification is the weapon by which the assertion of
Christ's uniqueness must be protected against encroachment by
so-called human merit: only Christ is righteous. Moreover, in
many of the passages where Luther calls justification the cardinal
point, the word "justification" is doing service for a far wider area
than the dogmatic tradition comprises under this head. It serves
for the whole wealth of our relationship of unity with Christ by
faith. Luther readily identifies St. Paul's "sole theme of the righteousness of faith" with St. John's "consistent stress upon the article of Christ's person, office, and kingdom." [68] Hence the pecul-
iarly dogmatic form into which the doctrine of justification is cast
for polemical purposes is an inadequate key to the richness of Luther's faith. Not justification, but Christ alone, is the material
norm of his theology and the lifeblood of his faith.

65. *21,* 488, 27ff.; *40/I,* 165, 13.

66. E.g. *30/II,* 650, 19.

67. This point is cogently stressed by Carl Stange, *Der johanneische Typus der
Heilslehre Luthers* (Gütersloh, 1949), pp. 9ff.

68. *21,* 376, 3.

If the uniqueness of Christ as only lord of righteousness is the ground of Luther's onslaught on good works,[69] it is also the ground of all his other barbs. Everything is excluded which attempts to encroach upon the person, office, or accomplishment of Christ. Reason and scholastic talk, councils and canons, popes and bishops, monks and masses, holiness and humility, Arians and Sacramentarians, fanatics, infidels, antinomians, Turks [70]— all these are assailed for usurping or despising the all- and only-sufficiency of the Son of God. The identical ground of all these attacks, and the key question for "trying the spirits," is this: "Is it Christ?" [71] I am not, my works are not, nor are pope, nobility, or emperor. Fasting, rosaries, and pilgrimages are not, nor are the Fathers and the saints; the Blessed Virgin herself is not. Only Christ, with His Word, baptism, and supper, must be all. (These external ordinances are our means of clinging to Christ alone, because in the hands of the Holy Spirit, Who directs only to Christ, they are what we actually have of the man Christ in the Church. To deny them is to deny Him, for they are His.) In short, "all light, wisdom, and teaching apart from Christ must cease, or be found in Him alone." [72]

If this negative application of the canon of faith seems to occupy a prodigious bulk of Luther's literary output as a doctor of, the Church, its positive application retains the primary place. The task of the words in preaching is to point only to Christ; the task of the words in confession is to hazard everything on Christ; the task of the words in prayer is to seek God and every necessity solely through Christ; the task of the words in temptation is to cling utterly to Christ. "This should be the Christian's only skill, to learn Christ aright and distinguish Him from all thought, existence, doctrine, and life, and everything that man can lay hold on, and so to cling to Him alone by faith and say with all the heart, 'I know nothing and want to know nothing in godly matters but

69. E.g. 10/III, 155, 8; 10/III, 168, 12; 21, 435, 1ff.; 506, 26; 27, 184, 12; 28, 61, 9ff.; 40/I, 301, 25; II, 11, 18.

70. E.g. 12, 548, 14–36; 33, 529, 13; 45, 667, 1; 46, 673, 20; 21, 435, 27; 25, 64, 30; 33, 562, 35.

71. 20, 723, 8; 40/I, 240, 29.

72. 22, 242, 5.

only my Lord Christ, Who alone is to be all that concerns my salvation.'"[73] A Christian is not saved except through Christ alone, Whom it cost His all.[74] Only Christ has freely kept the law whole and entire: no man takes this distinction from Him.[75] Only Christ's death and Resurrection fulfill the law—not ours.[76] Forgiveness and eternal life are therefore in Christ alone.[77] "For just as what is offered to us is not the law or any of its works, but Christ alone, so nothing is required of us but faith which lays hold of Christ and believes that my sin and death are condemned and obliterated in Christ's sin and death."[78]

The true worship of God is therefore to adore Christ in such a manner that we see nothing in heaven or earth apart from Him.[79] Faith ascribes to Him the entire agency, merit, and power, and utterly excludes every conceivable element which is not from Him.[80] He is the *fac totum;* He is unique; He is all in all.[81] If we have Christ, we have all.[82] "Lord Christ, I hold to Thee, for Thou art the only one."[83]

73. *45,* 511, 4.
74. *10*/III, 168, 15.
75. *10*/I/2, 364, 20; *20,* 266, 7.
76. *20,* 264, 11; *25,* 35, 1.
77. *21,* 218, 30; *31*/I, 256, 25.
78. *40*/I, 273, 30.
79. *40*/II, 304, 34; cf. *25,* 35, 21.
80. *21,* 218, 30.
81. *42,* 612, 29; *22,* 220, 9; *10*/I/2, 128, 25.
82. *20,* 375, 14; *31*/II, 768, 7.
83. *33,* 109, 18.

# 4. *The Atonement: Christ's Going to the Father*

Our study of Christ's uniqueness has carried us from Luther's declaration that Christ, as the one sent from God, is the only preacher, to the confession that Christ, as the one Who went to God, is the only savior of men. This "going to the Father" Luther sets apart from Christ's ministry of preaching, as a distinct phase of His mission. It consists of His suffering, Resurrection, and Ascension—"that Christ took our sins upon Him; willingly died on the cross, was buried and descended into hell because of them; yet did not remain in subjection to sin or death and hell, but passed through them by His Resurrection and Ascension, and is now at the right hand of God as mighty Lord over all creatures." [1] The titles of Christ which declare the significance of this history must now occupy our attention.

Here, however, some prolegomena are called for. Since this "going to the Father" constitutes Christ's accomplishment of the atonement between God and man, the question about Luther's "view of the atonement" arises. The continuing discussion of this question has had to take special account of Bishop Aulén's little book [2] rehabilitating what he calls "the classic idea" of Christ's victory; and Scandinavian Luther research in particular has had a field day integrating this "dramatic" conception with Luther's "dualist" motifs, ingeniously explaining the persistence of apparently Anselmic language by pointing to the tyrannic role of the

1. 46, 44, 6 and 28.
2. Gustaf Aulén, *Christus Victor: An Historical Study of the Three Main Types of the Idea of Atonement* (New York, 1961).

law in Luther's doctrine.[3] The more biographically oriented German tradition has laid greater weight on the need for expiation of guilt in the monastic crises of the young Martin Luther and the role of the cross in meeting that need.[4] But perhaps the very variety of the answers to the question about Luther's view has obscured the suspicion which must rest upon the question itself. For Luther has no theory of the atonement.

If "view" is taken to mean "theory"—some sort of coherent explanatory discourse about how the atonement works—then the question about Luther's "view" is a false one. And if the proffered answers are to this form of the question, they are correspondingly false. That is to say, Luther's sermons abound in the motifs which figure in the historic atonement theories—patristic, classic, dramatic, or Western, Latin, and penal; objective or subjective. Shallow comparative study might suggest that Luther held all the great schemes—or that he was a confused thinker who really grasped none of them. In fact, Luther is not attempting what the theologians attempted for dogmatic or apologetic purposes, and it is impossible to equate his result with theirs. The logical structure of his doctrine differs from all of them and therefore may not be typed with any of them. Doubtless it can be typed with the Scripture, which also propounds no theory.

We must allow Luther's own words about the atonement to define his "view," and not some superimposed cognitive pattern. For theories of the atonement do tend to conform to a pattern of explanation, whether understanding that explanation is regarded as identical with faith or whether explanation by necessary reasons of what was previously accepted by faith is regarded as an advance toward the knowledge of God. (Aulén draws a distinction between the religious motives of the Greek Fathers and Anselm's preoccupation with rational demonstration.[5] Leaving aside the emotive intention of this distinction and the injustice it does Anselm, Aulén fails to recognize that an a priori pattern of ex-

3. See the survey by Carlson, *The Reinterpretation of Luther,* esp. p. 62.
4. E.g. Heinrich Bornkamm, *Luther's World of Thought* (St. Louis, 1958), pp. 156ff.
5. *Christus Victor,* p. 45.

planation already emerges during the patristic period and during
the currency of the dramatic idea of atonement. The classic idea
can be as much an atonement theory as any other explanation.)
But Luther does not hope to explain Christ's accomplishment, for
it exceeds comprehension: understanding and faith are incom-
mensurates, and the need for faith is so all-important that the
need for understanding is altogether overwhelmed by it.

How, then, does Luther's language about the atonement work?
Luther's teaching moves between two poles (we have already noticed both in the course of this study). On the one hand, he can
say that a hundred thousand Christs might have been crucified
without avail if men remained ignorant of the use of His
Passion.[6] At the other extreme, Christ's atonement really availed
in such a way that mankind no longer stands beneath God's
wrath on account of original sin (the decisive issue is now the
faith of Christ),[7] and the man Christ is indeed lord over death,
the devil, and all things. These two poles are related as follows.
The history of Christ's going to the Father is the history of a real
and unique accomplishment. As such, it is capable of factual description. In this sense the gospel is "only a chronicle or history
about Christ, who He is, what He did, said, and suffered." [8] That
history was undertaken by Himself, yet not for Himself: it was
undertaken for us.[9] Hence the purpose of preaching Christ and
Him crucified is that men shall discover that He lived and died
and rose for us.[10] "The words OUR, US, FOR US, ought to be
written in golden letters—the man who does not believe them is
not a Christian." [11] This discovery is the use of the Passion. The
devil can preach the facts, but only the Holy Spirit preaches that
Christ died for us.[12] In this sense the gospel is "not just a historical record of Christ's life, death, and Resurrection, but spells out
their power and blessing." [13] Yet the resulting useful distinction

6. 26, 40, 10; cf. 20, 778, 3.
7. 46, 41, 19; cf. 20, 638, 30; 22, 224, 27; 25, 417, 20; 47, 106, 12.
8. 10/I/1, 9, 16; cf. 29, 657, 2ff.
9. 40/I, 448, 14; 46, 337, 12ff.
10. 18, 692, 20; 34/I, 318, 16; II, 509, 4; 40/I, 299, 9; 52, 229, 4.
11. 31/II, 432, 17.
12. 10/I/1, 71, 3; I/2, 24, 3; 214, 8; III, 137, 27.
13. 21, 216, 19; cf. 12, 518, 11.

between "first faith" (*fides historica*) and "second faith" (*usus passionis*) [14] ultimately breaks down, since the man who does not know that this history was accomplished for him does not properly know the facts themselves: that it was accomplished for us is one of the facts. It is so both because the promise of God and Christ's own declaration are part and parcel of the history, and because the identity of the person undergoing this history is inseparable from the history itself.

Yet all men do not receive this *pro me*. It is those who know themselves cut off from God who need a mediator. It is those whose enmity against God makes them tremble at His holy wrath who need a reconciler. It is sinners who need a mercy seat, slaves who need a ransom, prisoners who need a deliverer. Only the timid and affrighted conscience knows how to say, "Christ died for me." He needs no theory of the atonement to interpret to himself what the "for me" means.

Yet theology is in present danger of converting even this "for me" into a theory of atonement. If it does so, it again eclipses the uniqueness of Christ's accomplishment, which alone gave substance to Luther's "for me." It is not adequate to say that because a discourse about the atonement is applied exclusively to evoking faith, and the context for discovering the use of that discourse is in man, the language of the discourse is imagery, metaphor, or myth. Some of it certainly is: when Luther takes over from the tradition certain bizarre figures of Christ's double-dealing with the devil, he expects to be understood figuratively. But in the case of talk about "satisfaction" or "victory" (to take two perennial examples), the situation is not as clear. Presumably someone who cannot readily utilize the legal context of "satisfaction" talk, or the hostile context of "victory" talk, is not necessarily disqualified from figurative use of this language, when it is preached, as an access to faith. But this is not the normal use of this language as Luther preaches it. The normalcy of the Christian response to which Luther urges us includes the appropriateness of biblical language both to our own need and to the actual accomplishment of Christ.

In short: we can neither understand nor explain the mystery

14. 31/II, 431, 33.

and the fullness of Christ's atonement. We cannot fathom how "the Son of God loved me and gave Himself for me." We cannot comprehend how the fullness of the Godhead could dwell bodily in a man. We cannot conceive how one Who knew no sin could become sin for us. This marvelous, unaccountable love is as inexplicable as it is ineffable, yet it is just here that the soul finds its rest. For Christ has given us means by which we may remember and learn that it was for us—the Word, preached and read, and the sacraments of His death and burial.

Accordingly, Luther does not use soteriological titles as fixed dogmatic categories. In his preaching, the great classic and biblical motifs of Christ the savior overlap each other in a manner which at first sight makes the sort of analysis we shall attempt seem impossible. But Luther's purpose is to teach his hearers a biblical vocabulary for faith, by which the reality of Christ's atonement (that He can and does save) and its individual application (that He is my savior) may be confessed. If Luther's preaching of the atonement seems in danger of becoming an undifferentiated string of traditional motifs, bound together by no more cogent principle than rhetoric, he nevertheless succeeds in fulfilling his purpose coherently for two reasons. First, even though it is the exception, rather than the rule, when he explicitly educes the content of these motifs, such specific expositions are by no means totally lacking; and when he does engage in such exposition, he inculcates a lively awareness of their meaning without becoming theoretical in the slightest degree (a feat which few more systematic theologians have accomplished). Secondly, close attention reveals that even though these titles overlap, Luther constantly groups and associates them with certain aspects of Christ's accomplishment. They gain their content and richness from this pattern of constant association; for normally these associations are far from indiscriminate, even where they have become automatic. And the underlying cause of this consistency is evidently Luther's extraordinary familiarity with the Scriptures. His words about the atonement (while occasionally influenced by the dogmatic tradition) are in most cases the reflection, quotation, or paraphrase of some biblical passage or passages.

God has not given us language about Christ such that it will mislead us.[15] Luther, without espousing any theory, places wholehearted reliance upon the congruence of scriptural language with Christ's achievement. Indeed, it is only when we have learned the art, from the sole available source of God's own chosen, true, and appropriate words, of referring our salvation only to Christ Who died, that we may then draw figure and illustration from every quarter to refer to that one object. So Luther preaches of Christ's going to the Father; and with these lines laid down to guide us, we may turn to the detail of his teaching.

## Mediator, Reconciler

First, then, Christ is our mediator. Only rarely does Luther offer any christological account of Christ's qualification for this role. One explicit exception praises God for "setting between us one Who is God and equal to God, man and equal to man. For we are men and He is God, and where the two oppose each other, man must be smashed in pieces—he cannot withstand. This God has averted by setting one in the mediator's place Who is true God and man: through Him are we to come to the Father."[16] Not only is such an account rare, but Luther sometimes uses "mediator" without any technical content, merely as a synonym for "savior."[17] Characteristically, however, the title has two main associations for him: Christ's work of reconciliation and His present office for us at God's right hand.

The purpose of Christ's ministry was "that we should know that He is our mediator: for everything He does, He does in order to bring us to the Father."[18] On the one hand, this involves "making men sweet to the Father."[19] We have not kept the commandments of God, Who is eternal righteousness and purity, and hates sin. We are therefore His enemies by nature; but when we creep to Christ and believe that He is our shepherd, bishop, and mediator with God, He steps between, drowns sin

15. *45, 548*, 10.
16. *10/III, 161*, 21; cf. *41, 194*, 20.
17. E.g. *17/II, 431*, 36; *21, 482*, 10; *40/I, 246*, 15; *47, 108*, 16; etc.
18. *15, 470*, 14.
19. *28, 127*, 12.

and wrath in Himself, and covers us with His innocence.[20] This
is to believe in Christ: "I believe in Christ when I believe that He
is a gracious God to me, has taken my sins upon Himself and has
reconciled me with God the Father, that my sins are His and His
righteousness mine, that here there is a mingling and exchange—
that Christ is the mediator between me and the Father." [21] Because we are in Christ, and Christ in us, the wrath and displeasure that stood against us has vanished, for Christ is our dear
bishop and mediator before God.[22] He was set apart for reconciliation: in that He reconciles the Father, His kingdom is solely forgiveness and grace.[23] As mediator, Christ "was sent to pay for
sins," "was sacrificed for your atonement," "bore all punishment
for you," "took upon Himself our misery and sin." By this means
He "appeased God's anger." [24] In a way which makes the search
for dualisms a complicated irrelevancy, Luther movingly places
this appeasement in the context of God's love: "All that Christ
does and suffers for our sake was ordained by the Father's good-
will: that He, the true and faithful mediator, might thus cancel
all God's wrath and displeasure, and make our hearts sure of His
fatherly grace and love. For how could He still be angry with us
and wish to damn us, when He has given His only Son so earnest
a command to empty Himself of all His divine glory and power,
and for our sakes to cast them under the feet of the devil and
death? 'But oh! that the world' Christ says 'only knew and believed that I do this not for Myself but out of a great love, stak-
ing My body and life on obedience to the Father.' For the man
who can believe that is already saved, and has escaped from
devil and death." [25]

Thus the other aspect of the mediator's reconciling work is to
show us that we have a gracious God. God before seemed a
judge; but now through Christ, the ascended mediator, we know
God as Father. The purpose of Christ's reconciling action is that

20. 10/III, 136, 2; 21, 329, 28; 45, 148, 39.
21. 10/III, 125, 25; cf. 10/III, 127, 5.
22. 45, 601, 6; cf. 40/II, 302, 22.
23. 21, 493, 30; 49, 252, 1.
24. 21, 546, 2ff.; 33, 85, 6–22; 46, 24, 23.
25. 21, 477, 25.

we should no more fear the Father. Christ is mediator of the knowledge that I am loved.[26] He reveals His own love for us; and then, as we discover that His love and God's are one, we "climb to the Father through Christ. . . . Begin with His love and then you will come to the Father," Who took the very first step in loving us before we loved Him.[27] The human heart cannot free itself from horrible unbelief and a damned conscience, nor is it able to expect all grace and mercy from God except through Christ, God's appointed and attested mediator.[28] But the proper remedy for an accusing and timid conscience, lest it despair, is the preaching of the gospel, which leads us to Christ as the one Whom the Father has given us to be our mediator.[29] In Him, God's sheer grace, mercy, and love are revealed: "for Christ shall be called, and is, the atoner and mediator between us and God, and therefore, in faithful discharge of His office, constantly pictures to us poor sinners the Father's immense, heartfelt love toward us; so that everything we see and hear of Him we may know and accept as flowing from the Father's heart. And just as we look to Him for all love and every good, help and comfort (as indeed He has assured us by His words and works, body and life), so we should look for the same things and nothing different from the Father." [30] The gospel declares the grace and forgiveness of God through the mediator, Christ, for our consolation and peace of conscience *coram Deo*.[31]

Luther is swift to contend that popish doctrine doubly distorts the reconciling role of Christ the mediator. It robs it of both its uniqueness and its efficacy. There is no mediator but Christ, Luther insists.[32] The Father is known solely in the mediator and cannot be met apart from Him; [33] except through this one mediator Who was sent to pay for sins, men cannot be saved.[34] But the

26. *46, 718,* 38 to 719, 1; *28, 127,* 13; *10/III, 158,* 27ff.
27. *10/III, 158,* 30 to 159, 3.
28. *21, 455,* 33; *22, 392,* 23.
29. *17/II, 431,* 34.
30. *46, 94,* 17.
31. *21, 538,* 34 to 539, 2; *31/I, 243,* 12.
32. *12, 267,* 33; *29, 10,* 1.
33. *46, 19,* 21; *97,* 1.
34. *10/I/2, 171,* 25; *46, 24,* 22.

"popish rabble" opposes the doctrine of salvation by Christ alone
by setting up pilgrimages, monkery, private masses, holy orders,
and ascetic lives against the mediator sent by God.[35] They con-
tradict the Scripture's clear statement that "there is one mediator
between God and man, the man Christ Jesus" (I Tim. 2:5).
"They will not concede that Christ is our only mediator before
God, that He alone delivers from sin and death, and that our own
works and deeds cannot achieve this."[36] Again, these practices
not only deprive Christ of His uniqueness but convert Him into a
tyrant and a tormentor: "we all feared Christ and fled from Him
to the saints, and implored Mary and others for help in time of
need, and treated them all as holier than Christ. Christ was only
the hangman, but the saints were our mediators . . . Christ says
He is not judge, but mediator."[37] Luther fears for the fate of
those who lean on St. Barbara, St. Dominic, or St. George, or shelter under Mary's cloak: "for all their fine show of worship, they
change the Son and His love into judge; and why, then, did God
give Him to us as mediator and high priest?"[38] To abandon
Christ the mediator and seek to mediate between oneself and
God by works, fasts, cowls, and tonsures is to fall, like Lucifer,
into horrible despair.[39] And into Christ's mouth Luther puts the
words, "Do not picture Me thus as a judge—instead of invoking
the saints, call on Me, your true mediator and saint."[40] Here we
must set the teaching of the Spirit against the teaching of the
schools.[41]

The second chief association of the title "mediator" for Luther
is Christ's present ministry for us. He is lord by His Passion, by
which He has ascended to the Father, has reconciled us to God,
and now sits at God's right hand as our mediator.[42] In this sense

35. 25, 37, 11; 45, 717, 25.

36. 46, 655, 23; 45, 571, 16.

37. 47, 100, 3; cf. 20, 637, 22ff.; 25, 65, 25; 30/II, 506, 23; 40/I, 93, 12; 326,
17.

38. 47, 198, 25 and 30.

39. 40/I, 77, 17.

40. 33, 88, 15; cf. 12, 266, 1.

41. 10/III, 161, 14 and 16.

42. 10/III, 129, 27; 17/I, 254, 10.

"mediator" is often coupled with "high priest" (or "bishop") in declaring that even Christ's enthronement is for our sake.[43] Christ is "not sitting idle in heaven."[44] As our mediator, He makes intercession for us and beseeches the Father to send us His Holy Spirit for our strength and consolation.[45]

Because we have such a mediator at the right hand of God, our own prayers are heard. Prayer must be through Christ, who always remains the only mediator for all men.[46] This is what it means to pray "in Christ's name": to be sure that He is such a mediator that all things are given to us through Him, and apart from Him is nothing but wrath and disgrace.[47] Therefore we know that our prayers are heard only for the sake of our mediator and high priest, but that in Him they are made acceptable.[48] It is true that now we have been given the right to come directly to God with our prayers; yet direct prayer means not that we no longer need a mediator but rather that Christ is a mediator, not of fear, but of freedom and comfort before God.[49]

## Priest, High Priest

"Priest" and "high priest" are used with "mediator" in each of the contexts we have just examined—of the work of reconciliation, both in its Godward and its manward aspects;[50] against popish practices;[51] and of Christ's heavenly intercession for us, His sending the Holy Spirit, and His providing access for our prayers to the throne of God.[52]

Apart from its occurrence as a synonym for "mediator," Luther's use of "priest" is largely confined to the theme of the royal

43. E.g. 25, 65, 26; 33, 101, 33; 310, 15; 41, 191, 18; 45, 730, 22; 46, 85, 20; 47, 198, 34.
44. 45, 555, 1; cf. 34/II, 509, 10.
45. 41, 149, 24; 45, 567, 28.
46. 32, 427, 21; 46, 97, 27.
47. 17/I, 252, 4.
48. 46, 85, 20; 97, 16; Tr, 4, 541: 4841.
49. 34/I, 398, 15.
50. 33, 101, 33; 40/I, 301, 16; 45, 730, 23; 47, 198, 34.
51. 10/I/1, 722, 15; 17/II, 16, 35; 33, 310, 15.
52. 21, 363, 20; 28, 59, 16; 45, 555, 2; 46, 85, 20.

priest "after the order of Melchizedek." The promise to Abraham of a seed Who would rule and bless the nations led David, in Psalm 110, to identify the Christ clearly as both king and priest like Melchizedek;[53] and the Epistle to the Hebrews in turn "made a whole sermon" out of Psalm 110:4.[54] The prophetic tradition also pointed forward to a time when the kingdom and the priesthood would be reunited in one person, superseding and fulfilling the shadows and symbols of Aaron and the levitical priesthood.[55] The very name "Christ" means "a mediator, priest, and pastor Who is to sacrifice for us as His priestly office demands."[56] Christ's declaration, "for their sakes I sanctify Myself" (John 17:19), is in Luther's eyes an explicit appropriation to Himself of Old Testament priestly consecration.[57] "Therefore let Aaron give place, and worship under the law yield as shadow yields to substance."[58]

We may say that the office of a priest is to present worship and offering; and Christ fulfills this office par excellence. His words "are the highest service and offering before God." Indeed, He Himself is the sacrifice He presents. As high priest, acting for us in discharge of His priestly office, He gives Himself on the cross, offering God not money, not cattle, but Himself: "He is priest and offering together."[59] And as priest forever, His offering is eternal in its validity and effect.[60] Or we may say that the task of a priest is to bestow blessing. "As the priest, so the blessing"; therefore the temporal blessings of the levitical priesthood have been superseded by the spiritual blessings of Christ, whereby men are freed from sin and death and their hearts purified.[61] Most often, however, Luther describes the priestly role as threefold: to teach, to sacrifice, and to pray.[62] "Christ was consecrated

53. 43, 244, 6.
54. 21, 376, 22; 41, 173, 26.
55. 23, 586, 1; 17/II, 227, 31; 25, 411, 12; 41, 185, 27ff.
56. 33, 310, 15.
57. 28, 173, 9.
58. 42, 545, 23.
59. 45, 683, 13; 40/I, 301, 16; 41, 192, 35; 28, 174, 6 to 175, 1.
60. 17/II, 230, 10; 42, 538, 1.
61. 17/II, 228, 26; 41, 183, 18; 42, 540, 32; 43, 263, 32.
62. 25, 16, 18; 41, 183, 29; 42, 537, 35.

high and most exalted priest by God Himself. According to the high priest's office, He sacrificed His body for us; secondly, He prayed for us on the cross; and thirdly, He preached the gospel and taught all men to know God and Himself." [63] This threefold rubric is the pattern of Luther's extended treatment of Psalm 110:4: the office of coming from God with His Word and returning to God in sacrifice and prayer makes "priest" "the highest and most glorious name and title to be named or praised on earth." [64]

This royal priest, then, possesses total power and must bestow His eternal gifts on us, whose priest He is. And if He is the priest Who brings all to grace, I may ignore popes, priests, and works, for "these are the words of life: that Jesus is the Christ, my high priest and king, Who sacrifices His blood for me, reconciles me to God, and intercedes for me." [65]

### Propitiator, Propitiation

" 'He is the propitiation for our sins': the words are so slight and meager, the substance so overwhelming, that no one could speak in this way unless the Holy Spirit moved him." [66] When Luther calls Christ "our propitiator," [67] he retains the sacral associations of the term: Christ is the place of atonement and forgiveness, the mercy seat under the new covenant.[68]

To be a propitiation, Luther says, means to make satisfaction.[69] Christ is Himself the expiation: [70] "He does not *exact* propitiation—He *is* the propitiation." Our sins are greater than could be expiated by any human expiation; [71] Christ makes us clean not by works but by His own blood.[72] This propitiation is universal

---

63. *12*, 307, 27.
64. *41*, 183, 29ff.
65. *41*, 195, 8; *33*, 311, 14.
66. *20*, 637, 15.
67. E.g. *40/II*, 13, 15; 79, 31.
68. *31/I*, 423, 6.
69. *20*, 638, 19.
70. *8*, 114, 18.
71. *20*, 638, 9f.
72. *25*, 418, 4; 419, 28.

in its potency. "There is no opportunity for the thought: 'He is the propitiation for Peter's sins and Paul's—if only He were for mine!' It says, 'for the sins of the whole world.' For this, there is sufficient propitiation in Christ, even if the world were far greater than it is, for He has shed His blood so abundantly that it would suffice for many, many, worlds." [73]

Because of the eternal power and efficacy of this high priestly atonement, the Christian has constant access to the throne of grace. This is Luther's primary association whenever he uses "propitiation" of Christ: there is in Christ continual forgiveness for all the persisting sin in the Christian and in the Church.[74] The more aware Christians become of their weakness and sin, the more they take refuge in Christ, their mercy seat.[75] And because the holiness and righteousness of Christ the propitiator vastly surpasses the sin of the whole world, the Christian's sin is not mortal, the Church is made holy in spite of its weakness, and we are made righteous even in this present life.[76] Accordingly, Christ's role as propitiator is intimately connected with His present priestly office of intercession.


## Intercessor, Advocate

The content of Christ's heavenly intercession receives relatively minor treatment. Luther seems readily to associate the office of advocate and intercessor with the clause of the creed, "sitteth at the right hand of God the Father Almighty." [77] Even His heavenly session is "for us." [78] There Christ, both God and man in equal power and majesty with God, takes our part and is therefore the sole ground of reliance and hope.[79] "Is it not a great thing that the High Majesty Himself intercedes for me—indeed,

73. 20, 638, 30ff.
74. 20, 636, 24; 26, 222, 3; 31/I, 423, 7.
75. 40/II, 108, 28.
76. 40/I, 445, 14; II, 79, 31; 86, 15; 96, 29.
77. E.g. 46, 557, 9; 601, 7.
78. 34/II, 509, 10.
79. 33, 283, 37; 46, 601, 7.

gives Himself to be mine?" [80] Christ actually confesses sin before God, not for Himself, but as our intercessor and advocate before the Judge, and Himself makes satisfaction. He makes the very best plea on our behalf: He offers His blood for us. "As an eternal mediator and high priest, He prays and intercedes with the Father for those who believe, because they still have remaining weaknesses and sins." And what Christ asks must come to pass. When He prays, "Forgive them," we are forgiven; when He says, "Grant them pardon," we are pardoned.[81]

Christ's prayer is likewise the sole ground of our prayers: "He says to me that He wants to be my paraclete. If I come to the Father through Him, I come because by His own right He has gone to the Father, and because by His mercy He has shared this with me." [82] It is typical of Luther that, rather than expatiate on the possible content of Christ's heavenly intercession, he takes the prayer of John 17 as the archetypical instance of Christ's advocacy. "We already have Christ's prayer in which He interceded for us with the Father: He offered it once, but it is eternally efficacious, and because of it our prayers are pleasing and acceptable to God . . . His and our prayers must be one." [83] In this—"the high prayer of our salvation"—He interceded for His disciples in their person and their office, and prayed that they should remain steadfast in the Word.[84] This is a prayer which must certainly be answered, because Christ's obedience and His Godhead constitute a double claim on heaven, as His present enthronement declares.[85] How may we be sure that we are the subject of His advocacy? Christ offered His great prayer "for those who shall believe in Me through their word" (John 17:20). "This qualification applies to me—Christ prayed for me. He has prayed for us: in all John's gospel there is no more precious saying than this." [86] Even if we feel sin, then, Christ does not accuse us but

80. *12*, 490, 9.
81. *44*, 507, 34; *25*, 65, 26; *21*, 363, 20; *20*, 637, 2.
82. *20*, 639, 9.
83. *46*, 97, 20 to 98, 7.
84. *28*, 131, 3; 155, 9; 200, 10.
85. *28*, 128, 6.
86. *28*, 181, 14.

intercedes for us. Faith must lay hold of this "intercedes," so that when, in the deed, it feels Christ accusing, in hope it awaits Christ's interceding for it.[87]

"What does this advocate do? He is a champion in Whose presence the very angels stay their laughter; but His office is to be my paraclete, comforter, and counselor: 'Father, by Thy grace show compassion on him, for I have shed My blood for him.' Which one of us would not rejoice if we believed this?" [88]

### Savior, Helper, Deliverer

Needless to say, by far the most frequent and the most general soteriological title is "savior" (*Heiland*). It is used so broadly in its constant occurrences that quotation becomes superfluous. Yet even in this case, where the scriptural usage itself is not very specific, certain patterns of biblical speech are impressed on Luther's vocabulary.

Our Lord's name, Luther says, "is rightly called Jesus, which means savior: for we call one 'savior' who saves, redeems, brings salvation, and is of help to all men; and such a one is called 'Jesus' in Hebrew." [89]

> As often as not, Luther couples "savior" with other titles: "God and savior," probably suggested by the usage of Psalms, Isaiah, and the epistle to Titus (e.g. 45, 483, 25; 528, 10); "lord and savior," following II Peter (e.g. 10/III, 129, 32; 46, 542, 19); "head and savior," reflecting Ephesians 5:23 (e.g. 45, 711, 13); "mediator and savior" (e.g. 21, 365, 28; 40/I, 90, 24); "savior and redeemer" (e.g. 44, 587, 3; 45, 717, 21); "savior and helper" (e.g. 17/II, 214, 31); "savior and high priest" (e.g. 40/II, 118, 13); "savior and comforter" (e.g. 40/II, 42, 8); and especially in the commentary on Galatians, "justifier and savior" (e.g. 40/I, 255, 20; 679, 35; II, 183, 28).

Like the early Church in its preaching (Luke 2:11, John 4:42, Acts 5:31), Luther also uses "savior" as an assertion of Christ's

87. 25, 12, 7f.: ". . . in re sentit Christum accusantem, in spe expectat Christum interpellantem pro se."

88. 20, 634, 17.

89. 10/I/1, 518, 9.

messianic claim. He is "Messiah and savior." [90] But Luther, like the early Church, reinterprets Jewish conceptions about Messiah's role in the light of the history of Christ. The Jews thought the Messiah should be the world's lord; actually He was sent to be the world's savior. It was the promised savior that the faith of the patriarchs anticipated.[91] The Messiah came not to liberate Israel from political oppression but to save His people from their sins.

This early became the dominant Christian sense of "savior"; and so with Luther in a majority of cases the title is used of the atonement—in all its aspects.

> Christ is "the savior of souls" (36, 287, 29). He is "savior, priest, and intercessor" (45, 727, 24); we are accepted "for the sake of this savior and mediator" (21, 365, 28f.; 482, 9f.). He is the savior of sinners because He bears and atones for sin in His death (e.g. 21, 292, 30–37; 31/II, 434, 15; 45, 519, 32; 592, 17; 46, 580, 1; 47, 105, 6; 111, 28), and thus blots it out, abolishing its condemnation (e.g. 12, 544, 31; 21, 359, 27ff.; 46, 41, 34; 47, 105, 42), and removing the might and the fear of death in His conquest (e.g. 10/I/2, 236, 25f.; 45, 499, 14; 519, 32; 599, 10; 46, 603, 27).

This work of salvation is of universal significance. In many places Luther employs St. John's phrase, "the savior of the world" (John 4:42, I John 4:14),[92] and makes much of the text, "God sent not His Son into the world to condemn the world, but that the world through Him might be saved" (John 3:17). That Christ was sent as savior indicates, on the one hand, that the world was damned and cursed before,[93] but, on the other, that now we may be sure of the love and mercy of God. "Savior" is therefore a name of consolation for Luther. Time and again he declares that Christ is not a judge but a savior [94] Who brings us comfort and assures us that God is not angry with us.[95] Therefore the con-

90. E.g. 45, 716, 36; 717, 21; 46, 574, 19; 699, 38.
91. 46, 699, 23f.; 637, 9f.
92. E.g. 20, 391, 38; 769, 16; 33, 309, 39; 310, 3; 45, 543, 31; 46, 577, 35; 693, 26.
93. 20, 751, 14–19.
94. E.g. 10/III, 163, 22 to 164, 2; 33, 540, 10ff.; 549, 1; 45, 550, 3; 47, 106, 19; 110, 10.
95. 10/III, 164, 1; 46, 588, 3.

science rejoices when Christ is known as savior: "the highest of all joys is that joy the heart possesses in our savior Christ." [96] When Luther speaks devotionally, the name "savior"—often "my dear savior," "our faithful, loving savior," "sweet savior and high priest"—springs to his lips.[97] Now it is possible to confess, "Jesus is my savior, He is gracious," and so our hearts are not fearful or confounded before Him. "How can you love Christ unless you are convinced that He is your treasure and savior, life and consolation?" [98]

> A vital element in the meaning of "savior" for a Christian's devotion is the awareness of Christ's daily protection in this mortal life (e.g. *21, 336, 32ff.; 471, 31f.; 45, 483, 25; 604, 11*). "Christ is presented to us as a most loving savior and helper in every need" (*17/II, 214, 31*). "Helper," (*Helffer*) is chief among a small group of synonyms for "savior" in this sense (e.g. *33, 52, 17; 541, 40; 545, 29; 36, 346, 12; 47, 100, 9; 102, 13f.; 105, 30ff.; 198, 26*). They are applied much less frequently but perform the same task as "savior." Christ is our "deliverer" (*Nothelffer*) in the work of salvation and in the tribulations of life (*43, 253, 6; 44, 524, 6; 47, 100, 10*). Another synonym is *Seligmacher* (*33, 85, 19; 46, 776, 7*), which conveys the sense of eternal blessing, but whose use is so close to *Heiland* that it defies translation when Luther uses both words at once (as he does, e.g., in *17/II, 433, 27; 47, 69, 38; 115, 24*. As an instance of the difficulty of translation without banality or redundance, cf. *33, 393, 33*; "So wird er auch ein Heiland genennet, das er kan selig machen . . .").

Inevitably, the pedal note of Luther's doctrine is sounding in the case of "savior" too: he asserts constantly that Christ is the only savior, of the world and men.[99] "I cling to this man and confess Him alone as our savior"; "there is no savior besides." [1] If Christ is not lord and savior, we are lost.[2] "What is the new cove-

---

96. *22, 426, 40; 431, 1ff.; 49, 260, 34.*
97. E.g. *21, 336, 33; 28, 192, 13; 40/I, 92, 13; 45, 467, 16; 46, 584, 5; 655, 8.*
98. *25, 63, 16; 45, 595, 22.*
99. E.g. *28, 599, 6; 33, 48, 31; 560, 34; 40/I, 679, 35; 45, 491, 17; 46, 584, 13; 588, 3; 786, 29; 47, 110, 4.*
1. *33, 666, 19f.; 22, 427, 9.*
2. *46, 652, 26f.*

nant? To possess Christ. What is Christ? The savior Who carries our sins away and gives gifts to men. If He bears me on His shoulders, I shall fare well."[3] We confess, "He was yesterday, He is today, and He remains my savior—to the grave and from it, to the last day and to eternity."[4]

In short, Luther says, Christ is more than savior: "He is salvation and life in person." He alone is our salvation and the salvation of all men.[5] True, He looks more like an accursed sinner to reason; but this very estate is the ground of faith, for it was in His earthly history that Christ was made "our life, light, and salvation—here everything happened that we are to believe about Him."[6] And the faith that knows the use of this history exclaims, "He is my life, my salvation, and my wisdom."[7]

## Redeemer, Ransom

Luther's use of "redemption" terminology is generally more informed by Deuteronomy, the Psalms, and the prophets, where "to redeem" means "to deliver," than by the levitical usage, "to free by repayment." Thus Luther describes Christ's arduous redemptive work as deliverance from death, sin, the devil, and hell, and their destruction.[8] He is not only our redeemer in fact (פֹּדֶה), but our liberator and just avenger by right (גֹּאֵל). For the devil and death overreached themselves when they killed the innocent Son of God, Who now rightfully shatters their power and redeems us for Himself.[9] The redeemer is He Who can do for us what we are utterly unable to do for ourselves.[10] Thus Moses' brass serpent is "an allegory of Christ's office of redemption": our redemption does not lie in our own hands, but in looking to this

3. 20, 771, 3.
4. 47, 195, 13.
5. 47, 88, 35; 33, 20, 21; 54, 4.
6. 10/I/1, 201, 13; I/2, 305, 36.
7. 47, 81, 36; 82, 10.
8. E.g. 10/I/2, 235, 27–32; 14, 30, 13; 31/I, 145, 35; 45, 554, 4; 47, 178, 11; 228, 39; etc.
9. 44, 697, 23.
10. 47, 172, 9–21.

"serpent." [11] Luther early uses God's declaration, "I am thy redeemer," and St. Paul's affirmation of "Christ our redemption" to
establish that we are justified by a righteousness which remains
alien to us; and he scores his papal opponents for mouthing the
title *Redemptor* without realizing its content.[12] Christ alone redeems from sins; there is no other redeemer.[13]

Redemption in the sense of deliverance is Luther's most frequent association, but not at the expense of omitting other scriptural emphases, particularly the designation of Christ as ransom
in the light of the levitical practice of redeeming the firstborn,
and hence the apostolic doctrine that redemption is by His blood,
by the laying down of His life. Christ's death is our redemption.[14] In a passage which deserves some prominence in the study
of Luther, he declares, "As I have often said, faith alone is not
enough before God—a price is also involved." [15] What is the cost
of our salvation, he asks? "God has so loved us that He let it cost
Him His only beloved Child. He has submitted Him to our misery, hell, and death, and let Him drain them dry—that is the
means of our salvation." [16] For the gospel is nothing else but
"that this Christ is God's Son, sent by the Father to be the offering and payment for the sin of the world by His own blood, and
thus to appease God's wrath and to reconcile us in order that we
should be redeemed from sin and death and obtain eternal righteousness and life through Him." [17] In a startling phrase which
completely transmutes Anselm's doctrine of the abundance of
Christ's merits, or Thomas' *superabundans satisfactio*,[18] Luther
avers that "just one droplet of His blood helps the whole world,
for this person is very God." [19] What is the treasure with which

11. *21*, 550, 19; *25*, 477, 13.
12. *7*, 809, 23ff.; *45*, 722, 30.
13. *25*, 466, 30; *31*/II, 353, 19.
14. *45*, 707, 7; *43*, 28, 15.
15. *10*/III, 161, 11; cf. *8*, 112, 2.
16. *10*/III, 162, 11; cf. *29*, 576, 17.
17. *21*, 435, 1.
18. Anselm, *Cur Deus homo*, Bk. II, xix (*S. Anselmi opera omnia*, ed. F. S.
Schmitt [6 vols. Edinburgh, 1946–61], 2, 129ff.); Thomas Aquinas, ST III, Q. 48,
a. 2.
19. *47*, 172, 15.

we are redeemed? "Not corruptible gold or silver, but the precious blood of Christ, the Son of God. It is so precious and noble a treasure that no human imagination or thought can conceive it—so precious that one drop of this innocent blood more than suffices for all the world's sin." [20] Luther dispatches the Schoolmen's question, "Whether Christ merited anything for Himself?" [21] Christ holds this payment price for me, not for Himself: He was not born, nor subject to suffering and death, in order to become God's Son, which He was already. But He did so in order that I might become God's son, through Him.[22]

As in the case of "mediator," it is a rare exception when Luther relates redemption to technical Christology. Any attack on the christological dogma, he says, "must nullify our redemption and the forgiveness of sins," for Christ must be God in order to overcome sin, death, devil, God's wrath, and eternal damnation; and He must be man in order to suffer [23] (an argument vaguely parallel to Athanasius in some respects, yet markedly different in omitting any notion of the sanctification of humanity by the Incarnation).[24] This account forms part of Luther's rather technical 1538 exposition of John 3:13—a verse, he says, which describes "the work of our redemption in three propositions: that Christ descended from heaven, resides in heaven, and ascends back to heaven. The first states Who the agent is, the second what He did, and the third why He did it." [25] Luther tantalizingly omits to execute this explicit homiletic scheme!

In a reflection of the traditional practice of dividing dogmatic topics according to the parts of the creed, Luther sometimes contrasts "God the creator" and "Christ the redeemer"; [26] and he

20. 12, 291, 10.
21. E.g. Peter Lombard, *Sentences* III, xviii, 1 (MPL CXCII, 792); Bonaventura's commentary on this locus: *In Sent.* III, xviii, 1–2 (*Opera theologica selecta* [4 vols. Florence, 1941], 3, 371ff.); Thomas Aquinas, ST III, Q. 49, a. 3.
22. 47, 172, 17.
23. 47, 52, 22.
24. Athanasius, *De incarn.* 9 (MPG XXV, 111–12). Cf. Ernst Wolf, "Asterisci und Obelisci zum Thema: Athanasius und Luther," *Evangelische Theologie, 18* (1958), 481ff.
25. 47, 49, 37.
26. 47, 179, 28; 190, 27.

makes the distinction live by saying, "Now God is not to be known as creator, but as the One Who sent His Son for our redemption . . . to help the world from its sin and death. We must learn to know the Father, the almighty God and creator, in this form, namely in His Son, as savior and redeemer." [27] To know Him is to know that we are forgiven; for "the forgiveness of our sins is not for one or two thousand years, but instead an eternal redemption, a salvation, joy, life, forgiveness of sins without any measure." [28]

## Sacrifice, Satisfaction, Substitute

In recent decades Luther's understanding of sacrifice in relation to the doctrine of the Eucharist has received persistent attention.[29] The result has been a far more positive appreciation of the sacrificial nuances he retained in his thinking about the sacrament, at the same time as he strove against the "sacrifice of the mass" as a blasphemous denial of the sufficiency of Christ's sacrifice. Simply because the ground of Luther's sacramental revolution was indeed the perfection of Christ's sacrifice of Himself, recent study of this question has inevitably (if incidentally) also reexamined Luther's exegetical labors on the theme of sacrifice as a central element in atonement. Nevertheless, this is a theme of sufficient weight with Luther to deserve still more attention for its own sake.

Luther's chief exegetical insight into the role of sacrifice is that there are two quite distinct classes of sacrifice described by Scripture—propitiatory offering and thank-offering—and that the first of these is strictly a class of one, Christ's offering of Himself being the unique and only sacrifice of atonement.[30] "Behold the Lamb of God" (John 1:29) was John the Baptist's challenge to

27. 45, 717, 28.

28. 47, 197, 29.

29. E.g. Yngve Brilioth, *Eucharistic Faith and Practice, Evangelical and Catholic* (London, reprinted 1956); Hermann Sasse, *This is My Body: Luther's Contention for the Real Presence in the Sacrament of the Altar* (Minneapolis, 1959); Gustaf Aulén, *Eucharist and Sacrifice* (Philadelphia, 1958).

30. E.g. 6, 368, 26ff; 17/II, 206, 31; 26, 220, 21; 42, 537ff.; cf. Pelikan, *Luther the Expositor*, pp. 237ff.

the Jews to "contrast the true lamb and Moses' lamb, which in
the Mosaic law was commanded to be slaughtered and eaten . . .
The paschal lamb of the law was certainly a fine mime for the
children, and an exercise designed to remind you of the real
Lamb of God; but you extracted your own conclusion that such
slaughtering and sacrificing would remove your sins. You dare
not think that! Your lambs will never do that—only this Lamb
of God will. Those lambs were supposed to be only puppets by
which the people were to remind themselves of the true paschal
lamb that should one day be sacrificed." The sacrifices of the law
were men's lambs; Christ is God's lamb. God prescribed that He
"should be sacrificed and roasted on the cross for our sins . . .
God made Him a lamb which should bear the sins of the whole
world." [31]

> Here is the proper paschal lamb
> Which God Himself entailed;
> Who on the cross, in love aflame,
> Is roasted and impaled.
> His blood is painted on our door,
> The slayer, death, must pass before;
> Our faith he cannot plunder.[32]

This, says Luther, is the foundation of all Christian teaching.
He who believes it is a Christian; he who does not believe it is
not a Christian and will receive his due. The ground of this claim
is the utter seriousness with which he takes man's sin.[33] This eloquent sermon on "Behold the Lamb of God" deserves to be a
locus classicus for his handling of this deep concern. He speaks
here of sin as the evil of our nature, as hostility and blasphemy
against God, as transgression, as burden, and as bondage.[34] But
the principal theme is the disposing of sin—sin-bearing, the essence of the idea of sacrifice.

We may digress momentarily to notice a warning from the pen

31. 46, 676, 32 to 677, 19; cf. 25, 411, 12; 31/II, 433, 1.
32. 35, 444, 13.
33. 46, 679, 9; cf. 21, 211, 17.
34. 46, 679, 22ff.

of Gustaf Aulén. He says, "Every attempt to prove that Luther's teaching contains an idea of 'satisfaction' other than that involved in the triumph of Christ over the tyrants is doomed to hopeless failure." [35] But at the risk of the futility Aulén predicts, Luther's own words seem to make the endeavor inevitable. For to Luther sin-bearing (the sacrifice motif) and atonement or payment for sin (the satisfaction motif) go hand in hand. We may say that when Luther mentions one, he normally mentions the other in the same breath. "Because no man fulfills God's commandment or can be sinless before God, and therefore all men are under God's wrath and subject to eternal damnation by the law, God has found a remedy for this evil: He determined to send His Son into the world, that He might become a sacrifice for us and make satisfaction for our sins by the shedding of His blood and His death, removing from us the wrath of God which no creature could reconcile." [36] "He had to take our place, become a sacrifice for us, bear and atone for the wrath and curse under which we had fallen." [37] Again, "He offers Himself as a sacrifice by the shedding of His blood and His death in order to pay for our sins." He was sent by the Father "as a sacrifice and payment for the sin of the world by His own blood." Since there was no hope of redemption through any creature in heaven or earth, "the Son of God had to take our place and become a sacrifice for our sins, in order thereby to appease God's anger and make payment for us." "Christ has offered Himself once for us, and has thereby made satisfaction for sins." [38] The same association appears in even more concise forms: Christ must be crucified and become "a sacrifice for the sins of the world," take our sins upon Him and make Himself "a sacrifice to the everlasting wrath of God which we had merited by our sins." [39]

This relationship between sacrifice and satisfaction is the key to the whole question of the disposing of sin. The proper function

35. Aulén, *Christus Victor,* p. 118.
36. *21,* 358, 34.
37. *21,* 259, 9; cf. *21,* 234, 17; *40/I,* 448, 23.
38. *21,* 363, 14; 435, 2; 547, 36 to 548, 4; *25,* 411, 17.
39. *21,* 545, 19; 546, 29.

of the law is to apprise man of his sinfulness, his disobedience, his estrangement from God, and his eternal condemnation for sin. "In short, the law shows me what I am, it reveals sin and burdens me with it." The law deposits this sin on our shoulders. If it remains there, we are damned. But by the same token, we cannot throw it off.[40] It is clear from this account that the fact that we are sinners is not at issue: the issue is whether we must bear this sin. For the person who bears it must pay for it.

Now, as soon as human reason, in its "hideous and terrible blindness," hears this, it rushes off after its own solutions. It declares, "I will reform and become pious; I will atone by performing good works"—a solution which, on the one hand, ignores the pollution of the whole world by sin, and on the other, tries to atone before God with deeds which belong only to the realm of this world and actually "leave sins unborne and unpaid." [41] Or it does what the Jews did with the Mosaic ceremonies, or the papacy with the mass—attempt to make a sacrifice of atonement (instead of a sacrifice of thanksgiving) out of ordinances designed to direct faith to the one perfect sacrifice of atonement, the Lamb of God.[42] Or it runs to the saints and invokes the aid of the Virgin, saying "Intercede for me before your Son, show Him your breasts"; it calls on (the nonexistent) St. Christopher or St. Barbara for their intercession and even tries through monkery to be its own savior.[43] But all of these are disqualified from being our sin-bearers, for if sin rested on me and all the world, we should be lost: the burden is too great.[44] That is to say, there is no one but Christ who is able to make satisfaction for the sins of the world. No works or masses or purgatory have rendered satisfaction for sin; it is impossible to declare at once that Christ is our satisfaction and that these other things also satisfy for sin: "as to satisfaction, Christ is our only savior." [45] Looking back almost in disbelief at his monastic life, Luther exclaims, "We set our filth

40. *46*, 679, 25; 680, 1.
41. *46*, 679, 35; 682, 18.
42. *17*/II, 206, 24; *31*/II, 9, 24ff.; *42*, 539, 34.
43. *20*, 623, 15; *46*, 679, 28.
44. *46*, 683, 24.
45. *47*, 115, 31; cf. *26*, 220, 21; *31*/II, 433, 11.

and stench alongside the sacrifice of Christ the lord!" But, he says, "He has given for me not St. Francis or any other monk or the mother of Christ or St. Peter or an angel or cowls and tonsures, but a far more precious treasure. Salvation and deliverance from death demand a greater service than any man or angel could perform—only God's only-begotten Son can do it." [46]

Since there is only one Who can render satisfaction for the sin of the world, there can be only one atoning sacrifice, one sin-bearer. Therefore the search for other sin-bearers is futile. If we ask these other "saviors" to take the burden of our sins, in fact we keep the burden on our own shoulders. For in the last analysis, "there are only two resting places for sin: it either rests on you, weighing you down; or it lies upon Christ, the Lamb of God. If the load is on your shoulders, you are lost, but if it rests on Christ, you are free and saved. Now choose!" [47]

For the sinner the site of this issue is his conscience. It is in his conscience under the law that he feels "sin at his throat, driving him and pressing down on him." [48] To know freedom from this tyranny of law, sin, and the devil in an accusing conscience, a man must know that Christ is his sin-bearer. "For there is no other consolation in heaven or earth to strengthen us against all attacks and temptations, especially in the pangs of death." But he may know this consolation, because the ordinance and promise of God is that Christ assumes "the sins of the whole world, from Adam to the very last person." [49] The Lamb takes on Himself and pays for "not some, but all the sins of the world, great or small, few or many." [50] Therefore every man or woman without exception is guaranteed forgiveness. "Nothing is missing from the Lamb—He bears all the world's sins from its beginning, which means that He bears yours too." Refusal to believe this is not Christ's fault, but the fault of our unbelief, and leads to condemnation.[51] Here, as at so many crucial points in Luther's teaching, we discover the correspondence between our con-

46. *47*, 146, 38; 84, 34.
47. *46*, 683, 28; cf. 40/I, 438, 24.
48. *46*, 679, 36; cf. 10/III, 159, 29.
49. *46*, 678, 21; 677, 27 (cf. *20*, 638, 29; *31*/II, 434, 2).
50. 10/I/2, 207, 5.
51. *46*, 683, 8 (cf. *20*, 639, 5; *47*, 105, 1ff.).

science and our standing before God. To refuse Christ is to insist upon bearing our own sin—that is, since the person who bears sin must pay for it, to insist upon paying for our own sin, even though Christ has already paid with His blood for it. Conversely, to be oppressed, burdened, and accused in conscience by the weight of sin is to have refused the offer of God's mercy, "Behold the Lamb of God!", and to ignore His promise, "Through My Son I shall cancel My charge against you." [52]

One is almost tempted to reverse the priorities of Aulén's warning. Luther is firmly convinced by St. Paul's dictum, "the sting of death is sin, and the power of sin is the law" (I Cor. 15:56). It is because men are sinners against God that the law is a tyrant. It is because the law pronounces condemnation against sin that death is a tyrant. But now Christ and His gospel have replaced the law, which is therefore no longer a tyrant; He has borne our sin and its condemnation, so that even death itself is no longer a tyrant. In this way, Christ's triumph over the tyrants is an aspect of His sacrifice, its pivotal consequence, out of the richness of His love and the merciful forgiveness of God. He is "the savior Who removed sin, bore it on His shoulders, and bolted the gates of hell . . . Christ removed the sin of the world so completely that it is utterly canceled, utterly forgiven." [53]

Forgiveness remains at the center of Luther's gospel.[54] The wealth of biblical and traditional teaching about the sacrifice of atonement provided him with the most adequate expression of this mercy of God. In this connection, Luther's relation to Anselm, for instance, must be described in a manner quite different from Aulén's description. Some very able scholarship has sprung to Anselm's defense against the attacks leveled by Ritschl, Harnack, Aulén, and other critics,[55] and his evangelical purpose and his awareness of the mercy of God should no longer be in

---

52. *47,* 104, 33 (cf. *29, 576,* 24).

53. *47,* 105, 6; cf. *42,* 146, 38ff.

54. *15,* 703, 24; *22,* 389, 38; *29, 572,* 20.

55. E.g. John McIntyre, *St. Anselm and His Critics* (Edinburgh, 1954); Eugene Fairweather, "Incarnation and Atonement: An Anselmian Response to Aulén's *Christus Victor," Canadian Journal of Theology, 7,* no. 3 (1961), 169ff.; the same author's "Introduction to Anselm of Canterbury," in *A Scholastic Miscellany: Anselm to Ockham,* Library of Christian Classics, 10 (London, 1956), pp. 54ff.

question.[56] A theme that has accordingly received particular attention is Anselm's concept of *iustitia dei*, which he built upon the foundation of Augustine's notion of *iustitia*[57] and used (in Eugene Fairweather's words) "to interpret the whole sweep of God's plan for the resurrection of man to the true order of his creaturely existence."[58] As George Heyer points out, the effect of such an insight for a correct reading of Anselm is that "no merely juridical interpretation of justice will be adequate."[59] However, the young Martin Luther was heir to a dogmatic tradition in which a sternly juridical interpretation of *iustitia dei* was tantamount. His breakthrough to the knowledge that he was forgiven came with the discovery that the punitive view of God's justice he had been taught was a distortion of the gospel.[60] He proceeded to discover Augustinian insights into the meaning of *iustitia* which Anselm, *mutatis mutandis,* had also appreciated.[61] (A case might even be made for the proposition that the Reformation did not so much outmode Anselm's view of atonement as restore and purify some of its pristine perspective.) Luther's understanding of Christ our righteousness goes far beyond Anselm; yet if Luther's doctrine is immeasurably richer because he found his "necessary reasons" in the Word rather than in dialectic, it remains true that he shares common ground with Anselm.

By his rediscovery that the righteousness of God is an utterly different righteousness from any that obtains under all the law of

56. George Heyer, "Rectitudo in the Theology of St. Anselm" (doctoral dissertation, Yale University, 1963; University Microfilms, 1963), pp. 207–13; but for some of Anselm's difficulties at this point see ibid., pp. 34–40. For a briefer statement, see Heyer's "St. Anselm on the Harmony between God's Mercy and God's Justice," in Robert E. Cushman and Egil Grislis, eds., *The Heritage of Christian Thought: Essays in Honor of Robert Lowry Calhoun* (New York, 1965), pp. 31–40.

57. Robert Crouse, "The Augustinian Background of St. Anselm's *Justitia,*" *Canadian Journal of Theology, 4,* no. 2 (1958), 111ff.

58. Eugene Fairweather, " 'Iustitia dei' as the 'Ratio' of the Incarnation," in *Spicilegium Beccense,* Vol. 1: *Congrès international du IXe Centenaire de l'Arrivée d'Anselme au Bec* (Paris, 1959), p. 329; quoted in Heyer, "Rectitudo" p. 205.

59. "Rectitudo" p. 206.

60. *54, 185,* 17; cf. Karl Holl, "Die 'Justitia Dei' in der vorlutherischen Bibelauslegung des Abendlandes," in his *Gesammelte Aufsätze zur Kirchengeschichte* (3 vols., 7. Aufl., Tübingen, 1948), 3, 171ff.

61. E.g. *21, 259,* 9ff.

this world—that it is rather Christ's own righteousness, offered to us in the gospel and dwelling in us by the Word and faith [62]— Luther adds a new dimension to the nature of the satisfaction: "Our salvation, and the article of justification before God through Christ or satisfaction for sin, cannot be divorced from the person of Christ, Who is God. For He alone and no other has made satisfaction for sin in eternity." [63] In one sense it is true that Christ has done for us something we ought to have been able to do but could not.[64] But He does not merely compensate for our inability, or discharge our obligation of reparation; He does infinitely more. "What does the work or even the potential of all mankind amount to in achieving or meriting so great an issue as forgiveness from sins and redemption from death and everlasting wrath? How can it compare with the death and shed blood of the Son of God?" [65] The Passion and death of Christ are of infinite worth, and "satisfaction" understood merely as a quid pro quo is clearly inadequate to describe Christ's achievement.[66] Here is yet another reason why in all God's universe there can be only one sacrifice of atonement. There is strictly no forensic analogy. For "if you have sinned before men in this realm, you must pay and atone before the judge. But before God and in Christ's kingdom this is not the requirement. For there all satisfactions are rejected: instead you must have Christ, Who did not sin but made satisfaction for your sins." [67] This is God's own promise, ordinance, commission, and command: Christ suffered "not because there was any such requirement upon Him, but because it so pleased the Father." [68] God recognizes no other satisfaction.[69] "According to the law and justice, your sin should certainly remain your burden; but by grace sin was cast upon Christ the Lamb." [70]

62. 40/I, 305, 30ff.
63. 47, 113, 38.
64. 10/I/2, 220, 36.
65. 21, 218, 37.
66. 25, 52, 33; 21, 264, 27.
67. 33, 281, 13 to 282, 20.
68. 10/I/2, 236, 29.
69. 46, 679, 19; cf. 23, 555, 36ff.
70. 46, 683, 32; cf. 31/II, 432, 23.

This is the sacrifice of which Isaiah 53 speaks, the sacrifice of
atonement which God Himself provides.[71] A spiritual interpretation of the story of Abraham and Isaac according to the analogy
of faith would instruct us thus: "Whoever would come to God
must rise above human understanding and thinking to God's
Word, learn to know and apprehend God from this source. There
—if his conscience is to stand before God—he must offer by faith
before Him the sacrifice given for us by God as a sacrifice, Christ,
the Son of God." [72] This is sheer forgiveness. This is the inexpressible, incomprehensible love of God to which we must ascend
through Christ our passover, sacrificed for us.[73]

"One has sinned, another made satisfaction. The one who sins
does not make satisfaction; the one Who makes satisfaction does
not sin. It is an amazing doctrine." [74] This is the *mirabilis transla-
tio* in which the Christian religion consists: "The love of the Son
of God is so great toward us that the greater the filth and stench
upon us, the more He gives Himself to us, cleanses us, and takes
all our sin and wretchedness, lifts them off our shoulders and lays
them on His own back . . . What does it mean that the Son of
God should be my servant, and so utterly debase Himself that He
should take the burden of my misery and sin—yes, the whole
world's sin and death? He says to me, 'You are no longer a sinner,
but I am. I step into your place—you have not sinned, but I
have. The whole world is in sin, but you are not in sin—I am. All
your sins are to lie on Me and not on you.' No one can grasp this:
there in the life to come we shall gaze forever blessed upon this
love of God. And who would not gladly die for Christ's sake?
The Son of Man does the basest and filthiest work—not just wear-
ing a beggar's tattered coat or old trousers or washing us like a
mother washes a child, but He bears our sin, death, hell, our
wretchedness of body and soul. When the devil says, 'You are
a sinner,' Christ interrupts, 'I will reverse that, I will be a

71. 31/II, 433, 1ff.; 46, 682, 1.

72. 21, 377, 18; cf. 43, 234, 14–22. David Lerch, *Isaaks Opferung christlich
gedeutet* (Tübingen, 1950), pp. 156ff., describes the Reformers' exegesis of Gen.
22 in relation to the tradition.

73. 21, 211, 31.

74. 31/II, 339, 27: "Ita haec religio Christiana: Alius peccavit alius satisfecit.
Peccans non satisfacit. Satisfaciens non peccat. Mirabilis est doctrina."

sinner, you shall go free.' Who can be thankful enough to our Lord God for this mercy?" [75]

## Victor, Destroyer of Sin

What must surprise anyone familiar with the stress in modern Luther studies upon the proclamation of Christ's victory is how rarely the theme receives extended treatment in his preaching and exposition.

It is true that some of the best known passages in Luther dramatically portray Christ triumphing over the dark forces of our bondage: such rich oratory lends itself to quotation. It is also true that his Easter hymns of victory are among his most popular. As a result, it has been too easily assumed that this is the constant refrain of Luther's gospel of salvation. In fact, in his preaching Luther gives far greater weight to the themes we have already discussed. The exaggerated impression that it is otherwise may be enhanced by the undercurrent of joy in deliverance never long suppressed in his preaching. But his gospel is everywhere a gospel of joy, whether victory is mentioned or not.

To retain a correct perspective, the place of forgiveness at the heart of this gospel must never be forgotten. It is one of the dangers of an overly dualistic scheme that this perspective is dimmed. There are two other dangers. To press Luther's dramatic motifs into a dualistic mold may obscure his insistence that in every moment of our being—even in our bondage to the devil and death—it is God only with Whom we have to deal. When this is obscured, the simplicity of his message is lost and the place of God's wrath in the list of "tyrants" (the law, sin, death, hell, the devil, and God's wrath) becomes a problem—a problem within God, as if He could not let His left hand know what His right hand was doing; and then the *deus absconditus* becomes a *deus ex machina* to resolve an unnecessary and speculative conundrum. These were connections Luther himself never made, and we shall avoid pitfalls if we remain within the limits of his express concerns.

Perhaps the most explicit development of the victory idea is to

75. *46*, 680, 31 to 681, 16.

be found in Luther's exposition of the words, "Be of good cheer, I have overcome the world" (John 16:33). This is a text, he says, which we should write in golden letters upon our hearts.[76] Luther explains the indicative in closest connection with the imperative: "A Christian should steep himself in the thought of Christ's victory, in which everything is already done and we have everything we need. From now on we live only to show forth the victory that Christ has won and given to us, and to bring other people to it, exhorting and attracting them by word and example. For this victor has accomplished everything, so that we can do nothing, cancel or crush the devil or overthrow death—they are all laid low already. Our suffering and fighting are not the real battle, but only a prize or morsel of the glory of this victory. For our suffering—yes, the suffering and blood of all the martyrs and saints—would not gain us the victory: the task of crushing sin, death, and hell and trampling them underfoot is beyond us . . . The battle must be already won and the victory achieved if I am to have comfort and peace. Christ says, 'I have done it already, just accept it and use the victory by singing about it, glorying and making a show of it—just be men of good cheer.'" [77]

The victory is complete already. It is Christ's accomplishment, and Christ's alone: He has trampled devil, sin, death, and hell underfoot and gained the victory over them through His Resurrection and Ascension. In His own person and by His own power and authority, He is the only sin-slayer and death-devourer (*Sundewurger, Todfresser*). But this is the vital qualification: all this was for us.[78] " 'Yes,' you say, 'it is all very well for You to say You have overcome. Others, too—like Peter and Paul. But where do I stand?' 'Well,' Christ answers, 'I am certainly not saying this to you for My own benefit. Do you not hear? It is meant for you. You must know and take comfort that I have overcome the world not for Myself—for I had no need to descend from heaven, since I was lord of all creation beforehand, so that the devil and

76. *28, 68, 14.*
77. *46, 110, 24.*
78. *21, 217, 29; 40/I, 356, 32; 25, 53, 21 note; 22, 287, 21; 21, 484, 11; 45, 519, 32.*

the world could certainly not touch Me! But I have done this for your sake, for your sake I am speaking to you and want to comfort you. This is the reason to take it to heart and consider that I, Jesus Christ, have conquered and won the victory.' " [79]

The point of declaring the atonement in terms of victory is unequivocally stated to be the consolation of man's conscience. Perhaps nowhere does Luther more plainly demonstrate the ultimate unity of the objective and subjective facets of the gospel—of "first" and "second" faith. Because He was God, Christ (and Christ only) "trampled down sin, death, and the devil by the exalted work of His death and Resurrection." [80] If He were only man and not God, Christ could not have overcome; [81] but now the historic event of His Resurrection and Ascension have declared His victorious lordship over them.[82] Because He was God, He won the victory. But also precisely because He was God, He had no need to win the victory on His own account. This was not a conflict which involved Him—"I was lord of all creation before hand, so that the devil and the world could certainly not touch Me!" [83] He involved Himself in man's conflict for man's sake, because He loved him.

The conflict is man's, and his antagonists are sin, God's wrath, the law, death, hell, the devil, and the world. Yet this battle is not somehow independent of sinful man's standing before God. The very list of "tyrants" itself indicates the nature of Luther's metaphor. If this were a battle between God and His enemies, man would have to appear along with sin, the devil, and the world in the list of God's opponents: man is God's enemy because he is willfully a sinner. The absence of man's name and the inclusion of God's wrath and His law establish that this cannot be God's battle; which is to say, the fact of man's sinfulness and his willfulness are not at issue here but are presumed. "Sin," in the list of tyrants, is not "servitude to sin" but "sin known" in the

79. *46*, 110, 1.
80. *49*, 266, 1; cf. 33, 608, 10.
81. *10/I/2*, 221, 26; *21*, 511, 26; *40/I*, 84, 26; *46*, 554, 23.
82. *12*, 508, 14; *21*, 400, 38; 484, 11; 33, 610, 35; *40/I*, 439, 26; *46*, 554, 26.
83. *46*, 110, 6.

sense of the penitential Psalms or Romans 7 (and, as we saw, may
be equated with "sin borne"). This knowledge of sin has its tyranny from the law, which declares God's wrath and eternal condemnation, and thereby places man in bondage to death and hell
and in thrall to the devil, prince of death and of this world. If,
then, sin is forgiven, the tyrants are instantly overthrown.[84]

Christ came into the world to tell us of the forgiveness and
love of God, and in obedience to the Father's command of mercy
to bear the sin, endure the curse, and thus abrogate the dominion
of death, hell, and the devil. These connections Luther draws
clearly. In one breath he says that Christ removed sin, bore it, de-
leted it, forgave it, and locked the gates of hell. Luther equates
"the power of this world's god and prince, the devil" with "sin
and death." [85] "When Satan's power has been crushed—that is,
when sin and death have been destroyed by Christ—what pre-
vents us from being saved?" [86] And we have already seen how
closely his use of "redemption" draws together deliverance from
bondage and ransom for sin.

In short, Luther's use of the victory motif, too, is applied with
singleness of purpose to the assertion of Christ's all-sufficiency—
not to the description of any cosmic dualism. In that this is his
purpose, it throws an interesting sidelight on Luther's relation to
the tradition. For the immediate source of his familiarity with traditional language about victory was in all likelihood Gabriel Biel
(transmitted both by Luther's reading in Biel and by Biel's disciple Bartholomaeus Arnoldi von Usingen, who taught Luther at
Erfurt). For Biel, Christ was the "invader," "burster," "destroyer"
of hell, Who by His greater might defeated the army of evil, captured its arms, and regained the spoils.[87] The victory of Christ
was sufficient to effect perfectly the liberation of those informed
by faith and love from the bondage of sin. The bondage of sin
here meant the inability not to sin. Hence the victory of Christ

84. 10/I/2, 221, 35; 33, 161, 39 to 162, 21.
85. 47, 105, 6 and 28; 46, 556, 26.
86. 42, 143, 1.
87. Gabriel Biel, Sermones de festivitatibus christi (Hagenau, 1510), 25 C,
26 D, 28 A; quoted in Oberman, The Harvest of Medieval Theology, pp. 269f.,
nn. 75, 77, 80.

was sufficient to remove this bondage, but not yet sufficient to perfect redemption; for the merit of Christ is "insufficient, nay, counts for nothing" unless the *viator*, by imitation of Christ, follows his Leader out of the shattered prison and "joins his merit to Christ's."[88] Such a doctrine, of course, is anathema to Luther. Any hint of human merit impugns the all-sufficiency of Christ. Yet Luther has taken over a body of imagery whose original intention he explicitly and vehemently rejects and by harnessing it to the assertion of Christ's unique all-sufficiency, exploits it for the gospel.

What happens to detail when traditional material is thus exploited provides an illuminating key to the changes Luther made in the structure of medieval doctrine. For instance, his reinterpretation of bondage of sin as sin's power to condemn rather than the inability not to sin drew specific challenge from von Usingen.[89] Luther completely transforms the issue: "If you commit fresh sin, simply say, 'Christ is the destroyer of sin,' and at once the sin is gone."[90] Again, Luther freely employs the notion, present in his reading both of Augustine and Biel,[91] that Christ's innocence is the cause of the devil's downfall: "He has condemned sin on the cross, for sin wronged Him when it condemned and executed Him. Accordingly He now gains authority over the sin of all the world and rightly and justly condemns it, because it tried to condemn Him." "Christ with His innocence has canceled sin." "Christ alone is just and holy, therefore death could not hold Him." "The prince of this world, the devil, is present in his cohorts and will seize Me and try to trample Me down unjustly. But his scheme will fail—I will overthrow him, and I will do it justly." "Sin fell upon Him to vanquish Him, but it lost the day: He devoured sin."[92] We shall see later how Luther bor-

88. Biel, 11 G, 13 H, 24 s.v. *consummatum;* quoted in Oberman, pp. 268f., nn. 70, 74.

89. Bartholomaeus Arnoldi von Usingen, *Libellus . . . contra Lutheranos* (Erfurt, 1524), fol. I 4ʳ.

90. 7, 810, 19; *47*, 81, 31.

91. Augustine, *Serm.* 134, iii. 4 and v. 6; *de lib. arbit.*, III, x, 31; Biel, 25 C, quoted in Oberman, p. 269, n. 78.

92. *21*, 477, 6ff.; 20, 431, 25; 31/II, 438, 12; 10/I/2, 284, 8; *12*, 565, 2.

rows some of the most bizarre patristic imagery in amplifying this theme of the *pugna mirabilis*, the *iucundissimum duellum*.[93] Yet again Luther shatters the quantitative implications of scholastic thinking about the atonement by insisting that the efficacy of Christ is utterly incommensurate with all the power of the tyrants: "He submerged and drowned all our sin and filth in the great ocean of His love." "One droplet of His blood helps the whole world, for this person is very God." Because He is in the Father, "all this man says and does stands and must stand in heaven before all angels, in the world before all tyrants, in hell before all devils, in the heart before all evil conscience and subjective notions."[94] The figures of this transformation must reveal their own inadequacy, pointing beyond themselves to an abyss of mercy and love that our minds cannot conceive, let alone our words formulate. "The gift is so great it swallows up death: the world's sin compared with this gift is like a droplet of water in a blazing oven. If sin is shifted onto Christ, it is swallowed up like a smoldering straw the moment it falls in the ocean."[95]

This transfer, this swallowing-up, takes place, Luther says, "when a man by faith receives this treasure and believes in the Son."[96] Once again Scripture dictates the pattern of Luther's associations. Faith is the victory which overcomes the world (I John 5:4), because to faith Christ gives the fruit of His triumph in the Word.[97] Therefore the Word looms large in Luther's employment of conflict imagery, as in that most notable of instances, *Ein' feste Burg:*

> And if the world, with devils filled,
> Would utterly devour us,
> Yet we are not with fear instilled,
> Success must still be ours.
> The prince of this world
> His venom has hurled;

93. 15, 518, 4; 40/I, 279, 25. See below, pp. 253ff.
94. 10/III, 157, 32f.; 47, 172, 15; 45, 589, 25.
95. 37, 413, 9.
96. 37, 413, 12.
97. 20, 774, 1–15; 776, 7.

Our faith has not budged:
His kingdom is judged.
A little word can fell him.[98]

The judgment already declared upon the prince of this world is executed by the office of preaching; the flock of Christ has no weapon against the principalities and powers but the Word in all its seeming weakness.[99] Christ ascribes such power to His teaching that it becomes an absolute ruler over the devil, death, and sin. "Since the Word sets before us Christ, it sets before us the one Who has triumphed over death, sin, and Satan. So the man who by this means grasps and holds Christ has eternal deliverance from death—it is a Word of life." [1] The promise of forgiveness shatters the tyranny of death, which the Christian must now see as God sees it—as a sleep and a doorway to eternal life: this is a favorite theme of Luther's.[2] For without fear, he says, death is no longer death.[3] In a thinly veiled paraphrase of Paul, he declares, "Christ's office was to overthrow death and release the dead from death. We believe He died for our sin and rose again that we, when we die, should also live as God's own and share the resurrection of the body." [4] This is why we must rejoice in the story of His Resurrection "as our treasure and salvation, by which we have peace and every good from God . . . For through His Resurrection He has conquered all things, and gives us for our own all that He has done and suffered." [5]

98. *35*, 456, 17.
99. E.g. *21*, 371, 29; *33*, 436, 26ff.; *40/I*, 580, 15; *45*, 509, 6ff.; *46*, 107, 23ff.; etc.
1. *17/II*, 234, 14.
2. E.g. *42*, 147, 3ff.; *47*, 712–15, passim; *Br, 6*, 103–04; *Tr, 1, 422:* 860; *Tr, 2, 416:* 2316a; *Tr, 3, 123:* 2970b; etc.
3. *43*, 218, 10.
4. *47*, 712, 23.
5. *21*, 293, 25 and 31.

# 5. The King of Righteousness

Christ our Lord, to Whom we must flee and from Whom we must ask for everything, is an endless well and fountainhead of all grace, truth, righteousness, wisdom, and life, without measure, end, or limit."[1] A sermon or meditation, Luther says, cannot exhaust or even contain the theme of Christ, the eternal righteousness: it requires an eternal skill which will not be mastered in this life or the next.[2] This is not the place to pretend that the subject can be comprehended in a neat outline of Luther's doctrine of justification. However, any study of his doctrine of Christ would be incomplete without some reference to "the righteousness of God which is by faith." Here, then, is not an outline of his doctrine of justification—the literature on this theme is too vast already—but a sketch of the shape of righteousness for Luther: that "mathematical point"[3] where Christ rules in the soul by faith.

Here we may recall Luther's insistence that justification is the magisterial doctrine, the chief article, the head and cornerstone of the Church.[4] But we have already qualified this insistence in two ways. First, we discovered that Luther often intends much more by the word "justification" than the formal or systematic content of "the doctrine of justification"; and secondly, we found that justification is only one aspect, however vital, of a far broader theme—the theme "by Christ alone." As a result, Luther rarely deals with justification as a separate locus, yet in another sense he

1. *46*, 653, 11.

2. 33, 107, 8.

3. *40*/II, 527, 9: Christ's perfect justice is contrasted with the relativity of worldly justice, a distinction based on Aristotle, *Nicom. Eth.* I.13.

4. 30/II, 650, 19; 39/I, 205, 2; 40/I, 192, 20.

deals with it constantly by speaking always of Christ, Who is our righteousness. In so speaking, for instance, Luther obviously feels no tension or inconsistency whatsoever between the teaching of St. John and that of St. Paul; furthermore, he finds the language of St. John so congenial that clearly he reads the Pauline idea of imputation in the light of the Johannine idea of coinherence, the Pauline phrase "in Christ" in the light of the prayer of John 17. The diverse emphases in the two apostles' accounts (and in all the Scriptures) draw together, as Luther demonstrates, to the "mathematical point" of eternal righteousness.

It is vitally important to discover this point of identity between Luther's two most frequent equations for righteousness. On the one hand, Luther declares, *Justicia est fides,* "faith is righteousness";[5] on the other, "Christ is our righteousness."[6] Chronologically, the first of these definitions receives greater prominence in Luther's early sermons, the second in his later sermons; but the truth of both is maintained throughout. And to separate the first from the second is to court disaster.[7]

It may seem at first sight, however, that Luther himself is inviting us to do so. How does a man know that Christ's invitation is for him? "He need only look at his own heart: if he finds it so apt that it delights in God's promise and holds fast to the fact that he is one of those invited to this meal, then he certainly is one—for as we believe, so it is done to us. Such a man from then on receives and helps his neighbor as his own brother, protects him, gives to him, shares with him, comforts him, and does for his neighbor only what he could wish for himself."[8] "To be able to attribute such glory to God is to possess surpassing wisdom, surpassing righteousness, religion, and sacrifice. You can see from this what great righteousness faith is, and by contrast what great sin unfaith is. Thus faith justifies because it renders God His due: whoever does this is righteous."[9] Or this: "A true master—the

5. 7, 56, 11; 7, 810, 5; 10/III, 129, 25; 133, 9; 33, 86, 7.
6. 31/II, 768, 9; 33, 107, 8; 631, 33; 40/I, 65, 17; II, 183, 3; 46, 44, 31.
7. 19, 495, 4.
8. 17/II, 434, 26.
9. 40/I, 360, 32.

man who justifies God in His words—regards God as true in
His majesty and in His Word. Such faith drives the devil from his
own and other people's hearts—drives the devil out of his heart
and enthrones God in his stead. It is another thing, this faith, from
what people imagine. It must be a living document, seal, and signet, so confident that one would leave all for it . . . It redounds
entirely to our good. For if we regard God as true, we receive
righteousness and eternal life from Him." [10]

Such descriptions of the manner of faith perhaps sound as if
faith is the analytic ground of man's justification—as if Luther
has subtly redefined the Augustinian doctrine by replacing *humilitas* with *fiducia,* which nevertheless forms the basis of a proleptic
judgment that man is righteous. But such a conclusion would be
erroneous for a number of reasons.

First and simplest, Luther's descriptions of the subjective manner of faith cover a wide, and apparently contradictory, range.
This is because he sometimes describes what the attitude of the
faithful man should be ideally and indeed occasionally is. But Luther is far too much of a realist (and far too affectively labile) to
pretend that the normal experience of Christian people is anything but a pale shadow of what it might be. Nor under the on-
slaughts of the world, the devil, and the flesh can "the little flock
of the faint-hearted" [11] keep the even tenor of its way: our weak
faith is too often a desperate clinging to Christ in spite of ourselves. Luther insists that the ups and downs, the strengths and
weaknesses, the joys and the *Anfechtungen* of experience cannot
be the basis of our standing before God; if they were, we should
be oscillating in and out of the state of righteousness with infinite
velocity, for we are always sinners.

Whatever faith may accomplish, the accomplishment is not
man's. "The heart is not the source of faith: no, it must possess
the Word of God." The initiative remains with God: this righteousness of faith is given to us from heaven. He works faith in us
"without our cooperation (*sine nobis*)." [12] In this sense we

10. 47, 185, 11: an unusual echo of the *iustitia passiva dei* theme of the Romans
lectures of 1515–16; cf. 56, 226, 23.
11. 46, 583, 13.
12. 10/I/2, 291, 26; 31/II, 182, 15; 33, 86, 12; 6, 530, 16.

should call faith "something done *to* us rather than *by* us (*magis . . . passio quam actio*), for it changes our hearts and minds."[13] It is the Word which God sent through Christ that evokes faith and makes us Christians: "Christ makes us righteous, for His Word imparts righteousness."[14] The new birth which begets righteousness before God is a living work of the Holy Spirit in men's hearts, "not through one's own human intention or act (for that is all flesh and cannot see God's kingdom); but through the Word of the gospel, which declares and reveals to the heart both God's wrath toward men for repentance, and His grace through the mediator, Christ, for consolation and peace of conscience before God." Faith is not a matter of human competence: it can be founded on nothing but the Word of God.[15] There is a sense in which faith is a work which man must do: but paradoxically, "faith is a divine work which God demands of us, yet at the same time He Himself must implant it in us, for of ourselves we cannot believe."[16]

The reason faith can be our work, yet not our work, is that faith consists in its object. Its efficacy rests not upon its strength (or even its existence) but upon that object. It does not reconcile us of itself, but clings to the reconciliation Christ has achieved. What remains, if the true object of faith is forgotten, is "merely froth, and uncertain opinions or dreams, a painted, contrived faith." To have faith and to rely on faith are two very different things.[17] Luther loves to illustrate the character of faith by the figure of an empty container. Faith is merely husk, but Christ is the kernel. It is a purse or coffer for the eternal treasure, an empty vessel, a poor little monstrance or pyx for gems of infinite worth.[18] In this respect all Christians are equal and alike. "Even if I am feeble in faith, I still have the same treasure and the same Christ that others have. There is no difference: through faith in Him (not works) we are all perfect. It is just as if two people

13. *42, 452, 23.*
14. *10/I/2, 30, 23; 33, 398, 13.*
15. *21, 538, 34ff.; 33, 476, 5.*
16. *33, 29, 14ff.* (cf. *165, 21*).
17. *8, 519, 19; 47, 21, 8; 26, 164, 40.*
18. *21, 487, 38ff.*

have a hundred gulden—one may carry his in a paper bag, the other store and bar his in an iron chest; but they both have the treasure whole and complete. So with Christ. It is the self-same Christ we possess whether you or I believe in Him with a strong or a weak faith. And in Him we have all, whether we hold it with a strong or a weak faith." [19] Luther never fails to indicate this equality in Christ, even where he is exhorting his congregation (as he so often did) to strengthen and exercise their faith. "Of what use is the present and gift of faith if it is nothing but such an empty vessel?" he asks. "Of what use, indeed, unless we see and comfort ourselves with what it grasps and holds—on this account alone it is precious." [20]

So it is that the vessel of faith is created in us by the external Word, and its contents, which alone make it precious, are nothing of ours. "What a heart that must be that can hold more than heaven and earth can contain! And so it must be obvious what an ineffably divine work faith is, that it can do something that is impossible for nature and all the world—it is no less a miracle than all God's miracles and works." If the vessel is so great a miracle, its content is greater: indeed, the gift is so great, and man's heart so small, narrow, and weak, that an incomprehensible infinitude of difference separates them. I find faith within me; yet Christ is not any part of me, any more than the sun is my eye, which wakes to see the daylight. In fact, the gulf is greater, for I cannot feel or perceive Christ with my reason, my sensation, or my soul. Christ is in heaven, at the right hand of God: He is completely outside me, entirely other than me. Yet by the miracle of regeneration through the Word, all things that are Christ's become mine in faith, and I discover that true righteousness lies outside me, in Christ alone.[21] Three parts, Luther says, comprise Christ's discourse to Nicodemus concerning the righteousness of man before God: "He has taught us about the Word, baptism, and the Spirit Who works through them; about the merit and sacrifice of Christ,

19. 33, 37, 22 (cf. 10/I/2, 82, 1ff.; 432, 36; 17/I, 436, 6; 28, 189, 18ff.; 46, 376, 16).
20. 21, 488, 27.
21. 21, 489, 24ff.; 33, 30, 15ff.; 31, 11.

for Whose sake God's grace and eternal life are given to us; and about faith, through which we claim them as our own." We must retain the unity of the whole discourse, Luther counsels, so that the end may coincide with the beginning.[22] That is to say, faith, the Word, and Christ belong together at the "mathematical point" of righteousness.

It is for this reason that faith alone is not sufficient for salvation.[23] If it were the case that justification rested solely upon the divine imputation or *acceptatio*, two anomalies would impugn the uniqueness of Christ. First, a faith other than faith in Christ's accomplishment— "I mean a faith in the gracious mercy of God, not reckoning sins"—would be a justifying faith. And secondly, because this was so, the whole history of Christ's "going to the Father" would be emptied of its eternal and only-sufficient significance. Therefore it is to hold God not as true but as a liar —not to justify Him in His words but to contravert Him—when one claims a righteousness of faith which is other than Christ's own righteousness. [24] For true righteousness, as Luther contended against Latomus of Louvain, must be not only "through Christ" and "from Christ" but "in Christ." [25] Christ is not only the effective cause but the formal cause of God's blessing—that is, He is the blessing itself.[26]

At this point Luther finds two passages of the Fourth Gospel particularly fitted to his contention. The first is the discourse of John 6 on the flesh and blood of Christ. A Christian says, "I know of no work through which I can be justified; but my life and righteousness consist in this one fact—that Christ has flesh and blood which are my soul's food and life." [27] Christ in this discourse wants to direct us away from all other righteousness. We must learn to distinguish His righteousness, His life, His being, and His work from all others.[28] The eating and drinking of faith

22. *21*, 551, 18ff.
23. *10*/III, 161, 11.
24. *10*/I/1, 468, 16ff.; 470, 11; *31*/II, 296, 21; *47*, 185, 8.
25. *8*, 111, 37.
26. *43*, 249, 25.
27. *33*, 212, 27.
28. *33*, 224, 19; 211, 26.

effects Christ's presence in us, so that we abide in Him with our sins and our feebleness, and He abides in us with His holiness, righteousness, wisdom, satisfaction, and life. Where we are lacking, He has abundance; where we are weak, He drowns our weakness in His strength; He cancels our sin by His righteousness; He devours our death in His life.[29] This is a food by which we are transformed into the eternal righteousness, for Christ declares, "I am full of righteousness, you are full of sin—take My righteousness as your very own." [30]

A second passage, which Luther finds even more congenial, is John 16:10. He revels in the paradox of declaring that righteousness is Christ's going to the Father.[31] "My works and Christ's going to the Father are as far apart as heaven and earth." [32] True eternal righteousness is placed entirely outside and above us, outside the sphere of our senses, where we can neither see nor feel it, but only grasp it by faith in the Word of the gospel which tells us that righteousness involves nothing at all in us either active or passive, but that Christ is our righteousness.[33] When Luther says that "the righteousness of the Father which is in Christ will swallow up our sins," or speaks of "the heavenly righteousness of the heavenly man," of the one given to be in us as our righteousness Who has the Spirit without measure and in Whom the fullness of the Godhead dwells,[34] it is perhaps not hard to see how Andreas Osiander was misled into the error of "essential righteousness"; [35] but Osiander basically misunderstood the equation of righteousness with Christ's *transitus ad patrem*. "For these words: 'because

29. *11*, 126, 9; *33*, 225, 18; *228*, 14; *230*, 25; *240*, 38.

30. *15*, 467, 17.

31. *12*, 546, 31; *17/I*, 245, 15; *21*, 361, 30; *28*, 47, 18; *34/I*, 365, 5; *37*, 76, 9; *46*, 43, 14; 375, 3.

32. *28*, 49, 22; cf. *46*, 45, 27; 375, 13.

33. *46*, 44, 23.

34. *10/III*, 125, 30; *47*, 173, 24; 196, 15–20.

35. Andreas Osiander, *An filius dei incarnandus, si peccatum non introivisset in mundum. Item de imagine dei, quid sit* (Monteregio, 1550); *Von dem einigen Mittler Jhesu Christo und Rechtfertigung des Glaubens* (Königsberg, 1551). See Wilhelm Möller, *Andreas Osianders Leben und ausgewählte Schriften* (Elberfeld, 1870), pp. 379ff.; Emanuel Hirsch, *Die Theologie des Andreas Osiander und ihre geschichtliche Voraussetzungen* (1919), pp. 71ff.; and of course, John Calvin, *Inst.* III. xi. 5–12.

I go to the Father,' encompass the whole work of our redemption
and salvation for which God's Son was sent from heaven, and
which He has performed and still does perform until the end—
namely, His suffering, death, and Resurrection, and His whole
reign in the Church. For this going to the Father means nothing
else but this: He gives Himself as a sacrifice through the shedding of His blood and death, thereby to pay for sin; and after-
wards by His Resurrection He overthrows and subdues sin,
death, and hell, and seats Himself alive at the right hand of the
Father, where He reigns invisibly over everything in heaven and
earth." [36] The righteousness comprehended in this going is not
simply a righteousness of divine essence but a righteousness of
which Christ had no need for Himself.[37] We must learn this *usus
ascensionis*: if He had died and risen for Himself, that would
have helped us not at all; but His Resurrection was not for Himself: it was for us.[38] Thus His Resurrection can be called the
righteousness of God.[39] "Now He has accomplished such a going
or ascending to the Father not for His own sake nor for His own
person. For that would not have helped us, and could not have
been called our righteousness. But as He came from heaven for
our sakes and became flesh and blood, so He has also returned
thither for our sakes, and there completes His victory over sin,
death, and hell, and takes His dominion whereby He redeems us
from all this, and gives us forgiveness of sins, power and victory
against devil and death. He reigns in such a way that His kingdom or rule is called—and is—righteousness: that is, the righteousness in which sin and unrighteousness before God are done
away, making people righteous and acceptable before God." [40]

One theme returns insistently. To say that "righteousness consists in this person Who went to the Father" [41] is to speak not of
Christ's "essential" righteousness but of His "actual" righteousness. That is, the merit of this righteousness is the historical ac-

36. *21*, 363, 10; *46*, 44, 6.
37. *12*, 546, 33; 547, 10.
38. *46*, 376, 1; *47*, 172, 18.
39. *39/II*, 237, 25; *40/I*, 64, 25.
40. *46*, 44, 13.
41. *46*, 375, 20.

complishment of the man Christ: "here everything happened that we are to believe about Him." [42] It is the events confessed in the second article of the creed which constitute our righteousness.[43] The fullness and grace of Christ, by which we obtain forgiveness, adoption, and life, are to be called His because "God finds in Him no sin, deceit, or falsehood, but sheer grace, truth, righteousness, and life: therefore He loves Him with heartfelt love." [44] By His obedience and righteousness He has become the abundant source from which we obtain righteousness. It is His death and Resurrection—not ours—which fulfills the law. "Our faith depends on Christ alone, Who only is just—not I; for His righteousness stands before the judgment of God against God's wrath and for me." [45] One part, therefore, of Christian righteousness is the possession of the Christ Who, by His active obedience, deserves to be called righteous. It is in relation to other men that Christ is called the only holy and righteous one: this is the meaning of St. Paul's words in Romans 5:19.[46] The other part of Christian righteousness (where Luther lays far greater stress) is the possession of the Christ Who, by His innocence, has borne away and canceled our sins.[47] Our justification in this case is identical with satisfaction for sins in the historic event of Christ's cross.[48]

Luther in this way reflects the twofold aspect of Christ's accomplishment described in Romans 4:25 (which he quotes in expounding John 16:10): [49] "Christ was delivered for our offenses and was raised again for our justification." Hence the recurrent couplets, "merit and sacrifice," "forgiveness and newness of life," "grace and gift." The gifts of Christ are twofold, Luther says, and there are two essential principles in Christian life.[50] Christ covers us with His innocence, and He bestows His righteousness upon us; He has kept what we have not kept, and He has paid

42. 10/I/1, 201, 14.
43. 37, 76, 12.
44. 46, 655, 1–5.
45. 22, 224, 21; 20, 264, 11; 25, 35, 1.
46. 46, 649, 23; 656, 34.
47. E.g. 20, 431, 25.
48. 47, 113, 38.
49. 37, 76, 16; 46, 375, 22.
50. 10/I/1, 107, 21; 31, 7; 21, 340, 8.

for the sins we have committed.[51] Correspondingly, justifying faith has a twofold fruit. It leads to forgiveness, the nonimputation of sins for Christ's sake;[52] and positively, it leads to union with Christ, Who Himself is our eternal righteousness, holiness, and life.[53] Faith possesses all that Christ is and has; it makes Christ and the believer "one cake," so that they own all things in common.[54] Needless to say, Luther's favorite expression of this oneness is the biblical image of the marriage between Christ and the faithful.[55] This marriage is a very unequal union—the bride an impure, filthy, wrinkled old outcast, the groom the eternal wisdom, truth, and light itself, a most comely youth. Yet His righteousness is incomparably greater than our sins, and His life incomparably stronger than our death.[56] What we bring to this sharing and exchange is our sin, bondage, condemnation, and death: Christ takes them and makes them His. What He brings is His righteousness, victory, Resurrection, and life: He gives them to us and makes them ours.[57] All that we are and do is in Him, and He in us; but all that He is and does is in the Father, and the Father in Him.[58] Therefore we know that the righteousness we possess in Christ is a righteousness according to the Father's will and heart,[59] a righteousness which, because it is ordained in His kingdom, is different, perfect, eternal, and pure [60]—"a new righteousness which endures forever in the life to come with God, as Christ lives and reigns on high forever." [61]

*Christ Our Holiness*

This, then, is the shape of righteousness: the grace and gift of forgiveness and newness of life, at that "mathematical point"

51. *21*, 329, 31; 363, 14; *45*, 153, 33; *46*, 649, 36.
52. *10*/III, 130, 24; *21*, 359, 10.
53. *10*/I/2, 31, 22; *40*/I, 284, 24; *43*, 249, 37.
54. *10*/I/1, 319, 13ff.; I/2, 233, 20; *20*, 677, 5; *47*, 172, 34.
55. E.g. *41*, 554, 20; *42*, 174, 6; *46*, 712, 31; etc.
56. *10*/III, 417, 20; see below, pp. 259ff.
57. *21*, 365, 4; *33*, 225, 20; 230, 30; *45*, 590, 1.
58. *12*, 487, 1; *28*, 188, 4; *43*, 582, 21ff.; *45*, 589, 39ff.
59. *17*/I, 246, 6; *21*, 362, 31; *25*, 37, 11; *45*, 589, 31; *46*, 656, 37.
60. *17*/I, 246, 11; *21*, 368, 5 and 30; *33*, 163, 38; 281, 23; *39*/II, 214, 7.
61. *21*, 365, 10.

where Christ our righteousness, through His Word and Spirit, dwells in us in His fullness by faith. Now, if Christ is our righteousness, and justification is by faith alone, so also He is our holiness, and sanctification is by faith alone. Christ's righteousness is constantly defined in opposition to all so-called human righteousness; and in the same way, the only true holiness stands over against every self-styled sanctity of man.

Sanctification for Luther normally does not mean the process of moral purification or improvement in virtue, which is its chief connotation in post-Reformation theology. Rather, in the biblically strict sense, that is holy which is set apart for the worship and service of God: "The word 'holy' means what is God's own, what belongs only to Him, or as we should say, 'consecrated.'" [62] It is the exception rather than the rule when Luther equates holiness with purity [63] or sharply distinguishes holiness from salvation. [64] Even when he speaks of the purported holiness of men, the word has religious rather than ethical content. He employs it of the piety of church saints and fathers, of the religious formularies of Jews and Turks, even of pagan idol worship, [65] and in particular, of the external show of sanctity in his contemporaries, both monastic and radical: [66] "May the merciful God preserve me from the Christian church in which everyone is a saint!" [67]

Holiness, then, is properly a cultic concept, and true holiness consists in the true worship of God. "God is 'the holy one of Israel' in that Israel has been chosen and sanctified by Him for His worship. God is thus called 'holy' *ab effectu*." And similarly under the new covenant, "our 'holy one' is Christ, sanctifying us by the Word of truth." [68] True worship now consists in faith in the Son of God, in Whom the whole cult is consummated. [69] "But there

62. *12*, 287, 25.

63. E.g. *17/II*, 199, 13; cf. Philip Watson, "Luther und die Heiligung," in Vatja, ed., *Lutherforschung Heute*, pp. 75ff.

64. *26*, 505, 18.

65. E.g. *33*, 186, 3; *46*, 23, 10; *766*, 30ff.; etc.

66. E.g. *20*, 678, 12; *33*, 560, 17; *50*, 625, 33; etc.

67. *46*, 583, 11.

68. *31/II*, 6, 17.

69. *14*, 582, 25; *25*, 411, 13; *28*, 173, 9.

are very many who fight this one true sanctification with another sanctity, fabricated and false—just as a pig is dragged unwilling to the washing which it regards as mire, but jumps happily into the mire, which is its idea of bathing." [70] Now there is but one purification, and that is in Christ. Before God we require a holiness which exceeds all the world's works.[71] The purification commanded by God is different from all the world's: it is purification by the blood of the Lamb of God, Who took away our sins.[72] Christ Himself is our purification.[73]

What makes the Church or its members holy is not the works and sanctity of all the saints; but Christ's blood is holy, His word, sacraments, and saving achievements are holy, and He rules in the Church and in our hearts by His Holy Spirit.[74] "One must therefore distinguish two kinds of holiness—or rather, to be holy may be understood in two different ways. On one hand there is the holiness from and through ourselves (like monastic orders and self-chosen spirituality). This is nothing but the word or name of holiness, but it is fundamentally false and a lie—nothing but sin and stench before God. For in us and from us grows nothing but unholiness and uncleanness . . . Therefore I will not call myself holy nor boast of holiness of myself or on my own behalf, or of any man; but I am holy because with unswerving faith and untroubled conscience I can say, 'Even though I am a poor sinner, yet Christ is holy with His baptism, Word, sacrament, and Holy Spirit—that is the only true holiness, God's gift to us." [75] Christ's little flock knows nothing of its own righteousness or holiness, but knows instead that He is in us with His life, His righteousness, and His holiness.[76] Luther regards sanctification as an alien possession in us, but one which, like justification, is ours perfectly by faith in Christ.[77] "I cling to the conviction that Christ

70. 31/II, 6, 19.
71. 33, 96, 32.
72. 47, 143, 12ff.
73. 47, 150, 12.
74. 17/II, 208, 1; 33, 288, 18; 531, 17; 538, 17; 40/II, 520, 38; 45, 615, 13ff.; 50, 628, 29ff.
75. 45, 616, 14.
76. 33, 77, 3; 225, 25; 241, 1.
77. 28, 173, 11; 34/I, 370, 15; 46, 583, 22.

alone is my righteousness and my holiness." [78] For Christ alone is pious before God and alone makes us pious. He is so holy that He sanctifies those who believe in Him, by forgiving their sins and bestowing His Holy Spirit. "Since we are baptized and believe in Christ, we are holy and just in Christ and with Christ, Who has taken our sin from us and has graced, clothed, and adorned us with His holiness." [79]

The most holy state on earth, then, is to believe that Christ sanctified Himself for us.[80] The progression is precisely the same in sanctification as in justification: to be holy is not to cleanse oneself from sin and live piously, but to believe; [81] this faith sanctifies because its content, Christ's Word and gospel, are holy and unite us to Him; [82] He thus sets us apart for God by washing us and bestowing His Spirit upon us through the priestly sacrifice and offering for which He sanctified Himself.[83] For a highest sanctification is that Christ sanctified Himself for us; indeed, there is no holiness but this. He is to be called the All-holiest, the sanctus sanctorum: He alone is the eternal source of all holiness.[84]

## Gift and Example

The twofold character of Christ's achievement for us in His going to the Father—the abolition of our sin and the bestowal of all that is His—corresponds to the great exchange that makes Christ and the Christian "one cake." [85] For we have made all the debit entries to the common account of Christ and His Christians, and He has put paid to them; but all the credit entries are Christ's. The accomplishment of Christ has these two moments, negative and positive. Philip Watson's suggestion that this two-

78. 32, 349, 1.
79. 10/I/2, 36, 15; 31/II, 689, 12; 40/II, 241, 15; 31/I, 167, 27.
80. 28, 176, 7.
81. 28, 177, 11ff.
82. 12, 287, 21; 28, 166, 2ff.; 175, 7; 33, 531, 1ff.; 45, 616, 3.
83. 28, 173, 1ff.
84. 20, 390, 7ff.
85. For this expression, see below p. 258.

fold emphasis corresponds to a distinction between justification and sanctification may be misleading. Justification and sanctification, he says, are two aspects or descriptions of one and the same work of God, but the stress in justification lies on forgiveness, in sanctification on renewal.[86] But this is to confuse the twofold character of the historic work of Christ with another, quite different distinction—Luther's distinction between the "alien" righteousness and holiness of Christ and the actual or empirical rectitude and piety of the faithful man. Luther's favorite expression for this difference is the couplet, "Christ as gift and example."

Our justification and sanctification before God are not only entirely dependent upon Christ but wholly comprehended in Christ's history. They are "alien" not only because they are not ours in origin, but because they are not in us at all.[87] They are perfect and entire in Christ and become ours because Christ is ours.[88] Their entirety and perfection are in no way qualified by the fact that God has begun and will complete a new creation in us: for the fullness of that new creation will be nothing other than the fullness of Christ, Who fills all in all. It is in this light that we must regard any empirical righteousness or holiness of the Christian man.

Such actual holiness is now possible; for even though in this life Christians remain bound in their sinful flesh and are therefore called saints only because of Christ's holy blood, yet it behooves them to manifest their holiness by their deeds.[89] To this end the work of the Holy Spirit in faith is the daily destruction, purging, and mortification of sin, and the renewal of heart, soul, body, work, and conduct, writing God's commandments on tables not of stone but of flesh.[90] Actual righteousness is also possible now: for even though God has declared that our works are not righteous before Him, yet as we shelter beneath the overarching righteousness of Christ, God accepts as pleasing even things which

86. Watson, in Vatja, ed., *Lutherforschung Heute*, p. 84.
87. *21*, 368, 1; 27, 146, 22ff.
88. *15*, 467, 16; cf. 20, 669, 15.
89. *17/II*, 208, 1.
90. *50*, 624, 30; 626, 15.

have no intrinsic merit.[91] Actual righteousness is not only possible but essential; for Luther never tires of saying (especially against the antinomians) that faith without works is dead.[92] But for Luther as for St. Paul, this necessity has to be asserted only because of the infirmity of the flesh: strictly, the question whether the child of God should do the will of God ought not arise. Since it does, however, Luther is swift to assert that this question must be divorced from the ground of our justification in Christ.[93] Whatever actual piety the Christian attains, faith accounts it as worse than nothing before God.

The new possibility of actual righteousness, however, introduces ambiguities at another level. Luther often speaks as if it is the Christian's new status in Christ which qualifies him to bear good fruit, even if externally his works appear no different.[94] In such a case the possibility of actual righteousness consists in the faithful man's performing perhaps the same works for a new motive—namely, with a conscience that is now freed from the law by faith in the gospel. Thus faith is the experience of that indwelling of Christ, by His Word and Holy Spirit, which makes actual righteousness a possibility—and an inevitable consequence.[95] But Luther sometimes speaks so graphically of the experience of Christ's indwelling, of the resulting transformation in "the very essence of the heart," and of Christ as the agent of the Christian's works,[96] that he may seem to envisage a virtual infusion of righteousness. While it is certainly true that Luther regards the first fruits of faith as a meager beginning of the Holy Spirit's daily transformation of the Christian into the image of Christ, the idea of infusion is patently foreign to his thinking. No, the Holy Spirit's means of indwelling are always the external Word and sacrament, evoking faith;[97] and faith, by its newfound liberty of conscience, begins freely to follow the command-

91. 42, 564, 30; 45, 661, 9–24; 46, 641, 35ff.
92. E.g. 20, 641, 3; 45, 702, 18ff.; 47, 114, 1ff.
93. 21, 364, 16ff.; 31/II, 433, 6; 43, 255, 36.
94. E.g. 45, 672, 15ff.
95. 21, 502, 36; 36, 281, 13.
96. E.g. 42, 452, 17; 45, 667, 20ff.
97. 17/I, 436, 10; 45, 614, 35; 617, 22.

ment of Christ.[98] The greater its confidence becomes, the more freely it so acts.[99]

In this way, one and the same faith attains both to the perfect righteousness of Christ and to the beginning of empirical righteousness; yet the two kinds of righteousness are to be strictly segregated. Put another way, the statement that the justified man is in process of becoming just (or the sanctified man holy) addresses nothing to the question of justification (or sanctification).

Characteristically, Luther uses some of his vocabulary in one way when he is making this distinction sharply, in another when it is not at issue. This is true even of the word "faith" itself: it is normally used in connection with both kinds of righteousness, but sometimes Luther speaks of faith as passive before God, and love as the spring of action;[1] of faith as belonging to heaven, and good works to the earth;[2] of the true following of Christ which is faith, and a second following which is works and sufferings.[3] Something of this potential ambiguity attaches to the titles now before us—Christ as gift and example; but they remain one of the simplest expressions of the twofold relationship that a Christian's faith bears to Christ.

"What is it to know Christ?" Luther asks. "Nothing other than to recognize Him firstly as a gift and present, and secondly as an example."[4] It may be that the positive valuation Luther places on both members of this pair has been obscured by his more striking reactions against the *imitatio Christi* piety of his immediate predecessors. To know Christ, he says in apparent contradiction of the statement we have just quoted, is not to know Him just as example, but to know why He was sent as God's gift; to know that He is all gift, and that the gift is true gold but the example is mere iron.[5] The point of these remarks is plain: the sta-

98. *40/I*, 234, 21.

99. *12*, 547, 14ff.

1. *10/I/2*, 240, 22; *17/II*, 74, 31; *27*, 186, 6.

2. *Tr, 2*, 408: 2291a.

3. *33*, 522, 39.

4. *10/I/2*, 247, 28; cf. *10/I/1*, 12, 15; *I/2*, 22, 6; *12*, 372, 9; *25*, 51, 19; *38*, 528, 5; *40/II*, 42, 19; etc.

5. *17/I*, 263, 26; *15*, 778, 3.

tus of the *viator*, as it was understood by the Schoolmen and the Brethren of the Common Life, has been drastically recast by Luther's distinction between the gift and the example. For the imitation of Christ is no longer the path which the pilgrim must travel to the eternal city: "that is not the way, the truth, and the life." [6] Our going to the Father is totally dependent upon Christ's going to the Father, and not at all upon the success of our own walk. The following in His footsteps that leads to God is not imitation but faith. Emulating His example cannot be a means of attaining life, for our life is already hidden with Christ in God. Still, when all this is said, the role of the imitation of Christ in the daily life of the Christian should not be denied, and Luther, so far from denying it, vigorously affirms it.

Inevitably, of course, Luther does describe Christ as gift far more often than as example. The gift of Christ is the vital thing, since there can be no following His example unless we are made new men. Therefore it is the gift, not the example, which is the *principalissima pars et summa in Christo docendo et cognoscendo.* The Son is God's "great and precious gift." [7] Such a rich giver must give us a gift ineffably excellent and great—"not great kingdoms, not one or many worlds full of silver and gold, not heaven and earth with all they contain, not the whole creation; but His Son, Who is as great as Himself: it is an eternal, incomprehensible present, just as the giver and His love are incomprehensibly great." [8] God gives us the very dearest thing He is and has. [9]

> The manner of this gift corresponds to the two parts of Christ's ministry, His preaching office and His going to the Father. Luther expounds the words of John 4:10—"If you knew the gift of God" —in terms of the treasure God has sent us in Christ's words (47, 227, 3ff.). But this "inexpressibly precious treasure" simply points to the extent of God's self-giving love. "Even if Christ did nothing better, it would be a treasure above all treasures if He merely

6. 45, 497, 11.
7. 25, 53, 4; 54, 16; 21, 494, 30.
8. 21, 483, 21.
9. 47, 97, 10.

greeted us—that would be honor and treasure enough. Yet here there is further treasure still: He brings us forgiveness of sins and redemption from death, devil, and hell, and makes out of us heavenly people, shedding light in our hearts" (47, 228, 36). If you would see the manner of God's gift, "look on Him in what He has done and suffered!" He submits to manhood, wrath, and ignominious death for us, and triumphs over our enemies in His exaltation: that is how this gift is bestowed. "All this He gave us that it might be our own, so that we might possess both Him and all that He achieved" (21, 484, 4ff.). Therefore, since Christ is given to me with all that is His, I simply let go everything that is my own (10/III, 154, 16).

Only faith can appropriate this gift—"a faith which does not look to its own works, nor at the strength or worthiness of its own trust—that is, its own *qualitas,* or inwrought or infused virtue implanted in the heart, as the blind sophists dream and deceive themselves; but one which quite outside itself holds to Christ and embraces Him as its own bestowed good, certain that it is now beloved of God on His account—not for its own works, worthiness or service, for all these things are certainly not the treasure which God gave, namely Christ, God's Son, in Whom we must believe." [10]

But "those who have their sufficiency from Christ must follow the example of Christ" in love toward their neighbors—not as servants but as heirs who have no need to acquire what is theirs already by birthright; not as heathen, in the hope of obtaining something by it, but as colaborers with the Father, extending the kingdom to the need of others.[11] This kingdom was instituted not that we might indulge our fleshly lusts but that, released from our captivity to the law (which prevented our sincerely performing any good), we might freely follow Christ's example by obedience and good works in the liberty of faith.[12] The relation between the gift and the example, then, parallels the relation between faith and love: "We receive Christ not only as a gift by

10. *21,* 488, 18.
11. *33,* 171, 13; *10/III,* 168, 19 to 169, 20.
12. *21,* 505, 26.

faith, but also as an example of love to our neighbor . . . Faith gives Christ to you with all that is His; love gives you to your neighbor with all that is yours." [13] These two things are "the two parts of Christianity," for though we are redeemed once, we are purified daily. [14] Here, this example of Christ is not merely a model but a sacrament, an efficacious example which accomplishes what it teaches. In our constant progress from faith to faith, and from love to love, "Christ is the sun, given as our example to imitate." [15] However, the flexibility of Luther's pastoral concern is revealed by his advice that the Christian should set Christ the gift before himself in times of affliction, and take Christ as example only in times of joy; but by the same token, it is the example and not the gift which should be declared to the stubborn and the self-satisfied. [16]

Thus Christ's sheep follow their shepherd in two ways: He goes before and does every good for the people, suffers every evil for men's sakes; and His sheep follow Him first by their faith and reliance and then by heeding His example, doing His works, and suffering as He suffered. [17] The fact that Christ is our gift is itself our chief example. For the Father and Christ are the noblest and most perfect examples of Christ's own command to love: the Father in giving Christ for us, Christ in emptying Himself of His divine glory and laying down His life for our redemption. [18] Here is yet another reason why the imitation of Christ ought not to be confused with the gift as the way of salvation: His example is far too sublime for us! [19] For instance, Christ's washing the disciples' feet is an incomprehensibly high example—an utterly humbling experience, when we see the divine majesty so debasing Himself. [20] The account of the foot washing is associated in Lu-

13. 10/I/2, 38, 3.
14. 20, 708, 5; 25, 54, 8.
15. 43, 274, 5; 15, 502, 22.
16. 40/II, 42, 25; 43, 15.
17. 27, 186, 5; 33, 522, 39.
18. 25, 62, 10ff.; 10/I/2, 42, 5; III, 169, 15; 45, 686, 12; 690, 23.
19. 45, 497, 33.
20. 20, 310, 26.

ther's mind with the institution of the sacrament, presumed but
not described by St. John; and as the sacrament is Christ's testament by which He seals to us the gift of Himself and all that is
His, so washing the disciples' feet is His example to show that
mutual, self-giving love must be the fruit of the sacrament.
"What an example the Lord has placed before our eyes!—but we
cannot equal it: our light against His light is like a burning straw
against the sun." [21]

Nor can we begin to equal Christ as the pattern of our sufferings. Luther knows that the external course of our life in this
world—the vicissitudes, trials, crosses, and duties of daily existence—are means by which God effects our conformity to Christ
at least as much as by our poor attempts at imitation.[22] Yet however much we are called upon to suffer, however intense, bitter,
and extreme our agony, our most grievous sufferings are nothing
in comparison with His: "The extent of His agony, the intensity
and bitterness of his sufferings, no one can comprehend; and if it
exceeds our comprehension, how much more does it exceed our
ability to imitate or experience." [23] Still, to suffer is to walk in
His footsteps, and it is by Christ's words and example that the
Spirit evokes faith rather than despair in us in our trials—indeed,
teaches us to rejoice in tribulations. For this reason Luther is very
much alive to exemplary encounters in the narrative about Christ
—instances of prudence, of boldness, and of great forbearance.[24]

The story of Christ is full, too, of examples of loving action. For
God uses the need of our neighbor to evoke in us love, joy, peace,
long-suffering, gentleness, and the rest: Christ presents Himself
to our loving concern in the guise of the poor, the naked, and the
hungry. His own actions, therefore, have the double impact of inviting our trust and prompting our love in response to His
example.[25] When Luther expounds a pericope about a miracle of

21. *15*, 497, 22ff.; 499, 7.
22. E.g. *10*/I/2, 251, 12ff.; *15*, 539, 25ff.
23. *21*, 300, 26 to 301, 15.
24. E.g. *17*/II, 233, 2; *33*, 317, 35; 407, 29; etc.
25. *37*, 507, 20.

healing, he adduces its exemplary character as a deed of love.[26] And he describes the miracle at Cana and the feeding of the five thousand as examples of great kindness and concern.[27]

In all these ways are we to be imitators of Christ (and of the saints, insofar as they are of Christ) [28] both in devotion to His teaching of faith and in emulation of His life. This is to know Him as gift and example.


### The Resurrection and the Life

The way is not imitation of Christ, but Christ Himself. He is the way, the truth and the life—three ways, Luther explains, of saying the same thing. For they refer to the one Christ and reflect our various reactions as we cling to Him for the passage or crossing to the Father. "As to the beginning, He is called the way; as to the middle and the journey, He is the truth; as to the end, He is the life." [29] Eternal life is the goal to which the gospel moves (John 20:31): the overthrow of death is the true office of Christ. He is the very essence of salvation and life.[30]

"Essence" here is more than a rhetorical expression for Luther: it is a technical term. The gospel's declaration that whoever believes in Christ has eternal life is *essentialis definitio:* only God can do such a work. That Christ "bestows eternal life, slays death through Himself, and saves all who believe in Him" establishes the divinity of the Son of God.[31] More than any other theme, it is the constantly recurring motif of "life" in the Johannine writings which provokes Luther to speak formally of Christ's divinity. (This, he claims, was St. John's purpose: he wished to "strike Cerinthus with thunderbolts.") [32] The chief such passage, of course, is the Prologue of the Fourth Gospel.

26. E.g. *8, 363, 19; 10/I/2, 383, 1; 17/II, 74, 20;* etc.
27. *17/II, 64, 30; 224, 4; 47, 221, 12ff.*
28. *46, 775, 3ff.; 781, 4.*
29. *45, 502, 6; 504, 32.*
30. *47, 712, 23; 88, 35.*
31. *47, 88, 39.*
32. *10/I/1, 197, 16 to 198, 16.*

Luther explicitly rejects as "idle hairsplitting subtlety" the idea of noetic emanation offered by Neoplatonic interpreters of the Prologue. The words, "In Him was life," have nothing to do with projection of *rationes seminales* as Augustine taught ( 10/I/1, 195, 14 to 196, 21; Augustine, *Tract. in ev. Ioh.*, I, 16–17; see also A. D. R. Polman, *The Word of God according to St. Augustine* (Grand Rapids, 1961), pp. 13ff.). No, the explanation is far simpler than Augustine's high-flown theory (27, 529, 9ff.). "It means, in the very simplest way, that He is the fountain and source of life, that all things that live, live by Him and through Him and in Him, and besides Him there is no life; as He Himself says in John 14:6, 'I am the way, the truth, and the life,' or in John 11:25, 'I am the resurrection and the life.' Accordingly, in I John 1:1, John calls Him 'the Word of life,' and in particular speaks of the life which men receive from Him, that is, eternal life. It was for this life that John set out to write his gospel" ( 10/I/1, 196, 24). It is rather interesting to find that by the time of his 1538 exposition of the Prologue ( 46, 567–648), Luther has become more sympathetic to Augustine's understanding of "life and light" in universal terms ( cf 10/I/1, 195, 14; 202, 2 [in 1522]; 27, 529, 9 [in 1528]; and 46, 561, 7; 562, 10 [in 1538]). Even so, however, he continues to read the Prologue in terms of the narrative it introduces (see von Loewenich, *Die Eigenart von Luthers Auslegung des Johannes-Prologes*).

"In Him was life" is spoken of the Word, Who is God, and in Whom resides the sheer life that cannot die.[33] Therefore the power to make alive is not ascribed to Christ's humanity, but the life is in the Word which dwells in the flesh and makes us alive by the flesh.[34] Since Luther certainly does not intend to suggest that life is a "something," this is another way of saying that the power to make alive belongs only to the living God. Therefore, that Christ has life in Himself (John 5:26) is an affirmation of His divine essence.[35] That He is the bread of life (John 6:35ff.)—a food that expels death and gives eternal life to him

33. *46*, 561, 21–32.
34. *10/I/1*, 199, 14; 208, 6.
35. *46*, 67, 9; perhaps his only recorded comment about this vital text, on which sadly there is no extant sermon.

who eats it—proves that He can be none other than the eternal God.[36] However genuinely human Christ's converse is with His disciples after the death of Lazarus, in His declaration "I am the resurrection and the life" (John 11:25), God speaks; for "these words are fitting to no one but the one true God."[37] He is equal with God; for knowledge of the Son and knowledge of the Father lead equally to eternal life (John 17:3).[38]

Whatever christological problems are raised by speaking of life as the definition of Christ's essence—and as we shall see very shortly, such problems do arise when, on the ground that "life cannot die," Luther claims that Christ the Word remained alive when Christ the man died[39]—He is not really interested, he tells us, in discussing "the resurrection and the life" under the rubrics of act or being. For no benefit accrues from dividing them—calling the life "essence" and the resurrection "act," or discussing them theoretically apart from the historical Christ. "He is the resurrection and the life; and He has resurrection and life. That is, the object of your faith is not in heaven: here on earth He is the resurrection. 'You must not separate Me and resurrection and life from one another. Rather, the person who believes in Me will both live and rise again.'" This is the issue. Academic discussion merely distracts us from the main point, which is that we be united with Christ by faith, and know Him to be our resurrection and our life.[40]

For the Resurrection was not for Christ's own sake but for ours: His Resurrection and Ascension are our comfort, life, bliss, our resurrection, and our all. If mortal man born of Adam is to enter heaven, One must come from heaven Who has eternal life in Himself; but to accomplish this, He had to take flesh and suffer.[41] Thus the Prologue, when it ascribes life to the Word rather than to the humanity of Christ, nevertheless proclaims that the life-giving Word makes us alive by means of His humanity.

36. *33*, 173, 16.
37. *47*, 715, 12ff.
38. *28*, 93, 1ff.; *111*, 3.
39. *10/I/1*, 208, 4; *47*, 54, 34.
40. *49*, 53, 11–39.
41. *12*, 546, 33; *21*, 546, 2.

Furthermore, its words are, "In Him *was* life," not "*is* life." The evangelist is not making cosmic propositions about eternity, nor is he describing the beginning of time, but he describes "the time of Christ's life or sojourn on earth, when the Word of God revealed Himself to men and among men. For the evangelist intends to describe Christ and the life in which He accomplished everything necessary for our life . . . We must seek Him as He was and as He sojourned on earth: there we shall find life." [42] This is the sense, too, of the following words: "and the life was the light of men." The life in the Word was not only for itself: [43] it went forth among men. He was the life: they lay in death; and the life in Him lightened men with His words and deeds.[44] "Life has been sent in such a way that it is manifested, so that we may acknowledge that we are in sin and death and under the prince of darkness, and so that the man who hears this announcement may fly for refuge to it, fling open the door and windows, and let in the life which has been manifested to make us alive." [45]

This life enlightens men through faith by two means: His words and His deeds. He comes to tell us that death shall no longer be death. "A life that ends in death is only a sham copy of life and the Holy Spirit; therefore I shall begin another life that soars over death." The voice of the shepherd, Who lays down His life for the sheep, assures His flock of eternal life.[46] He calls death merely a sleep, transforming its image from grief and tragedy into gladness, with the words, "Because I live, you shall live also." [47] The dying of Christians is no longer "tasting" or "feeling" death, because of Christ's promise.[48]

The deeds by which His life enlightens men are the events of His Passion and Resurrection (to which the raising of Lazarus is a fitting introduction).[49] His going to the Father was His ad-

42. 10/I/1, 200, 13; 202, 9.
43. 46, 562, 8.
44. 27, 531, 1.
45. 20, 607, 2.
46. 49, 52, 7; 15, 557, 9; 37, 74, 15.
47. 38, 489, 12; 47, 713, 21 to 715, 13; *Tr, 1*, 477: 949.
48. 17/II, 234, 36ff.
49. 47, 712, 9 and 16; 49, 50, 2 and 14.

vance from this mortal life, through death, into eternal life—an advance accomplished by His leap into the abyss of hell, and bursting its gates by rising again to freedom from death, in order to be our guide from death to life.[50] What does this Resurrection effect? We have already seen how Christ, by bearing our sins, drew the sting of death, and by His Resurrection triumphed over it, shattering its dominion. "The greatest weight and importance lies in this article; for if there had been no Resurrection, we should have gained no comfort or hope, and everything else Christ did and suffered would have been in vain." [51] By overthrowing death, Christ raised the dead from death. His Resurrection works the resurrection of the whole human race.[52] Furthermore, we shall see that this triumph declares Christ's exaltation by the Father to eternal lordship over death and all things.[53]

Word and work belong together if "faith's sharp vision" is to discern and take hold of life in the midst of death.[54] Conscious of this, Luther devotes careful attention in Eastertide to amassing the proofs of the Resurrection.[55] (Luther was far too alert to be caught on the horns of his own dialectic and faintheartedly despair the value of evidences!) Even as he does so, he is instant to urge his hearer on from the history to the use and fruit of the Resurrection. If we are to know its proper fruit, we must give heed to the words of Christ after His rising, when He made clear those figures that earlier His disciples could not understand.[56] For whatever systematic lines we may draw between Good Friday and Easter, there is at least a real disjunction to this extent: we could never have conceived of the riches of the glory of His inheritance that we have received from His fullness in the Resurrection and exaltation of Christ. This treasure is so great, Luther says, that we can never adequately preach it nor worthily grasp it

50. *13*, 273, 7; *41*, 574, 9; 575, 3.
51. *12*, 268, 21; *13*, 27, n. 2.
52. *47*, 713, 2.
53. E.g. *13*, 273, 20; *21*, 547, 11; *46*, 69, 30.
54. *33*, 114, 18; *28*, 465, 11.
55. *28*, 425–64.
56. *21*, 214, 6 and 19; *46*, 93, 1 and 11.

in our hearts. Yet Christ has shown us after His Resurrection how all Scripture and all creation speak of it.[57]

Christ's conversation in the garden with Mary Magdalene contains His first words after His return from the grave. As such, they have especial importance in Luther's estimation.[58] First, he asks, what sense can we make of Christ's telling Mary not to touch Him? Should she touch Him *after* He has ascended? Or does it mean that He would have to come down again before He could be touched? Obviously, after His Ascension, Christ could be touched no more; but His purpose with these strange words was to revolutionize her thinking—to show her that her immediate reaction to seeing Him alive was mistaken. She thought He had come back from the dead like Lazarus—back to the same life He had before. This was why she wanted to touch Him. But He, by forbidding her, taught her that He had risen to a new sort of life. *Non sic resurrexi ut sic vixi.* He had risen, in order that He might go to the Father.[59] Christ's Resurrection was a translation from the life of time, of sense, of nature, and of death to a new, immortal life and kingdom.[60] It is true that had Adam not fallen, we should have enjoyed life without threat of death; that Enoch and Elijah could be translated from this mortal existence to paradise without seeing death; that natural life is a beginning of eternal life if only death, the obstacle on the way, can be surmounted.[61] Yet in Christ, risen from the dead and exalted to the right hand of the Father, there is a new life, a new possibility, a new creation for man—a sharing in the divine life itself, so that "God lives in us, and makes us partakers of His life, to live through Him, and from Him, and in Him." [62] Christ says, "As I live because of the Father, so he who eats Me will live because of Me." Luther glosses, " 'The Father abides in Me; He is My life' . . . This life He has from the Father, His Incarnation ac-

57. *46*, 329, 2.
58. *46*, 330, 1.
59. *28*, 455, 9 to 456, 6.
60. *21*, 368, 24; *22*, 426, 19; *46*, 331, 4.
61. *41*, 574, 14; 10/I/1, 200, 3; *45*, 505, 33.
62. 10/I/1, 199, 25.

cording to the Father's will, His work of redemption, and His
Father's abiding in Him—all these things He gives to us when He
says, 'Just as I have life because the Father is in Me and gave it
to Me, so also you will have life because you are in Me and I in
you.' " [63]

But if Christ is now risen to a new, transformed, eternal life—if
Mary may not touch Him because He ascends to the Father—
how may we know that we, in the midst of death, can be partakers of His life? His next words to Mary were, "Go, tell My
brethren . . ." This is one of those texts, Luther exclaims, that
ought to be written with great golden letters.[64] It was directed
to Peter, who three times denied the Lord; to the disciples who
deserted Him in His need and suffering, who cowered in the
upper room not only afraid of the Jews but afflicted in conscience, knowing themselves utterly lacking in loyalty, perjurers of
their oath to stand by their Lord; and furthermore, to all those
everywhere who, in distress of conscience and fear of death, hear
the gospel; for He sends this word before Him, to those who are
not witnesses of His Resurrection.[65] Christ might well have said,
"Go to the perjuring, faithless miscreants who first denied and
forswore Me, then forsook Me without loyalty, and tell them that
they shall receive their due." Instead, the Son of God says "brethren." We are not worthy to be called creatures, let alone brethren. Before He had called His disciples "dear children" and
"friends," but now He uses the most glorious name of all and calls
us "brethren." Neither mind nor heart can comprehend how we
may be brothers of such a man, Who is lord over heaven, earth,
death, and all creation. On this hangs our highest comfort and
courage against sin, death, Satan, hell, law, and every ill which
befalls body or soul.[66] "I ascend to My Father and your Father,
to My God and your God." To be brothers means to share the
same heritage—to be coheirs, so closely united with Him that we
have one Father, one honor, one estate, a great, mighty, and eter-

63. 33, 231, 29.
64. 28, 457, 4 (cf. 10/I/2, 214, 21ff.; 29, 296, 6ff.).
65. 28, 458, 1.
66. 28, 458, 3; 46, 332, 4; 28, 458, 10f.; 10/I/2, 217, 9.

nal brotherhood.[67] He shows Himself to us not only alive but bearing this inexpressible treasure—a treasure of eternal life and glory now hidden in Christ until the resurrection of our bodies, but anticipated in that peace and joy in believing which is the power and fruit of the Resurrection in the midst of death.[68]

For we are in the midst of death. As Christ's going meant to die, and to pass through death to the Father, so faith, too, must travel the road through death to God.[69] We are buried with Christ in baptism; here all Christians begin to die, and they continue to die until they reach the grave. Yet the faithful man is prepared for death at any moment—today, tomorrow, or ten years hence—for in Christ he has already been carried to the other side. We regard as but one fact the Resurrection of Christ and the resurrection of ourselves. For by virtue of His rising, our resurrection from unbelief leads to resurrection from the dead.[70] Hence Christ's Resurrection is mightily effective in our trials and in the hour of our death. ("I am the resurrection and the life" was Luther's favorite verse for use in illness and impending death —his own and others.[71] But no one knew better how death was the fiercest trial of faith.[72] Cordatus records how Luther, convalescing from a strange illness in 1533, told his visitors: "God holds His hand over us and says, 'I live, and you shall live also.' If God lives, then we also shall live, even if we are dead." Then with a smile, he added, "Reason tells us that is a monstrous lie.") [73] Christ can give more life than death can strangle.[74] The tyrants, if they are to devour us, must begin with the one Who is up there; He is our head and firstborn, the bridegroom Who took a bride upon earth, and interprets His own ascending to mean that we shall ascend in Him.[75]

67. 28, 464, 35; 46, 336, 2ff.
68. 10/I/2, 303, 36; 28, 465, 23 to 466, 5; 33, 112, 1ff.
69. 10/I/2, 304, 21–32; III, 130, 23.
70. 45, 507, 9; 21, 267, 29; 49, 159, 24.
71. E.g. Tr, 4, 7: 3916; Tr, 5, 666: 6445.
72. E.g. 20, 774, 9; 33, 112, 28; 43, 218, 16; 45, 505, 10.
73. Tr, 3, 123: 2970b.
74. 41, 100, 27.
75. 45, 715, 19; 46, 635, 37; 47, 61, 21–35.

When we have rightly heard, learned, and known Christ's Resurrection, it quickens and fires our hearts, and bears in us new thoughts, new knowledge, new powers, it works life, joy, consolation, and strength.[76] Christ has power to refashion even our wretched bodies.[77] Therefore, whatever our fate—to be burned, beheaded, devoured, scattered in a myriad of pieces [78]—yet, like aged Simeon, we depart in peace and look to Christ: "I am a poor sinner and deserve to die, but I cling to Thee in the face of sin and death and will not let Thee go. I have taken hold of Thee, dear Lord Christ—Thou art my life. All who cling to Thee have eternal life and shall rise from the dead, for this is Thy Father's will." [79]

### Lord and King

The culmination of Christ's going to the Father is His exaltation to the right hand of God, to begin His eternal reign and dominion over everything in heaven and earth.[80] In this way Christians know that they, too, are to be lords over all God's creatures, for they can gladly confess, "My Lord Christ, Who is on my side, is lord over all things: what shall harm me? For the Father in His greatness has made Him lord over all creation, and all things must therefore lie at His feet." [81]

While in a majority of cases "lord" is used not as a title but as a name, yet together with "king" it often occurs appellatively as a messianic title in Luther's comments on the prophets and the narrative parts of the Gospels.[82] In Luther's view the kingdom of Christ was a major burden of the prophets of Israel. "First of all, the prophets proclaim and testify to the kingdom of Christ in which we now live, in which all believers in Christ have lived till now, and will live to the end of the world." [83]

76. 21, 224, 31.
77. 22, 372, 29.
78. 33, 112, 40; 49, 52, 20.
79. 33, 113, 22.
80. See Gottfried Forck, *Die Königsherrschaft Jesu Christi bei Luther* (Berlin, 1959).
81. 12, 578, 12.
82. E.g. 46, 700, 2; *DB*, 11/I, 401, 2.
83. *DB*, 11/I, 3, 16; cf. 13, 5, 10.

It is Isaiah who prophesies more clearly and diversely of Christ's kingdom than any other prophet; in fact, his chapter 53 proclaims Christ's kingdom as powerfully and plainly as if it had already arrived (*DB, 11/I,* 19, 27; *31/II,* 428, 10). Two chapters of Jeremiah, chapters 23 and 31, especially prophesy the person of Christ, His kingdom, the new covenant, and the superseding of the old (*DB, 11/I,* 193, 7; *20,* 549, 21ff.). Ezekiel teaches the kingdom of Christ in each part of his prophecy—in the vision of the four living creatures, in the promise of a new covenant and the ingathering of Israel, and in the computation of the temple (*DB, 11/I,* 395, 16; 401, 24ff.). Daniel declares with great clarity the time when Christ's kingdom will begin (*DB, 11/II,* 19, 10). Hosea prophesies powerfully and most consolingly about Christ and His kingdom, especially in chapters 2, 13, and 14 (*DB, 11/II,* 182, 22; *13,* 64, 24). Joel, Amos, and Obadiah all preach of Christ's everlasting rule (*DB, 11/II,* 212, 23; 226, 6; 250, 25). Micah points constantly to the future Christ and His kingdom, and uniquely predicts the place of Messiah's birth (*DB, 11/II,* 288, 19; *13,* 312, 24; 324, 29). Habakkuk insists that despite the vicissitudes of the Jewish nation, Christ's kingdom will surely come (*DB, 11/II,* 299, 3 and 7; *13,* 432, 35). Zephaniah prophesies "exceeding gloriously and clearly of the joyful and blessed kingdom of Christ to be spread throughout all the world," and though he is a minor prophet speaks more about Christ than most of the major prophets (*DB, 11/II,* 310, 20; *13,* 480, 2). Haggai, in his description of Christ as "the desire of all nations" (2:7), declares in a mystery that the Jewish kingdom and law shall have an end, and the kingdoms of the world shall be subjected to Christ (*DB, 11/II,* 320, 26; *13,* 540, 27). The prophet Zechariah depicts the King Christ entering Jerusalem on an ass and suffering betrayal, and so as He enters into His glory His kingdom comes to the Gentiles (*DB, 11/II,* 329, 24; *13,* 595, 23). Finally Malachi declares how soon Christ the lord shall come (*DB, 11/II,* 362, 6; *13,* 701, 1).

When this theme is taken up in the Gospels, "lord" and "king" are again used as messianic titles.[84] But as we saw earlier,[85] these messianic designations are applied to the reinterpretation of Messiah's role in the face of Jewish misconceptions. Christ came

84. E.g. *10/I/2,* 45n.; *22,* 393, 34ff.; *46,* 700, 2.
85. See above, p. 28.

as a spiritual king and preacher: His dominion was not merely
over the Jews but over all nations, a dominion exercised not by
the sword but by the gospel.[86] His kingdom consists in His
message.[87] He is a spiritual, not a secular, king and lord.[88]

This reinterpretation of Messiah's role forms a vital component
in Luther's law-gospel dialectic. It has been suggested that there
is a radical difference between Paul and Luther in their use of
this dialectic.[89] Paul, it is argued, was not confronting the quest
of the afflicted conscience for a gracious God; rather, Jewish-Gen-
tile relations within the primitive Church forced him to reflect on
the status of the Mosaic Torah in the new messianic age. Even
though he placed so high a value upon it, he was bound to regard
the Torah as abrogated now that its function as custodian was
complete. While it may well be the case that Luther makes Paul's
attitude to the law answer more questions than the apostle intended to address, it does Luther scant justice to suppose that he
does so inadvertently, a captive to his Augustinian heritage. On
the contrary, Luther is perfectly explicit: when Paul calls the law
a custodian until the time of faith, "he is referring to the time of
fulfillment when Christ came. However, it should be applied not
only to that time, but also to experience, because what happened
historically at the point in time when Christ came—His abrogat-
ing the law and bringing liberty and eternal life to light—the
same happens personally and spiritually to every Christian every
day. In him too the time of law constantly alternates with the
time of grace." [90] The law, precisely in the sense of the Mosaic
Torah, was custodian until Messiah replaced the old covenant
with the new.[91] But just because Christ's kingdom, when it came,
shattered any local, worldly, temporal preconceptions, and appeared instead as a universal kingdom over sin, death, and hell, it
cannot be confined in its liberating power to any one experience

86. *13*, 278, 14; *25*, 14, 3; *46*, 570, 34ff.

87. *47*, 178, 1.

88. *31*/I, 233, 19; *46*, 710, 14; *49*, 219, 12.

89. See Krister Stendahl, "The Apostle Paul and the Introspective Conscience
of the West," *Harvard Theological Review, 56* (1963), 199ff.

90. *40*/I, 523, 31.

91. *23*, 501, 19; 540, 14.

of bondage to the law. Nor, Luther insists, can Paul be read coherently as suggesting that its power is so confined.[92] Christ liber-
ates the captive conscience of the sinner before God as surely as
He puts an end to the ordinances of the old covenant—and this is
not merely an analogy. The kingdom of law which Moses established has actually been superseded in time by the kingdom of
Christ which God established.[93] Any attempt to reimpose the
sovereignty of the law in the spiritual realm—by the bishops in
their jurisdictions, by the spiritualists in their theocracies, or by
the tyranny of sin in the conscience—is therefore a denial of the
kingdom Christ established. It is a grave misinterpretation of Luther to read his law-gospel dialectic as if it were entirely an individual, conscientious, and purely theological distinction, while ignoring its all-important foundation in the historical progression of
the covenants.

The reinterpretation of the Messiah's role is thus also the exegetical basis of the distinction between the "two kingdoms"—the
worldly and the spiritual.[94] Once again, if its exegetical foundation is ignored, Luther's distinction comes to appear both naïve
and doctrinaire. But in context it insists, in the face of all our
human expectations, that the kingdom which Christ in fact established among men is a kingdom not of this world.[95] Its justice is
not the juristic righteousness of the world but the righteousness
from God, which is by faith.

Luther's terminology, like Scripture's, is interchangeable to
some extent when he speaks of the kingdom of God, the kingdom
of heaven, the kingdom of glory, or the kingdom of Christ. Nevertheless, he deals with three distinct concepts, which, for the sake
of clarity, we shall label consistently as the kingdom of God, the
kingdom of Christ, and the kingdom of the world.

92. 39/I, 48, 36ff., esp. Theses 4–34.
93. 49, 137, 19; cf. 13, 299, 11.
94. See, e.g., Harald Diem, *Luthers Lehre von den zwei Reichen* (München,
1938); Anders Nygren, "Luthers Lehre von den zwei Reichen," *ThLZ*, 74 (1949),
1–8; Gustaf Törnvall, *Geistliches und weltliches Regiment bei Luther* (München,
1947); Franz Lau, *Luthers Lehre von den beiden Reichen* (Berlin, 1952); Wingren, *Luther on Vocation;* etc.
95. 41, 541, 20ff.

By the kingdom of God, we mean that eternal Godship of God declared by the first commandment [96]—the almighty dominion of the creator of heaven and earth, in Whom all things live and move and have their being.[97] By the kingdom of Christ, we mean the invisible, spiritual rule of Christ by His Word and Holy Spirit —the kingdom of faith and grace.[98] By the worldly realm, we mean simply what the words say—earthly dominion and rule.[99] The world, of course, lies in the evil one and is at enmity with God, therefore opposing the kingdom of Christ,[1] but is neverthe- less subject to the kingdom of God and involuntarily serves the purpose of Him Who brings good out of evil. Oddly, then, the powers that be may be both tyrants and ordained by God (not that their tyranny is any less evil for that).

The theological affirmations that these labels are intended to protect are as follows: the first, that God is lord of all; the sec- ond, of what sort Christ's kingdom is—namely, for salvation; the third, of what sort it is not—namely, an earthly rule. Axiomati- cally, it is inherent in the kingship of God that both the other kingdoms serve the purposes of God.

Now as we have just seen, the contrast between Christ's king- dom and the kingdom of the world arises from the Christian rein- terpretation of Messiah's rule. "Christ is not a king as the kings of this world are; He wears no golden crown, He rides forth with no great pomp and circumstance." [2] No, this king is a teacher. He is to govern by the rod of His mouth.[3] Therefore the all-important theme of Christ as preacher sent from God is inextricably linked to the institution of the kingdom of Christ. At His baptism, where He was ordained teacher, He was ordained king: His preaching

96. *Tr, 1*, 358: 751: "Primum praeceptum est Deus ipse et regnum gloriae."

97. See Hanns Lilje, *Luthers Geschichtsanschauung* (Berlin, 1932); Seeberg, *Luthers Theologie*, Vol. 1: *Die Gottesanschauung bei Luther;* Peter Brunner, "Luther and the World of the Twentieth Century," in *Martin Luther Lectures, 5* (Decorah, Iowa, 1961), pp. 3ff.

98. *25, 7*, 26; *47, 47, 26; Tr, 1*, 358: 751: "Secundum est Christus et regnum fidei ac gratiae."

99. *45*, 602, 36; 603, 7.

1. *40/I*, 94, 22; *45*, 607, 26.

2. *12*, 317, 30; cf. *13*, 626, 1; *31/II*, 515, 21ff.

3. *40/II*, 264, 12; 279, 31; *46*, 730, 23.

ministry began after His baptism and pointed to Himself as God's anointed and as the man Who by His going to the Father would achieve the kingdom.[4]

Thus the scepter of Christ's kingdom is the gospel (for His is a kingdom of salvation).[5] The gospel describes how by His going to the Father Christ has borne away our sins, bringing forgiveness, freedom from bondage, and newness of life. So even though He was ordained king at His baptism, the actual assumption of His "real office and reign" awaited His departure from this world.[6] So, too, the way to His lordship may be identified with the cross [7]—the *regnum Christi in cruce* [8]—or with His Resurrection, by which He became king over death, and as a mighty lord snatched us from its jaws,[9] or with His Ascension, where His visible departure was an external sign that He assumed His active, powerful, and continuing spiritual kingdom.[10]

What is the extent of this kingdom? He is lord of all.[11]

> This is that dominion which the Scriptures foretold. He is the
> שֵׁב לִימִינִי of Psalm 110:1 (*Tr*, 6, 19: 6528)—"one word elevates
> Him to the position of glorious king—not over the mean palace in
> Jerusalem nor yet the imperial thrones of Babylon, Rome, Constantinople, or the whole world, however prodigious such power would
> be; not even king only of the heavens, the stars, and as far as the
> eye can see. No, this is far more exalted and momentous, for it
> means: 'Sit by Me on the lofty throne where I sit, and be My
> equal.' To sit by Him, not at His feet but at His right hand, means
> to possess the divine majesty and power itself . . . a king of inconceivable glory and ineffable might" (*41*, 86, 29). He is lord
> and king over all creatures, which must be subject to Him "until
> I make Thine enemies Thy footstool" (*10*/I/2, 295, 9; 29, 368, 12).
> Psalm 8 declares that God has made Him lord and ruler of the
> whole world—"of angels, men sin, death, world, devil, hell, and

4. *13*, 541, 1; *46*, 602, 31.
5. *5*, 63, 22; *13*, 608, 25; *21*, 387, 1–16; *25*, 7, 27; *41*, 123, 34.
6. *13*, 541, 1; *45*, 480, 3.
7. *10*/III, 129, 27; *15*, 506, 14; 536, 22; *41*, 235, 22.
8. *31*/II, 428, 8.
9. *21*, 295, 7; *33*, 310, 24 and 32.
10. *12*, 562, 15; *20*, 428, 10; *21*, 547, 13–21.
11. *21*, 378, 16; *22*, 431, 14; *33*, 608, 15; *41*, 112, 19; *47*, 47, 14.

whatever may be named, in heaven, on earth, and under the earth"
(45, 210, 35; cf. 10/I/2, 295, 14–21; 47, 199, 6). Psalm 2 proclaims
Him enthroned as king of all—the world is subject to no other
prince or king (10/I/2, 296, 28; 33, 28, 27; 40/II, 263, 29; 46, 575,
18). Psalm 118 praises God for His greatest gift to the world,
Christ and His kingdom of grace (31/I, 68, 24). He is "lord of the
law" (40/I, 566, 15; II, 31, 28); "lord of life and of eternal glory"
(21, 430, 20); "mighty lord over everything in heaven and earth"
(10/I/2, 303, 26; 21, 474, 9; 46, 21, 21); "lord of all angels" (45, 629,
7); "king of glory in a new and eternal life" (28, 64, 6). Moreover,
Christ is appointed judge: "He is lord of all and has authority and
power to condemn and punish with eternal fire of hell everything
that opposes Him, including the devil and his angels" (21, 371,
13). Christ is the lord of life and death (40/I, 240, 31).

In short, God has given all things into His hand. "He loved Him
so greatly that He has placed everything in His hands; that is, He
has made Him almighty. As St. Paul says, all the treasures of wisdom are in Him—God's highest wisdom, righteousness, and truth
are placed in the Son, and all has been given to
Him . . . Nothing is excepted in heaven and earth. All angels, all
men, leaves, fruit—all these are in His hands; He is almighty
God. God of course subjected oxen, and sheep, and all animals to
man (as Genesis 1 and other passages tell us), but it is not added
that man is to be lord over all. In fact, Adam did not actually attain to dominion over all the birds, fish, and beasts; but even if he
had exercised his rights over all these, he was still not appointed
lord over heaven and earth, over death and life, or sin and righteousness. But to this lord, Christ, everything is given without exception—whatever God has, Christ has also. Therefore as God
has given Him all things, so He has also invested Him with His
throne and His majesty." [12]
    Of course, the problem immediately arises: "How is such an ex-
altation possible? For God is a God Who will not give His glory
to another. "God makes no one such a king who is not God, for
He will not let the reins out of His hand—He alone will be lord
over heaven and earth, death, hell, devil, and all creatures. Since

12. 47, 198, 40 to 199, 18.

He now makes Christ lord of all created things, He must be God indeed." [13] If, then, He is God, His is the kingdom of God anyway: He was lord of all beforehand. If He is God, Luther asks, how could God give Him all? If he owns all, how can it be given to Him? [14]

Luther offers a number of solutions to this enigma. Some of them employ the christological dogma (and to these we must shortly devote more detailed attention).[15] Thus he suggests that the communication of properties provides the answer. "According to His divinity He does not receive anything; but in that God and man are one person, God gave all things to Christ. Since the Son was man, God gave to the man what was God's; and since it is now given to the man, it is by the same token given to God." [16] This explanation comes from the time after the sacramental dispute; before it he had said less technically, "From eternity the Father delivered all things to Him. According to His manhood He has appointed Him lord over all." [17] Only a few weeks before Marburg, Luther attempted a solution by distinguishing Christ's office from His essence: when Christ says the Father is greater than He, He means that God's kingdom is greater than the servile office He assumed for our salvation; but He is not speaking of His person or essence. In a 1537 gloss on the titles "lord" ( יְהוָה ) and "ruler" ( אָדוֹן ) in Psalm 8:1, Luther argues: "In that He is lord and God Christ needs no dominion, but in that He became man He does need it, or else He could not have the name and title of ruler . . . He is lord and God by His eternal and divine nature and essence; ruler by His human nature, His office and kingdom." [18] It is a moot point whether these suggestions solve more problems than they create: to this we must return. Suffice it to say here that the problem is not a merely verbal one for Luther. He is very much aware that to reduce any of the reality of Christ's enthronement as a genuine exaltation is to make the

13. 10/I/2, 295, 22–26; 296, 37; 40/II, 260, 27; 45, 208, 26.
14. 47, 199, 20.
15. See below, pp. 231ff.
16. 47, 201, 16.
17. 15, 536, 21.
18. 29, 368, 19ff.; 45, 208, 38.

scriptural account equivocal. (The avenue taken by some other expositors—namely, that Christ's lordship, which had always been His, was merely declared by the Resurrection [19]—is therefore not satisfying to Luther, especially since the declaration of His lordship is the Word of the gospel and is therefore the very real sword of a very real kingdom.)

The reality of Christ's exaltation is vital to the truth of our salvation, for it is inseparably linked to the reality of His self-abasement and self-emptying for our sakes [20] (not to mention the additional riches in glory of which it assures us). It is this consideration which leads Luther to turn characteristically from academic questions to evangelical concerns: he becomes impatient with even his own theoretical explanations. When Christ calls His going to the Father an occasion for joy "because the Father is greater than I" (John 14:28), "the question under discussion here is not whether Christ is God or man, or what His nature and essence is—whether according to His person He is greater or less than the Father—but rather He intends that His disciples shall not be afraid because He leaves them . . . 'Simply follow Me and cling to Me, and be unafraid when I go from you. For I go where I shall be great, and not in order to be there alone, but that I may serve you thereby and take you there later.' So He passes from the narrow exigency of His confinement into the broad heaven, from this dungeon into His great and lordly kingdom, where He is far greater than before. Before He was a poor, wretched, suffering, and dying Christ; but now with the Father He is great, lordly, living, almighty lord over all creation. I maintain that this is the whole meaning of this text: He simply speaks of His going from this life into the Father's kingdom. So we must not engage in sharp disputation over the divine essence of the Father and the Son. For in His essence He remains equal with the Father, eternal God, and yet cast Himself down from on high to the earth, into the lowliest and meanest office of all, for us, and went to His death; but through this very going overthrew death

19. For a discussion of the exegetical difficulties still centering on this point, see M.-E. Boismard, "Constitué Fils de Dieu," *Revue Biblique*, 60 (1953), 5ff.

20. 45, 633, 16; cf. Gottfried Forck, Königsherrschaft, pp. 38f.

and drew us up with Him to where His kingdom is the Father's kingdom, and the Father's kingdom is His." [21]

The very existence of the christological problem reveals that even His exaltation was not for Himself but for us. The Father places all things in His hands in order that we may know that all Christ does and wills is the act and will of God, the revelation of a profound love.[22] "The Scriptures begin gently and lead us first to Christ as a man, then as lord over all creatures, and then as God. Thus I come all the way to learning the knowledge of God." [23] All that we have learnt about Christ, as preacher, as the embodiment of the Father's will, as the only way to God, and as our savior, here crowds together as we learn that this man Christ is lord over life and death, over the world and all things, and our lord.[24] Everything is given with Him, Who is the only-begotten and beloved Son, heir and lord of all creation: therefore all creatures, angels, devils, death, life, heaven and earth, sin, righteousness, and all things present and future are subject to us too.[25] And this everlasting kingdom is ruled by His Word.

Here arises the extreme paradox of faith. We must, on pain of our soul's damnation, believe in the lordship of Christ.[26] Yet when we hear that all things are given into His hand, does not the very opposite seem to be the truth? [27] Before God, Christ is indeed lord of all; yet there seems to be nothing humbler in heaven and earth.[28] In relation to the kingdom of the world, Christ's kingdom is hidden, secret, spiritual, subject to the cross.[29] It has no might, no wealth, no population statistics. It does not regard the riches and power and position, nor yet the wisdom, piety, and virtue of the world, but is open to the weak,

21. *45*, 633, 1; 634, 1.
22. *15*, 506, 9; *47*, 203, 34–40.
23. 10/I/2, 297, 5.
24. *45*, 483, 7ff.
25. *21*, 438, 35.
26. *33*, 603, 31.
27. *15*, 506, 13.
28. 17/I, 276, 14; cf. *36*, 50, 9.
29. 10/I/2, 260, 18; *21*, 337, 8; 451, 9–31; 373, 1; *22*, 426, 24; *23*, 189, 8; *25*, 7, 26; *12*, 537, 28.

poor, blind, and sinful only.[30] Not only does the world refuse to recognize it, but the most eminent, wisest, holiest, and most zealous men persecute it as a destruction and subversion of sound government, both spiritual and temporal.[31]

Is then the kingdom of the world not given into Christ's hand? But when God declares that He gives Him all things, nothing is excepted.[32] In the purpose of God even the kingdoms of this world serve the kingdom of Christ. There is nothing to show for this affirmation but the Word of Christ, by which the kingdom grows throughout the world;[33] the sacraments and the office of the keys, by which Christ shows Himself to be lord of consolation for the weak, the sick, and the broken[34] (and therefore the tyranny of the pope in making out of the keys an empty show and worldly dominion is doubly reprehensible);[35] and the Holy Spirit and prayer, by which Christ reigns in our hearts in the midst of tribulation and sorrow.[36] But these things may be seen only by faith. God has indeed glorified Christ, but His glory is hidden to the world and reason, revealed only to faith (which ought to recognize Christ's glory shining in the Word, but because it is weak sees only through a glass darkly).[37] These things, so despised in the world, are the Christian's assurance that Christ's kingdom does tread down all evil, does storm the world by the gospel, does hold sway over this world's kingdoms too.[38] What is the significance of this affirmation for faith? What can it mean? It means for all the faithful that God orders the whole course of history for the sake of His Christians. This is the point of Luther's words, "We often undergo such terrible experiences that we imagine Christ has no kingdom at all; but even if the Turks were to succeed in conquering all kingdoms and kings"

30. 40/II, 196, 26; 10/I/2, 164, 24; 12, 532, 16 to 537, 15; 33, 509, 18; 36, 383, 31; 46, 701, 3ff.

31. 21, 369, 16ff.; 427, 17; 33, 111, 14ff.; 41, 105, 18; 41, 216, 18.

32. 15, 506, 12; 41, 96, 11; 47, 199, 7.

33. 12, 540, 1–15; 31/I, 232, 26.

34. 12, 532, 16ff.; 30/II, 468, 3; 45, 669, 31.

35. 49, 153, 28; 54, 250, 3.

36. 46, 74, 31 to 75, 5; 87, 10; 17/I, 194, 1.

37. 28, 194, 11 to 196, 13.

38. 33, 608, 10; 40/II, 200, 35; 45, 538, 8–38.

—this was in 1539, when it was a live possibility for Europe [39]—
"even then we must say that the Turk, too, is subject to
Christ." [40] All the political and civil history of this world is ordered for the propagation of the gospel. (The implications of this
faith for the mission of the Church in the world are boundless in
scope and power.) Yes, even the course of nature, the springing
up of corn in the field, are for the sake of Christendom.[41] For the
individual Christian this affirmation means that all things work together for his good, however desperately otherwise his outward
fortune may seem.[42] Though he lose his entire portion in this
world—"life, goods, honor, children, wife"—yet he possesses all
things in Christ the lord, Who gives him not only resurrection
and life but eternal lordship and glory.

For Christ's kingdom is an eternal kingdom of grace, governed
always by forgiveness.[43] Its motto is, "I forgive you your sins,"
for in it forgiveness of sins goes on unceasingly.[44] In these two
words Christ's whole kingdom consists. "It is an amazing thing
that Christ does not want sin, and yet there is no one in His kingdom but the sinner." [45] The self-styled saint He will not admit.
"My kingdom is a hospital for the sick, and I am the physician." [46]
It is a hospital for curing sins, for Christ's kingdom is not idle:
it scours clean.[47] It is a kingdom of mercy and grace, in which
there is nothing but a continual, patient, unwearying carrying
of the lost.[48]

An eternal difference separates Christ's kingdom from the
world's. Not only are their standards utterly different—their pow-

39. See S. A. Fischer-Galati, *Ottoman Imperialism and German Protestantism
1521–1555* (Harvard, 1959).
40. *47*, 207, 34; cf. *21*, 371, 35.
41. *45*, 532, 9.
42. *17/II*, 109, 14; *20*, 375, 1ff.; *32*, 500, 16; *33*, 114, 12ff.; *44*, 373, 19; *45*,
629, 6.
43. *21*, 261, 26; cf. *12*, 675, 4; *13*, 658, 28; *17/II*, 268, 31; *37*, 90, 16; *49*, 138,
32.
44. *33*, 509, 13; *15*, 727, 1.
45. *15*, 703, 24; 726, 10.
46. *33*, 510, 12; *23*, 691, 13 (cf. *15*, 726, 10).
47. *17/I*, 463, 3; *15*, 729, 18 (cf. *13*, 694, 23).
48. *10/I/2*, 366, 18.

ers, their purposes, and their modes of judgment [49]—but the one is eternal and the other passes away.[50] "The secular realm can do nothing at all to please God, make men His children, effect redemption from sin and death, or achieve eternal life: for it must all end with this life." [51] But the purpose of Christ's kingdom is to create a new, eternal righteousness by which all nature shall be transformed and renewed, and in which there will be no sin or death any more, but only a perfect divine work and life.[52]

One question remains. If God has given Christ a kingdom over all things, a dominion to which even the powers of this world are subject, what is the point of distinguishing the kingdom of Christ from the kingdom of God? It is not always important to do so: [53] faith confesses that God has committed His kingdom's destiny and power to the Son. The Son, therefore, is lord of nature, lord of both realms, lord of heaven and earth, the God to Whom we look for even our material well-being.[54] But the exercise of this dominion is known only by the Word. Christ's kingdom is God's in a way that the world's transitory kingdom can never be; yet the distinction is useful simply because it affirms once again that the way God has chosen and designated for our salvation is Christ and Him only—the man Christ as He walked this earth, and His external Word and sacraments by which He unites us to Himself. The kingdom of God is never in question—He is God over all—but whether we have Him as our God, whether we can please Him, depends solely upon Christ.[55] Christ's kingdom, by which He makes us pleasing to God, uses created means as it moves toward the consummation of all things. It uses flesh and blood to effect life; the external Word and sacraments to remake us; and prayer in the name of Christ to invoke the uncreated power of God's intervention now committed to the Son. "This is the work which He has begun by His going to the Father and in His own

49. 32, 204, 19; 33, 495, 28; 505, 29; 41, 92, 29.
50. 31/I, 218, 33.
51. 45, 669, 36.
52. 21, 368, 10.
53. E.g. 11, 249, 27; 17/II, 268, 27; 30/I, 200, 5; 36, 50, 20; 45, 634, 15.
54. 45, 655, 35; 46, 733, 1 and 12; 51, 22, 4; 47, 204, 31; 206, 17ff.
55. Tr, 1, 159: 369.

person has already perfectly accomplished. In this life He constantly propagates this kingdom by the preaching of the gospel and the work of the Holy Spirit in the believers until the last day; but in that life it will be lived and found perfectly in us." [56] The distinction between God's kingdom and Christ's, then, does not describe two distinguishable focuses of dominion in the Godhead. Rather, the distinction is in us, in our modes of apprehension.[57] "The kingdom of faith and the future kingdom of glory are one kingdom; they are distinguished in that what is offered to us through the Word here in the kingdom of faith—what here we receive and hold by faith—there will be unveiled to us." [58] Now we see Christ's glory in the Word—"through a glass darkly"; one day we shall see the glory of His divine majesty—"face to face." [59]

Meanwhile our citizenship is in heaven, where our lord has gone before to prepare an eternal home for us and where we shall enjoy His company eternally.[60] From there He shall return to judgment. Luther is convinced that such a culmination of worldly history is not only real but imminent.[61] The Christian yearns for that day. "Thy kingdom come," he prays: "Help us, dear Lord, and hasten the day of Thy second coming, so that we may be delivered from this evil world, the devil's kingdom, and redeemed from the terrible suffering we endure, inwardly from our conscience and outwardly from the wicked . . . that we may obtain bodies freed from all physical and spiritual distress and fashioned like Thine own glorified body, dear Lord Jesus Christ." [62] Thus as a bride looks forward to her wedding day with great longing, so the Church joyfully awaits Christ's advent.[63] We await the

56. *21*, 368, 17.
57. Cf. *14*, 27, 22ff.; *18*, 785, 20ff.
58. *45*, 230, 7.
59. *28*, 194, 11ff.
60. *45*, 484, 9 to 488, 37; *46*, 713, 11ff.
61. E.g. *10/I/2*, 95, 17; *47*, 621, 17; *Tr, 5*, 184: 5488; *Tr, 6*, 306: 6985. See John Headley, *Luther's View of Church History* (Yale Publications in Religion, 6, New Haven, 1963), pp. 224ff.; Paul Althaus, *Die Theologie Martin Luthers* (Gütersloh, 1962), pp. 339ff.
62. *41*, 317, 12.
63. *25*, 53, 3n.; cf. *10/I/2*, 109, 24; *22*, 372, 3–26.

judge from heaven, but without fear; for how can judgment terrify us when the judge Himself declares He has removed our sin? Who may judge the judge? [64] Just as Christ had nothing to fear from any judgment, neither do we, for the judge gives us His righteousness; and indeed, we shall judge the world and the ungodly with Him on the Judgment Day.[65] Yet this final judgment will be simply a declaration of the judgment that He has already made in the world: to the distressed, "Come to Me, all you who travail"; to the smug and self-righteous, "Depart from Me, you evildoers." [66] The promise of His coming is both a consoling promise of eternal glory and a most terrifying threat of eternal wrath.[67] Christ is not a judge unless He is refused; to those who do refuse, He is utterly intractible. For in that day it will be manifest that the light, because it is the light, judges the darkness of men's guilt.[68]

"Then in the world to come this light will cease and will be transformed into eternal glory, when, as St. Paul says, 'He shall deliver up the kingdom to God'; but now He rules through His humanity. When He delivers up the kingdom He will deliver up the light too—not that there are two sorts of light, or that we shall see something different from what we see now; but we shall see the self-same light and the self-same God that we now see by faith, but in a different way. Now we see Him dimly in faith: then we shall see Him without any concealment." [69]

### Heir and Head

Of all the medieval doctors Luther's favorite was easily Bernard of Clairvaux; for "even though he followed strictly the rule of his order, yet as death approached he praised the dear Lord more than all other teachers." [70] And Luther's favorite story

64. 10/I/1, 49, 19.
65. 20, 391, 20; 47, 103, 1.
66. 33, 564, 33; cf. 13, 503, 32ff.
67. 22, 411, 21.
68. 33, 540, 3; 47, 400, 37; 33, 543, 35ff.
69. 10/I/1, 223, 9.
70. 46, 784, 5; cf. 20, 746, 14; 40/I, 687, 19.

about Bernard is the legend of how the saint stood before the judgment seat of God and withstood the accuser by claiming Christ's "twofold right to heaven." [71] That is, Luther explains, "Christ can first of all claim heaven for His own person, for as Son of God He is the heir Whose inheritance was heaven. Secondly, He can claim heaven on the ground of His earning it by His suffering and death. And now He has given heaven to us—it belongs to me!" [72]

Christ is the only-begotten. He alone of all the children of God is Son by right and nature. But He has become our head, the head of all the children of God, so that in Him we too are adopted as God's beloved children. The knowledge and worship of God may be found only in Him, for God has made Him the head of all saints. Under this head God has included and united all things, so that he who does not believe in Him cannot stand before God, whatever other "righteousness," "salvation," or "wisdom" he may have; they are all condemned. At the same time, to receive Christ as head is to discover a flesh and blood that imparts life, banishes hell, and mightily repulses and casts out the devil and sin. [73]

So Christ, the only founder, lord and head of the Church, imparts to it all His goods, His eternal righteousness, holiness, and blessedness. [74] We must never divide Christ the head from His

71. Quoted, e.g., in 20, 624, 3; 32, 534, 20; 46, 580, 25; etc., from the *Legenda Aurea* CXV, which reads: "Once, being fallen sick, the man of God seemed about to breathe his last; and at that moment, being rapt in ecstasy, he saw himself before the judgment seat of God, and Satan standing opposite, pelting him with malicious accusations. When he had come to the end of his charges, and the saint was to speak in his own defence, fearless and unperturbed he said: 'I avow that I am nothing worth, and unable to obtain the Kingdom of Heaven by my own merits. For the rest, my Lord has won heaven by a twofold right, namely by inheritance from His Father, and by the merit of His Passion; whereof He is content with the one, and gives me the other. Therefore, by His gift, I claim heaven as my right, and shall not be confounded!' At these words the Enemy was overborne, the meeting came to an end, and Bernard returned to himself" (trans. Granger Ryan and Helmut Ripperger, *The Golden Legend of Jacobus de Voragine*, Pt. II [New York, 1941], p. 471).

72. 46, 784, 11.

73. 46, 637, 37; 9, 407, 8; 33, 28, 34; 219, 13.

74. 21, 321, 31; 46, 712, 31.

members;[75] and this unity has deep implications for those who are in Him by faith.

First, it means that the body will suffer the same fate as its head in the world.[76] As He was subjected to tribulation and suffering, so shall we be; as men rejected and scorned His teaching, so they shall reject ours; for "it is not fitting that the head wear a crown of thorns, and the members sit on a velvet cushion." [77] Christ our head makes our afflictions His own: He feels the evils which we, His body, suffer.[78] In a sense, now that He has been exalted above suffering, He must suffer through the afflictions of His members.[79]

But it also means that the members will do the same works that Christ their head began—indeed, works that are greater in their extent, though identical with His: "destruction of the devil's realm, deliverance for souls, conversion of hearts, victory, preservation of peace for country and nation, help, protection, and preservation for those in all manner of distress and need." [80] All these mighty works they derive from Christ their head by faith.

Within the fellowship of the Church it is Christ's desire that "You, as members of one body under one head, should show one another loyalty and kindness, friendship, service, and mutual help" and avoid "factions and schisms that destroy love"; for in gratitude for His own ineffable love, He would have those who are His friends to live in friendship with each other.[81] This unity of the Church, the reversal of Babel, is "Christ's new miracle." [82]

But most of all, the unity of the head with His members in the Church effects the great salvation that God has made the goal and aim of His Kingdom. For if the devil would devour us, he must begin at the top by devouring Christ our head! [83] There is

---

75. 45, 532, 4.
76. 46, 714, 33.
77. 21, 429, 18; 45, 711, 13; 33, 5, 1; 423, 7; 45, 715, 2.
78. 40/II, 172, 13.
79. 34/II, 219, 11.
80. 45, 531, 27ff.; 535, 17.
81. 45, 691, 9.
82. 42, 413, 34.
83. 45, 727, 25.

refuge from all the things that would destroy us only under this
one head. And God's purpose of infinite mercy is to gather His
Church under this head, Whom He loves, so that it too shall be
beloved.[84]

For there is intimate connection between Christ's place as head
of His body, and God's great mystery and plan to head up all
things in heaven and earth in Christ. "When God moves Christ
before our gaze He includes all creation, for God gave him everything in the world. God intends to declare, 'I shall show you that
head under which all things are gathered: this head is My Son.'"
Christ is God's heir Who fills all things by Himself.[85] Since the
heir is given to us, all things are given to us—we are His, and He
is God's.[86] What this will mean in the eternal life to come, we
cannot conceive; but we know that He will make us more re-
splendent than the sun.[87] For if we have Christ, we have fulfilled the law and conquered hell; we have come to the consummation, and not death nor sin nor devil can touch us; we possess
the one Who is the fulfillment of the law, of time, and of all
things. In this man all things are concluded and fulfilled. All that
He has is mine, and He has all things. I am His, and He is all in
all.[88]

## All in All

What, finally, can faith say but that Christ is all in all? "Christ,
all things are Thine—of Thy fullness have we received." [89] He is
the point at the center of the circle; from wherever we look, He is
the focus of our gaze.[90] If we seek the knowledge of God, Christ
is "the only one," the one Who is above all.[91] If we seek wisdom
or righteousness, here too He is the only wisdom and righteous-

84. *47*, 198, 29 and 16–23.
85. *47*, 203, 7; 205, 2.
86. *21*, 483, 35.
87. *47*, 13, 4 and 18.
88. *33*, 37, 3ff.
89. *21*, 318, 38; *46*, 101, 13; *31/II*, 768, 7.
90. *47*, 66, 21; *Br, 10*, 491, 95.
91. *47*, 194, 31.

ness and sanctification and redemption, and stands over all the issues of salvation.[92] If we seek life, that life is in Him.[93] I cannot even properly appreciate "the sun, the moon, the stars, trees, apples, and pears" until I discover that He is lord over them all and the center of all things.[94] In Him we possess all things—God, and all that is His, and all that we could in our hearts wish or desire—and outside Him nothing is valid, nothing is eternal.[95] He is the same Christ yesterday and today, the Christ of the past, the present, and the future, "Who was, and is, and is to come." [96] His is the new eternal kingdom in which He is all in all; from above He fills and rules all things.[97] "I am the beginning, and the middle, and the end of your salvation—I alone am all." [98]

92. 20, 728, 20; 31/II, 768, 9; 47, 194, 38; 196, 20.
93. 10/I/1, 202, 16.
94. 47, 203, 11.
95. 20, 375, 14; 10/I/1, 202, 15; 18, 779, 17; 33, 163, 21; 45, 488, 9; 594, 34.
96. 47, 146, 17; 163, 11.
97. 12, 530, 14; 21, 317, 23.
98. 45, 504, 35; 508, 2.

# 6.  Very God and Very Man

Every major facet of Luther's doctrine of Christ is now before us, with the exception of his reflection upon the christological dogma itself. Yet at no point has detailed attention to technical Christology so far proved necessary. On the two or three occasions when christological problems have appeared, Luther has characteristically resolved them by eschewing dogmatic technicalities in favor of what he calls a "down to earth" understanding—the significance of the scriptural account for saving faith.

Nevertheless, his works do contain substantial exposition of the christological dogma, and to this we now turn. But as we do so, the very fact that we have not had to attend before to these materials will force us to ask how far they are integral to Luther's teaching.

## Very God

Without any question, Luther holds the assertion of Christ's divinity to be integral to the gospel. Part of his especial fondness for the Fourth Gospel springs from the unique emphasis he finds in St. John on this article: "No evangelist speaks of this like St. John." [1] Throughout his Gospel, Luther says, "he stresses that Christ is very God, begotten of the Father from eternity, not made; and he wrote this Gospel in order to proclaim this article of faith." [2] The immediate occasion of St. John's writing both his

1. 28, 90, 4.
2. 47, 112, 4.

Gospel and his first Epistle was the denial of Christ's divinity by the heretic Cerinthus.[3] In opposition to this heretic he preached the divinity of Christ "in almost every letter, as none of the other evangelists do." [4] For the person who does not believe this article is eternally lost.[5]

The confession that Christ is very God is built on two inseparable premises: the Word of God, in Scripture, the preaching of Christ, and the apostles' testimony; and the history of Christ's life. First, "we can have no surer foundation for Christ's divinity than to wrap and bind our hearts in the declarations of Scripture." [6] Several of these declarations, Luther contends, are perfectly explicit, despite all the efforts of the devil and "his bride, Dame Witch, crafty reason" to evade them by pretending that Holy Writ never records that Christ is God.[7]

> The name "God" is used plainly and explicitly of Christ in St. Thomas' confession, "My Lord and my God!" (John 20:28). In Romans 9:5 Christ is called "God over all, blessed forever" (45, 546, 22). Luther is not unaware of the ambiguity of the latter text, but cites the patristic consensus in favor of his reading. (For the patristic interpretation of Rom. 9:5, see Otto Michel, *Der Brief an die Römer* [*Meyers Kommentar*, 10. Aufl., Göttingen, 1955], p. 197.) Luther finds another explicit designation in Acts 20:28, since he adopts a text which gives Paul's exhortation in the form, "Take heed . . . to feed the flock of God which He purchased by His own blood" (41, 273, 5). Titus 2:13, a potentially ambiguous text, is inescapable, Luther argues; for whether "the great God and our savior" all applies to Christ, or whether "the great God" refers only to the Father and "our savior" to Christ, in either case Christ is declared to be true God; for in the first case it is explicitly stated, and in the second the Father and Christ share a splendor and glory which God insists He will not share with another (10/I/1, 57, 5).

"My glory will I not give to another" (Isa. 42:8) recurs constantly as the major premise of Luther's favorite syllogism for es-

---

3. See Irenaeus, *Adv. haer.* I.26.1, III.3.4 (MPG VII/1, 686 & 851); Eusebius, *Hist. ecclesiast.* iii.28, vii.25.
4. 10/I/1, 197, 16; 20, 601, 16.
5. 10/I/1, 198, 17.
6. 10/I/2, 297, 3.
7. 45, 543, 21; cf. 20, 685, 21.

tablishing Christ's divinity from Scripture. For example: "Here (in Psalm 2:8) the Son is appointed lord of the ends of the earth, that is, of all creation. It follows consequently that He is by nature God. For the Lord says: 'My Glory will I not give to another.'" [8] The minor premise—God's glory is given to Christ—appears time and time again in the Scriptures: in Moses,[9] in the Psalms,[10] in the prophets.[11] The same is true of the apostles' testimony. St. Paul makes masterful use of the Old Testament in asserting Christ's deity, especially in Ephesians 1:20 and Colossians 2:9; [12] he takes passages which Moses applied to Yahweh and applies them to Christ,[13] and he always conjoins the Father and the Son in invocation, praise, and attribution of power.[14] Such passages are very frequent, Luther says, and deserve to be collected and studied: they form "an armor which cannot be pierced." [15] Most plainly of all, of course, the Johannine Prologue not only names the Word "God," but refuses the subtle Arian ploy of interpreting the term "God" as titular, rather than natural, deity.[16] For when John says that all things were made by Him, he establishes the divinity of Christ: [17] "if He is not made, but is Himself the maker, He must be truly God." [18] Creation is the domain of the one true God—no angel or other creature can claim this title.[19] Again, when the evangelist calls the people to whom Christ came "His own," he indicates His equality with the God Who chose the Jews for His own possession (Ex. 19:5, Deut. 7:6).[20]

The Prologue—"that beautiful, glorious testimony to the deity of Christ"—is the first in a series of passages where St. John con-

8. 40/II, 260, 25ff.; cf. 34/II, 57, 7.
9. E.g. 43, 251, 31.
10. E.g. 10/I/2, 295, 9ff.; 40/II, 269, 24; 41, 90, 3; 45, 244, 28.
11. E.g. 10/I/1, 600, 7; 13, 320, 37; 31/II, 89, 6.
12. 10/I/2, 295. 21; 45, 549, 30.
13. 41, 272, 16.
14. 25, 15, 34; 40/I, 79, 24.
15. 41, 273, 38; 275, 2; 40/I, 80, 18.
16. 10/I/1, 184, 19; 46, 552, 4.
17. 27, 529, 1; 46, 552, 36.
18. 10/I/1, 194, 21; 10/I/2, 295, 7; 46, 548, 15.
19. 46, 600, 35.
20. 46, 603, 2.

stantly reaffirms this article of faith.[21] When he speaks of the
"glory" of Christ, we are reminded of the ἀπαύγασμα of Hebrews
1:13, which also speaks of His divinity; but when he speaks of
this Word's dwelling among us, he refers to the life He led outwardly in this world. It is John's purpose that we may recognize
Him as God in this history.[22] He demonstrated His glory by His
deeds: He is God not only in His person but in His works.[23]

> Thus Christ's knowledge of the thoughts and hearts of men was
> a superhuman knowledge and demonstrated His deity (33, 291,
> 33; 46, 697, 12; 764, 21). His preaching evoked the confession that
> He spoke as God (33, 469, 12ff.). He performed mighty works and
> raised the dead, as no one but God can do; and His own resurrec-
> tion attested His divinity (45, 586, 31; 46, 636, 35; 759, 8). Further-
> more, the claim to Godhead was at the very heart of His own
> preaching. When He described Himself in "strange and heavenly
> words" as descending from heaven, ascending to heaven, and re-
> maining in heaven (John 3:13), He portrayed Himself as God, for
> it is God's nature to reside in heaven above (47, 49, 2ff.). When
> He claimed that He was before Abraham (John 8:56ff.), He meant
> that He was the one true God (17/II, 236, 20; 47, 50, 6). He de-
> manded equal honor with the Father, applied the first command-
> ment to Himself, and exercised the unique prerogatives of God
> (17/II, 233, 22; 27, 163, 8; Tr, 1, 159: 369). For who but God can
> forgive sins (15, 711, 27; 21, 296, 17; 40/I, 80,17; 45, 528, 5)? Who
> but God may claim, as Christ did, to answer prayer (Tr, 2, 16:
> 1265)? And who but God may call for faith in himself? It is God's
> exclusive privilege to be believed in (33, 160, 10; 38, 511, 38ff.).
> Christ made Himself equal to the Father in every respect—in life,
> possession, power, and majesty: "All that the Father has is Mine"
> (John 16:15). "He would not dare say this, nor would the Father
> tolerate it, unless He were true God" (46, 67, 20; cf. 45, 477, 29).

Very often Luther applies these arguments against the heretics
—against Cerinthus, against contemporary anti-Trinitarians, and
above all, against Arius (whom he calls "Narrius": [24] Narr is the

21. 46, 567, 37; 41, 273, 27ff.; 274, 36ff.
22. 10/I/1, 243, 13.
23. 46, 635, 1; 47, 89, 1.
24. 33, 128, 30.

German for "fool"). As antiheretical arguments, their form is instructive; for if they were intended as apologetics, they would simply beg the question. The pattern is consistent. Only God may be the object of faith; Christ is the object of Christian faith; therefore Christ is God.[25] Only the eternal God and Creator can grant eternal life; Christ offers eternal life to the faithful; therefore Christ is eternal God and Creator.[26] To send the Holy Spirit belongs to God alone; but this is Christ's promise; therefore Christ is truly God.[27] In its most extreme form the syllogism runs: the Christian faith confesses one God, Father, Son, and Holy Spirit; therefore if Christ is not God, the Father and the Holy Spirit are not God.[28] This form of argument (and instances could be multiplied) illuminates two aspects of Luther's relation to the dogma. In the first place, it reflects his exegetical insight that the antichrist arises within the Church,[29] that heresy is a matter of concern simply because it is within the sphere of faith, not outside it; and his refutations are virtually a challenge to those who abandon the Christian confession of Christ as God to relinquish the guise and name of Christianity too. Secondly, these syllogisms reveal that the positive function of the dogma in Luther's mind is that Scripture should be allowed to speak unequivocally when it speaks of Christ.[30] The decisive premise in each argument is the admission at face value of the truth of the biblical testimony to Christ.[31]

If this testimony is read without dissembling, it yields three creedal affirmations of the deity of Christ: Christ is the sublime majesty, equal with God; He is creator and preserver of all things; and He is eternally begotten of God.

First, Christ is coequal with the Father in every way, in glory,

25. 33, 160, 10; 45, 477, 29; 479, 36ff.; 50, 263, 4.

26. 17/II, 236, 18; 28, 90, 5; 33, 160, 11.

27. 21, 424, 4.

28. Tr, 2, 16: 1265.

29. E.g. 20, 669, 2; 26, 147, 27; 47, 181, 12; 51, 505, 29; cf. Karl Barth, Church Dogmatics, I/1, par. 2.1.3; and see Headley, Luther's View of Church History, pp. 184f., 208ff.

30. 50, 550, 11ff.; 605, 20.

31. 45, 544, 30 to 545, 39.

power, might, and authority. Before the worlds He dwelt in the highest divine majesty as eternal God, always beholding His Father and present with Him, ruling and working together with Him in equal power and might.[32] He is in essence one God with the Father from eternity. The Father is unbegotten, the Son begotten, not made, but they are one divine essence.[33] Struggling for an analogy to illustrate this unity of the divine essence, Luther points to the limbs as several parts of a single body, or better, to the unity in Christ of the individual members of His body, the Church—inadequate parallels of the confession that Father and Son are two distinct persons, but one single God.[34] This, too, is the plain intention of St. John as he talks of God the speaker of the Word, and of that Word as God, thus condemning the opposite errors of Sabellius, who mingled the persons, and Arius, who split the natures.[35] Christ is the divine majesty Himself.[36]

Secondly, He is the coequal creator of heaven and earth with the Father.[37] Luther underlines this affirmation by repeatedly applying to Christ the words of the creed's first article, "maker of heaven and earth." [38] Jesus Christ is the creator and preserver of all things with the Father, the maker of every creature, the one through Whom all creation is made, preserved, and governed, the coworker of God.[39]

Thirdly, He is the only-begotten, born before the world and all things created, begotten of the Father from all eternity.[40] Christ lives because of the Father: the Father abides in Him, and He in the Father, so that His eternal life springs from the Father's eternal begetting.[41] His "coming forth from the Father" means not only His coming into the world but His eternal generation, His

---

32. *8, 7, 23; 10/III, 129, 26; 21, 454, 20; 37, 41, 1; 41, 90, 10; 46, 553, 7; 47, 205, 26.*

33. *21, 474, 35; 42, 14, 8; 43, 88, 20; 46, 567, 35; 50, 276, 31.*

34. *28, 148, 1; 49, 237, 6ff.*

35. *10/I/1, 190, 16ff.; 46, 549, 1ff.*

36. *47, 213, 7.*

37. *18, 515, 37; 42, 14, 18; 46, 553, 4; 635, 36.*

38. E.g. *27, 533, 7; 28, 90, 16; 45, 629, 29; 46, 578, 39;* etc.

39. *46, 548, 28; 550, 21; 558, 20ff.*

40. *10/I/2, 202, 14; 40/II, 256, 29; 46, 94, 9.*

41. *33, 231, 14; 43, 88, 18; 46, 635, 26ff.*

procession from the Father "internally" in His divine essence.[42]

The sum of these dogmatic affirmations is that Christ may say, "I am God, and that in the fullest sense." [43] Now, as we have seen, Luther holds this article to be essential to salvation.[44] Moreover, the conviction of its truth is impossible without the agency of the Holy Spirit: "You will be a long time coming to God unless you believe that Christ is true God!" [45] It comes with rather striking force, then, when he remarks that this knowledge by itself does not help anyone. To believe in Christ "is not merely to believe that He is God, or that He reigns in heaven in equal power with God the Father—many others believe that!" [46] If this is the case, what role does this dogma play in saving faith? How can it be "the true skill and profoundest wisdom of faith to acknowledge this person Christ as God"? [47]

The faith of Christ, Luther explains, is not only to believe that He is God but to believe He is a gracious God to me—*my* God.[48] While it is perfectly good and proper to expound the deep and sublime article of Christ's divine and eternal Godhead, Luther prefers to remain "down here on earth and deal with the common significance of His office for Christendom." [49] The affirmations of Christ as God, creator, and eternal Son of the Father are for our souls' use. First, "if Christ is not true and natural God, begotten of the Father in eternity and maker of all creatures, we are lost. For what good would Christ's suffering and death do me if He were only a human being like you and me? We must have a savior Who is true God and lord over sin, death, and hell." [50] When the vital article of the eternal generation is lost, "the whole gospel becomes mere history." [51] Moreover, when we confess Christ's divinity we know that, possessing Him, we possess God Himself;

42. *28*, 65, 16ff.; *46*, 98, 20.
43. *33*, 591, 27.
44. *10/I/1*, 198, 17.
45. *27*, 533, 6; cf. *46*, 54, 21.
46. *17/I*, 255, 11; *10/III*, 125, 23.
47. *33*, 176, 42.
48. *10/III*, 125, 25; *33*, 166, 20.
49. *46*, 98, 18; cf. *93*, 18.
50. *46*, 554, 21.
51. *40/II*, 259, 28.

but he who refuses Him as God remains without God.[52] Christ's own discourse constantly separates and then conjoins the Father and Himself, in order to distinguish the persons but to identify their essence and work and honor. Therefore, though the persons are different, they must be one in our hearts: we know no other God but Christ.[53] Christ elevates Himself to the level of God not to usurp the true God's honor for Himself but to show us where we must properly place our trust, lest we fail to find the true God.[54] For Christ has served us by His whole life, and Christ is God; thus the discovery of His divinity is the one thing needful, for it reveals God's attitude of grace and mercy toward us.[55] Christ not only is true God, but also forgives our sins and reverses our misery: since He is in God, and God is in Christ, we know that we have a gracious Father, eager to help and save us.[56] It is the creator of heaven and earth Who tells us not to fear, but assures us that having made all things from nothing, He can change our worthlessness into greatness.[57] The Son Who lives because of the Father promises us in turn that we shall live because of Him, sharing all that is His except His eternal divine essence, and to this extent He will make us partakers of His divinity.[58] For Luther the dogma of the divinity of Christ proclaims that "our salvation is to be attributed solely to the Son; and the glory belongs to the Father, Who speaks of the Son through the Son." [59]

### True Man

The confession that Christ is very God occupies a substantial place in Luther's preaching and is certainly germane to his gospel. The confession of the true manhood of Christ receives far

52. *45*, 488, 9; *33*, 256, 6.
53. *45*, 551, 30.
54. *45*, 480, 13.
55. *10/III*, 158, 27; *45*, 549, 14.
56. *45*, 527, 11ff.; 587, 19ff.
57. *45*, 629, 29; *46*, 105, 20.
58. *33*, 231, 32; 235, 16.
59. *33*, 165, 32.

less attention; but this alone is not sufficient warrant for suppos-
ing it incidental to his doctrine of Christ. For here the issue is totally different. Whereas faith's most outrageous claim is that a
man is God, Luther sees no problem in the assertion that the man
is a man.[60]

In most cases, therefore, Luther mentions Christ's true humanity only in conjunction with His deity—in the phrase "true God
and true man." For the rest, he is prepared to allow the evidence
to speak for itself. Whatever else Luther's calling himself an Oc-
camist may imply,[61] he certainly espouses the unmetaphysical,
common-sense, descriptive semantics of the Terminalists. "You
can tell that Jesus Christ is true man because you can hear Him
and see with your eyes that He speaks as a human being." "He let
Himself be seen, heard, and touched; He ate, drank, slept,
worked, suffered, and died like any other human being." Eating,
drinking, sleeping, resting, having a home, walking, standing—
these are all human conduct and deportment. Christ had flesh
and blood, body and soul, like every other man. "He had eyes,
ears, mouth, nose, chest, stomach, hands, and feet, just like you
and I have. He took the breast; His mother nursed Him as any
other child is nursed." [62] In fact, for thirty years His life was un-
remarkable. His boyhood conduct was like any other boy's. He
was subject to His parents and obeyed their commands; and then
in adult life He attended to His physical wants, had citizenship
like anyone else, carried out a human vocation as preacher, was
the best of friends to His disciples, and generally deported Himself as any human does—with this one exception, that He was
free from sin.[63]

Not only the outward course of His life but His inner feelings,
too, were human. He knew worry, weakness, and timidity; He became poor, frail, and humble; He suffered the pangs of fear, sad-

60. *41*, 89, 16.

61. See the entries under *Okkam* in 58/I, 259–61 (Gesamtregister); cf. Paul
Vignaux, "Sur Luther et Ockham," *Franziskanische Studien,* 32 (1950), 21ff.;
Gerrish, *Grace and Reason,* pp. 43ff.; E. Gordon Rupp, *The Righteousness of God*
(London, 1953), pp. 87ff.

62. *33*, 115, 26; *46*, 69, 28; 10/I/1, 243, 19; 199, 6; 236, 11; *46*, 634, 15.

63. *46*, 599, 5; 10/I/1, 243, 8; *33*, 251, 40; *46*, 32, 6; 634, 17; *47*, 131, 31.

ness, anger, and hatred.[64] He was filled with grief and anxiety at
the approach of death and felt wretched, lonely, and forsaken
when even His own friends left Him in His extremity.[65] We saw
earlier that it often suits Luther's purpose to stress those emotions
and afflictions which Christ shared with the unhappy side of
human existence. In some of Luther's predecessors this bias was a
corollary of the need to maintain the dogma while describing a
Christ Who, in everyday terms, was not very human at all. But
with Luther the bias is partly homiletic, partly an intuition of
the agony of the sinless Christ in bearing man's sin, and partly a
profound sympathy with the figure of Christ opposed by the
whole world, from a man who in less measure also knew the bitterness of standing alone.[66] Luther does succeed in revitalizing
the somewhat Apollinarian Christ of the scholastic tradition. He
pictures one Who is unquestionably human: "He ate, drank,
slept, awoke, was tired. He was sad and happy, He wept and
laughed; He hungered and thirsted, froze and perspired. He chat-
ted and worked and prayed. In short, He required all the necessities and sustenance of this life, and died and suffered like any
other man, sharing fortune and misfortune." [67]

Luther simply points out that the historical figure described in
the gospel performs all those functions we call human, and which
allow us to distinguish a man from other beings. If, then, the
Scripture is unequivocal, there is really no question that Christ is
a man. The order of discussion is always from the concrete reality, the history of Christ, to the creedal proposition, His possession
of human nature. The phrase "possessing human nature," therefore, is in no sense substantial, nor is it a metaphysical abstrac-
tion, but is simply a complicated equivalent of "being a man."
The importance of this order is illustrated when Luther declares
(in a manner exactly parallel to the passages just quoted) that
Christ's humanity is evident from the fact that He was crucified
and died: suffering and dying pertain to men. "The fact that He

64. *43, 131, 1; 47, 212, 18.*
65. *41, 573, 17; 46, 102, 35; 52, 735, 23.*
66. *40/I, 567, 26; 52, 735, 8–18; 46, 103, 3ff.*
67. *46, 598, 32; cf. 17/II, 244, 5.*

is to be destroyed and die is proof of His humanity." "It was necessary for Him to be true man in order to suffer." [68] When this
proposition is stated in the form, "Christ was crucified according
to His humanity," [69] nothing different is intended: the order of
discussion has not been reversed, so there is no implication that
Christ's person is divided or that His person did not really die.

Because the humanity of Christ ought to be self-evident (even,
he implies, to reason: after all, even the Jews admit they crucified
a man),[70] Luther's systematic arguments in support of the
dogma are sporadic and undeveloped, and appear only as antiheretical polemics. The objects of these polemics are the Manichaeans in most cases, and occasionally Marcion, the Valentinians,
and Apollinaris.[71] ("What a very strange game they played!") [72]

The chief, and most effective, of these arguments is again the
perspicuity of Scripture. Luther amasses biblical parallels (such
as Psalm 78:39, Matt. 24:22, John 3:6 and 17:2) to establish that
"flesh" in biblical parlance means "complete human being," in opposition to the Manichaean notion of Christ as a phantom, a
"moon-child," a mere refraction of the divine light through the
humanity of Mary.[73] Against the Apollinarians' allegation that the
divine Logos replaced the human soul in Christ, Luther scoffs
that they might as logically omit His body as His soul, since
"flesh" does not mean "body" either; besides, Scripture uses the
word "flesh" for "living body," and thus "flesh" means body
and soul together.[74] Furthermore, he contends, Christ uses the
name "Son of Man" in order to declare that He is a true and natural man, with flesh and blood like us.[75] (In practice, Luther himself far more often uses "Son of Mary" when he wants a christological title to express Christ's humanity.) [76]

68. 47, 71, 38; 46, 759, 18; 47, 52, 30 (cf. 20, 359, 1).
69. 10/I/1, 208, 8; 47, 87, 12.
70. 47, 175, 7; 46, 759, 27.
71. E.g. 10/I/1, 236, 5; 26, 501, 24; 27, 519, 4; 33, 189, 1; 45, 543, 14; 46,
555, 13; etc.
72. 50, 268, 4.
73. 10/I/1, 236, 7; 27, 519, 5; 46, 555, 17; 633, 21.
74. 46, 631, 36ff.
75. 21, 546, 25; 33, 201, 3; 254, 1.
76. E.g. 45, 556, 27.

A different sort of argument makes a brief appearance when Luther says that if Christ is deprived of His humanity, we are lost, on the ground that if He is not real and natural man, He is not our flesh and blood, has nothing in common with us, and we can therefore derive no comfort from Him.[77] This notion at first sight appears to reverse the order of discussion I have outlined—to employ the dogmatic definition as an a priori explanation of the history. It could perhaps be construed as an echo of the Cappadocian idea that what is not assumed is not restored;[78] yet Luther's explicit rejection of the realist view of human nature ("a common humanity which is in all men")[79] makes this parallel unlikely. Instead, it appears that several stages in Luther's train of thought have been telescoped: in fact, the order of discussion is still a posteriori. Our community with Christ, which Luther here declares to be necessary, is the fruit of the salvation Christ has brought us. This salvation in turn rests on His death and Resurrection: the vital intermediate premise takes the form, "If Christ were not true man, He could not have suffered and died to achieve our salvation."[80]

Christ became man because of sin, as the creed declares. It was for us He became man, and on account of our sins was subjected to the law and God's wrath. "His flesh and blood, born of the Virgin Mary, was given because He had to bear the cost of death and endure hell in our stead, on account of sins He never committed, as if they were His own; which He willingly did and received us as brothers and sisters."[81] The positive form of Luther's argument against the heretics, then, is the confession, "I believe in Jesus Christ, the only Son of God, Who sits at God's right hand as my advocate. He is of my flesh and blood—yes, He is my brother. For us men and for our salvation He came down from heaven, and was incarnate, and died for our sins."[82] Now, if the question is asked, "Why was it necessary that Christ should die

77. 46, 556, 7.
78. E.g. Gregory Nazianzus, Ep. 101, 7 (MPG XXXVII, 182).
79. Tr, 5, 653: 6419.
80. 46, 555, 29.
81. 47, 205, 27; 21, 484, 5; 17/II, 434, 6.
82. 46, 557, 9.

for our salvation?", no a priori explanation is possible. Instead, the answer is God's Word and action in Christ; its necessity consists for us in the fact that it happened, according to the promise of God. All heresy consists in making Christ and His Word and cross dispensable; the ultimate blasphemy is denial or infringement of the unique and all-sufficient necessity of the history of Christ.

This history, as we have seen repeatedly, has two moments, Christ's office of preaching and His going to the Father. In both of these the history is a human history. Christ's calling as preacher is the function of His human office, not of His divine nature. Because we could not endure the awful majesty of God, He sent us His Son, "Who will be a human being and will speak to you in human speech and words." [83] The accomplishment of our salvation is likewise in Christ "as He was and as He sojourned on earth": [84] He was human in His death (as we have just seen), in His Resurrection,[85] and even in His exaltation. For it is as man that Christ now rules in heaven as lord of all.[86] "This man sits above in divine majesty, even though He is my flesh and blood, my brother." [87] It is not only as God that He is lord of all: "even according to His humanity everything is subject to Him, angels, sin, death, world, devil, hell, and whatever may be named in heaven, on earth, or under the earth." [88] In the light of this stress on the humanity of Christ (a stress continued strikingly in his insistence on the external Word and sacrament), it is doubly noteworthy when Luther asserts without compunction that Christ must be more than man, different from other men, and that His humanity by itself could have accomplished nothing.[89] Christ's human words come with divine power because they are sent by God; Christ's human deeds are the very means of our redemption because of the grace, mercy, and power of God. It is in these dy-

83. 33, 358, 1; 47, 38, 24.
84. 10/I/1, 200, 13; 202, 9.
85. 22, 426, 18.
86. 19, 491, 17; 21, 231, 12; 40/II, 261, 21; 41, 91, 11; 49, 527, 20.
87. 41, 99, 31.
88. 45, 210, 34.
89. See below, p. 214.

namic terms that Luther approaches the confession of Christ as
very God and very man: the fact that God is the focus of our
faith in Christ does not reveal a basically monophysite tendency
(as it might if an abstract God of immutable essence replaced the
Father of our Lord Jesus Christ). On the contrary, it is the
Father Who wills that we should look to the humanity of
Christ.[90] Indeed, only flesh and blood is visible. To love Christ is
to love Him in His humanity obedient to the sacred cross. If we
are to come to God, we must come first to the man, then to what
the man means for us, and thus only to God.[91] Illumination must
come in this life, through faith in the man Christ—through the
humanity, by the divinity.[92]

This is why Luther can say of St. John both that he teaches
Christ's humanity throughout his Gospel, and that he speaks of it
very little.[93] For in one sense the fundamental place of the manhood of Christ, the historical datum of His life among us, goes
without saying; in another sense it is the sole ground and hope of
our oneness with God, the whole content of the gospel. "The
Word became flesh" is the sole pivot of all our comfort and joy
against sin, death, devil, hell, and despair. That Christ conde-
scends to assume, not the noble, glorious and holy nature of angels, but our flesh and blood, our poor, feeble, and corrupt body
and soul—our "poor bag of worms"—is the ineffable token of
God's mercy to wretched human beings.[94] It is our abiding consolation that He wanted His Son "to become our brother, and to
endow us with the immeasurably great honor of having a God
born and made man in our own flesh and blood." [95] Luther re-
counts the fable of the coarse lout who refused to genuflect or remove his hat at the *Incarnatus* in church, but remained standing
without reverence until the devil struck him on the head and
cursed him with the words, "Hell devour you, you boorish ass! If
God had become an angel like me, and we sang, 'God was made

90. *1*, 274, 33; 39/II, 25, 18.
91. *33*, 191, 27; *12*, 578, 5; *10/I/2*, 297, 5.
92. *10/I/1*, 222, 19.
93. Cf. *47*, 72, 12; *Tr*, *5*, 209: 5516.
94. *46*, 627, 11; 624, 20ff.
95. *43*, 252, 32.

an angel,' I would bend not just my knees, but my whole body to the ground!" [96] The most precious treasure and the highest consolation that Christians possess is that "the Word, the true, natural Son of God, has become man, complete with flesh and blood like any other man; and that He became man for our sake, so that we should come to great glory, and with our flesh and blood, skin and hair, hands and feet, stomach and back sit up in heaven as God does. Thus we may boldly defy the devil and whatever else assails us. For we are sure that our flesh and blood belong in heaven, heirs of heaven's kingdom." [97]

## Very God and Very Man

The attempt to isolate Luther's teaching on the divinity of Christ from his teaching on the humanity is finally unsuccessful —itself a sign of Chalcedonian health in one direction, at least. The truth of each nature is differently apprehended; but the subject of the dogma is the man, the historical personality, Who is confessed to be God. The characteristics of Luther's approach to the dogma are therefore already before us. But the usual form of the dogma is a twofold confession, in the manner of the Chalcedonian decree: "very God and very man"; [98] "two natures united in one person"; [99] "God and man in one person"; [1] "essential, natural, true, complete God and man in one person, undivided and inseparable"; [2] "Christ our savior is the true Son of Mary and the only-begotten Son of God, and yet there are not two sons, but only one Son of God the Father and of the Virgin Mary"; [3] "true God of true God, and true man of true man"; [4] "begotten of the

96. *46*, 627, 13; other versions in *49*, 569, 28; *52*, 39, 5.

97. *46*, 631, 27.

98. E.g. *10/I/1*, 213, 23; *10/III*, 162, 1; *40/I*, 560, 27; *45*, 548, 17; *46*, 599, 40; etc.

99. E.g. *33*, 79, 19; *46*, 568, 24; *47*, 199, 26; etc.

1. E.g. *33*, 115, 8; *43*, 251, 33; *46*, 69, 35; *47*, 53, 15; etc.

2. *26*, 326, 30.

3. *47*, 51, 32: in the first clause I have followed the emendation suggested by the Weimar editor, and read "of Mary" in place of the original's "of God."

4. *27*, 529, 1.

Father in eternity, and conceived by the Holy Ghost, born of the Virgin Mary in time." [5] Luther's language obviously reflects the *Chalcedonense* [6] and other creedal formulas of the christological settlement; and he often cites the ecumenical creeds as worthy bearers of the truth about Christ. [7]

This article, he says, is essential to salvation. He echoes the *quicunque vult* of the "Athanasian" creed: "whoever does not have this belief will never be saved," and affirms that "this article is the foundation on which our eternal well-being and salvation are founded." [8] For this reason the apostles stress it continually, and we should imitate them in this, retaining it in its purity against the devil's rabble and the heretics. [9] Once again, Scripture is the chief resource. "The patriarchs possessed considerable light and knowledge about the two natures in Christ," Luther believes. [10]

> Sometimes the grammar itself establishes this truth, as when Psalm 8:1 joins the divine name "Yahweh" with the human epithet "ruler" (*45*, 207, 31); Psalm 68:24 joins "my God" with the earthly title "my king" (*8*, 25, 15); the tetragrammaton is applied to the human champion of God's people in Micah 2:13 (*13*, 273, 23); or the Lord of Hosts is sent by the Lord of Hosts in Zechariah 2:8–9 (*13*, 572, 6). Luther never misses an opportunity to use the by now familiar argument that exclusively divine functions are predicated of someone who is plainly a man. Thus "the seed of Abraham" is obviously Abraham's human descendant, but His work of releasing all nations from the curse and bestowing blessing is God's unique work (*20*, 550, 1; *43*, 251, 33). "Shiloh" means "son of the womb" and therefore a man; but Shiloh is to be the devourer of sin and death, and is therefore also God (*44*, 805, 26–37). Christ is promised from David's lineage, yet is to reign eternally, as only God shall (*10/I/2*, 409, 25; *13*, 320, 37; *45*, 155, 35). This

5. *34/I*, 436, 9; *40/I*, 568, 13; *47*, 52, 37.

6. Text in Eduard Schwartz, *Acta conciliorum,* 2/I (Berlin and Leipzig, 1933), pp. 322ff., and standard English sources.

7. E.g. *33*, 115, 13; *45*, 543, 35; 548, 23; *50*, 268, 16; etc.

8. *46*, 602, 21 (cf. *39/II*, 97, 9); *46*, 557, 31.

9. *33*, 115, 4; *45*, 543, 7.

10. *44*, 805, 38.

king is the eternally begotten Son of God, but He is appointed by
God and set to rule upon Zion, a physical place, and therefore He
is also a man, a creature (40/II, 250, 20). The judgment committed
this king (Who must be man in order to receive it from God) is
God's own inalienable judgment—the judgment over sin, death,
and all flesh declared by the first commandment, "I am the Lord
your God" (49, 14, 5ff.). Micah says of the man Who was to be
born in Bethlehem that "His origin is from of old, from ancient
days," establishing the "cornerstone of Christian faith, that Christ
is God and man" (10/I/1, 600, 19).

Among the apostolic writers, it is St. John who bears the most
powerful witness to this belief. To establish its truth is the constant object of his Gospel; the Prologue, especially, is "all armor"
and the chief foundation of the doctrine.[11] Luther's exposition of
the Fourth Gospel's method at this point is particularly revealing
of the order of his christological thought. St. John, he says, always links the two natures, divinity and humanity, together. The
very words, "The Word became flesh" are a prime example: this
Word, which he had named "God," he now names "flesh"—true
man of our very nature.[12] John 3:14–16 provides another example: what Christ says first about the Son of Man—that He must
be lifted up—He now says about the Son of God; we hear first
that Mary must give up her Son, and then that God's great love
has led Him to give us His Son. "God's Son and Mary's is but one
person: He applies both natures to the work of salvation and redemption from eternal death." [13] Christ intends to indicate the
same conjunction of the two natures in His own person with the
"well-chosen words" of John 6:62: [14] "What if you were to see
the Son of Man (that is, Mary's Son) ascending where He was
before (that is, as eternally God's Son)?"
But since frivolous spirits are wont to distort these clear words
of Scripture, the Holy Spirit has erected safeguards against arbitrary interpretation by describing Christ both by name and by

11. 10/I/1, 246, 20; 47, 78, 7.
12. 47, 76, 31; 46, 624, 18.
13. 47, 71, 36; 76, 21.
14. 33, 254, 1.

activity.[15] The extraordinary contrast between the discourse that ends the third chapter of St. John's Gospel and the narrative that opens the fourth provides a paradigm: "John wanted to describe this very carefully, so that we could see how differently Christ lived according to each of His two natures. He is life itself, and yet He dies. He is everything, and simultaneously He is nothing. Because He is everything, He certainly ought to be worshiped, since the words, 'He who believes in the Son has eternal life' (John 3:36), speak of His majesty—if He can give eternal life, He is surely God, for no creature or angel can claim this power, but only the Son of God Who has in His hands the same power as His Father, and therefore the person who believes in the Son and worships Him has eternal life; yet for all this He is also Mary's Son, and not only that, but here He is in flight, and eventually lets Himself be killed. So St. John constantly sets side by side Christ's eternal omnipotence and His exceeding weakness." [16]

St. John's skill in this juxtaposition is revealed in two further passages, the story of Lazarus (chap. 11) and the discourse on prayer (chap. 14). The same man Who had fled from the threat of stoning (John 8:59) now braves that same threat to return to Bethany (John 11:8-9). He speaks of "our friend Lazarus"—humanly, as if He and Lazarus were simply neighbors. He is a good friend: He comes at the request for help, which is human sentiment, love, and pain, like ordinary human intercourse. Now, notice the nice balance between the human and the divine in Christ's responses: "Lazarus is dead," "I am going there," "I am glad for your sakes," "Jesus wept"—all of them human words and responses; and then "Lazarus sleeps," "I shall awake him," "Believe in Me," "I am the resurrection and the life," "Lazarus, come out!": here the one almighty God is speaking.[17] So also in the discourse on prayer: the repeated words, "Whatever you ask in My name, I will do it," are the words not of a mere man but of God (for only God has power to grant what we ask); yet the words immediately following, "I will pray the Father," are the words of

15. *45, 545, 32.*
16. *47, 209, 6.*
17. *47, 715, 6ff.; 49, 51, 37.*

a man (albeit those of God's Son, Who prays). "First He speaks as God, then as man. So I learn my article that Christ speaks as God and man." [18] This discovery that Christ speaks as both God and man is the powerful evidence on which the doctrine of the two natures rests. For "if Christ were to speak as God all the time, we could not prove that He was true man; but if He were always to speak as a true man, we could never discover that He is also true God." (Luther's choice of "prove" and "discover" here is significant.) Although in His one person He is both God and man, He speaks now in the fashion of the one, now in the other, in rapid succession, both in the same sermon and even the same sentence.[19]

Paradoxically, Luther is here returning to an understanding of the apostolic testimony which had lain submerged possibly since the days of the Arian controversy, an understanding whose reliance on the actual experience of the men who had been with Jesus was never so keenly felt as by Luther, and before him, by the exegete whom Luther most detested—namely, Origen ("the third evil angel of the Apocalypse"!).[20] Origen had educed precisely the same sorts of evidences and concluded, "Since, then, we see in Him some things so human that they appear to differ in no respect from the common frailty of mortals, and some things so divine that they are appropriate to nothing else but the original and ineffable nature of Godhead, the narrowness of human understanding can find no way out, but overwhelmed with stupefied admiration, it does not know where to escape, or what to cling to, or in what direction to turn. If it thinks of God, it sees a mortal; if it thinks of a man, it discovers Him returning from the grave, having overthrown the kingdom of death, bearing its spoils. Therefore we must contemplate the sight with all awe and reverence, that the truth of both natures may be demonstrated in one and the self-same being." [21]

Origen expressed precisely Luther's order of thought. The dis-

18. *Tr*, 2, 16: 1265.
19. *45*, 555, 32ff.; cf. *10/I/1*, 148, 19; 279, 4.
20. *DB*, 7, 410, 34.
21. Origen, *De princ.* II, vi, 2 (MPG XI, 210).

tinction between the two natures is made on the basis of two sorts of discourse, two sorts of action. The resulting discovery that the one figure of Christ is both divine and human defies all rational attempts to grapple with it, let alone comprehend it. This last point, impressive from Origen's lips, receives predictably eloquent treatment from Luther. "This is too profound for reason to fathom—no doctor or wise man of the world has ever been able to explain it." [22] Reason finds it ridiculous: when consulted, it dismisses the article as impossible. "But what is my wisdom compared to the wisdom of God? So I gladly remain a fool, and let myself be captured: I surrender. That Christ is God and man is contrary to all our reason and intellect—we would conclude there must be two persons together in the one being in Christ! 'I do not understand it,' you say. No, but give thanks for it!" [23] Luther is perfectly aware of just how great a surrender of worldly wisdom is required by this faith. Even the axioms of philosophy have no relevance here.[24] Satan is capable of making this doctrine sound like utter stupidity; but we are dealing with a God Who is totally incomprehensible, Who holds the whole heaven in His hand, and shall we imagine we can grasp Him in our tiny understanding? No, here we must simply close our eyes, tell wisdom "Desist!", and hear what the Lord says.[25] The world scoffs, "How can God and man be one, since God's nature is eternal and man's is mortal?" If this were within our comprehension we should not need the word of Christ; but reason is blind, and Christ will tell us how to believe.[26] This means, "Believe it, and away with your presumption! Don't be clever and rationalize: but close your eyes and put down your cups, stop murmuring and believe the Word that Christ sets before you, when He says He came from heaven —that is, that He is God's Son, revealed to the world, and Mary's." [27]

For however plainly the history of Christ evidences His two-

22. *33, 79, 18;* cf. *10/I/1, 239,* 15ff.; *39/II, 98, 13; 45, 155, 38.*
23. *33, 611, 39; Tr, 2, 16: 1265.*
24. *39/II, 7,* 24ff.; *100, 13* and passim.
25. *28, 90,* 14ff.; *36, 408, 29; 47, 52, 33.*
26. *47, 178, 30.*
27. *33, 125, 21.*

fold activity as God and as man, yet faith is required if this article is to be confessed. Reason penetrates only as far as the human
in Christ; and indeed, Luther admits, the human in Christ is so
obvious that the divine may be quite overlooked. His external
mode of life was so perfectly human that He would remain unrecognized as God if it were not for the Word.[28] It was for this reason that Christ prayed the Father to glorify Him—that is, to
make it manifest that He was true man, born of the Virgin, and
true God, born before all ages, so that His disciples might confess
Him thus. The Holy Spirit must accomplish this through the
preaching of the gospel.[29] "So this is the chief article for us who
are named after Christ. The right and true Christian faith (and
there is absolutely no other faith) is this, that Christ is very God
and man; and this is the only saving faith. Whoever wants to believe another, let him go and see how he fares! If reason will not
believe that God could become man, let it do as it pleases! But
we Christians believe it because God's Word says it; and for faith
nothing is impossible."[30]

Faith believes, nor questions how; we shall have to ask in a moment whether Luther refrains from asking how. But first, if this
article may be confessed only by faith, a difficulty arises. There
are obviously those who retain this belief but who, for all their orthodoxy, lack what Luther regards as saving faith: the papacy is
a prime instance. Luther approaches this paradox from two apparently different directions, but finally is making a single assertion.

One approach is to say that this article is essential but not sufficient. " 'To believe in Christ' does not mean merely to believe
that He is a person Who is both God and man—that does not help
anyone." But that He is the Christ sent from God for our salvation, and that returning to the Father He accomplishes that salvation: this is saving faith.[31] Luther therefore elicits another twofold pattern from the pages of the gospel. Christ must be con-

28. *47*, 175, 7; 715, 6; 10/I/1, 243, 21.
29. *28*, 110, 3; 33, 125, 11; *46*, 759, 32.
30. *46*, 599, 38.
31. 17/I, 255, 11.

fessed first as true God and true man: this confession excludes
the heretics, and without it, heresy is swiftly rampant.[32] Secondly, Christ must be confessed as the only savior: this excludes
the pope and his monks, who concede the article but want to
earn their own salvation. "What does it profit you to confess Him
as God and man, if you do not also believe He has become all
things and done all things for you?"[33]

His second approach is the accusation that the pope and his
theologians say they believe Christ to be God and man, but effectively deny it by their doctrine of salvation. The Jews and Turks
deny Christ's divinity; "still, they are better than the pope, who
professes belief in the deity of Christ only with lip-service, but
denies His power."[34] Even if the papists confess that Christ is
God and man and that He suffered, they cannot mean it seriously, because they think nothing of the Resurrection and eternal
life.[35] What is gained, Luther asks, if Christ is not what the heretics make of Him, if He means nothing more to us than to
them, and does no more for us? "What is the use of condemning
heretics and knowing Christ correctly, if we have no different faith
in Him than they? If I can obtain grace by my works, I see no
reason to make Christ necessary; nor is it necessary for Him to be
God and man; in short, all that is written about Him is unnecessary—it would be enough to preach God alone!"[36] To deny
Christ's unique sufficiency for salvation is to give the lie to a pro-
fessed faith in the dogma, for "it is impossible to separate God
from man in the person of Christ, and it is accordingly impossible
to separate our salvation—the article of justification before God
through Christ, satisfaction for sin—from the person of Christ,
Who is true God and also true man that we might be saved
through Him (since otherwise His humanity would have brought
us no benefit). For only He, no one else, made eternal payment
for sin."[37]

32. 33, 125, 8.
33. 50, 269, 8.
34. 33, 124, 9.
35. 50, 269, 32.
36. 10/I/1, 237, 21.
37. 47, 113, 34–42.

These two approaches, first separating living faith from the christological article and then declaring such a separation impossible, are another form of the distinction we examined earlier between "first" and "second" faith—a distinction useful for thought but ultimately invalid in the nature of the gospel. It is a distinction which gives rise to some ambiguity in Luther's use of "the person of Christ" as a technical term; [38] but in any case Luther's concern in the matter is plain enough. He wants his congregation to know the use of this confession in the way of salvation.

First, because Christ is God and man, we can be sure that when we deal with this man, we deal not with a creature but with the very God Himself: this is what "in the unity of the person" means. We see the eternal, creating Word before our eyes. If we do not see the unveiled Godhead, we do see the person Who is God, for Christ is undivided God and man.[39] Furthermore, we here deal with God as His presence may be endured: His deity is incomprehensible, but here in Christ is God as He may be known, His majesty wrapped in His manhood. The fanatics want to rise above the humanity and deal with the naked divinity; but with God the two are one person. No one should be so foolish as to deal with God apart from Christ or with Christ apart from His manhood.[40] For this is the further vital importance of this dogma: even if the humanity without the divinity could not have profited us or won us salvation, nevertheless the divinity will not and cannot be found outside the humanity. "In Christ we find both the terrible and sublime majesty, which is able to save us, and the frail humanity by which we can approach Him and cling to Him." [41]

So it is that the man Christ is the quintessence of God to us, and the fullness of His grace and love poured out on our behalf. "If the weight of my treasure consists in the fact that Christ, true God and true man, died for me, then it outweighs all sin, death, hell, all misery and sorrow, and cancels them. For if I know that

38. See below, pp. 223ff.
39. 20, 603, 5ff.; 39/II, 106, 9ff.; 47, 638, 17.
40. 28, 487, 2ff.
41. 10/I/1, 208, 23; 20, 605, 9; 47, 213, 39.

He Who is true God suffered and died for me, and this same true man also rose from the dead and ascended to heaven, I know for a surety that my sin was blotted out and death overthrown by Him, and that God is no longer disposed toward me with wrath and displeasure; for I see and hear nothing but tokens and deeds of mercy in this person." [42] Luther vitally builds his central doctrine on the confession of Jesus Christ, very God and very man.

## More than Man

Because Luther's approach to the definition of "nature" is functional rather than structural, the confession that Christ is very God and very man may be cast in the form, "Christ is more than man," without danger of Apollinarianism—that is, without risk of denying the real humanness of Christ; indeed, "Christ is more than man" becomes a statement of the obvious. "Christ is not merely a man, but there is more to Him than this . . . He is truly a man like other men, yet at the same time He is more than man"—simply, of course, because He is God. "Christ is not mere man, but true God and man at the same time." [43]

This mode of expression does not appear very often in Luther's preaching, but the contexts in which he finds it useful are worth notice. The most obvious of these we have heard several times already—namely, the assertion, "If Christ were only man, His suffering would have been useless; for no man's suffering has the power to overthrow my sin and yours, death, the power of the devil, God's wrath and eternal damnation. Therefore He had to be God, and yet also true man so that He could suffer." [44] If the devil could persuade us to regard Christ as only a man, we should be lost, for "if He were only man like other saints, He could not deliver us from even one sin or extinguish a single skerrick of hell fire with all His holiness, blood, and death." [45] Even a man wholly pure and without blemish could not have subdued

42. 45, 559, 19.
43. 47, 152, 6; 63, 25; 40/I, 127, 22.
44. 47, 52, 26.
45. 45, 559, 17.

sin, death, and the devil without God's unique almighty power.[46]

But the glory of the gospel is that Christ, and Christ alone, can deliver us. Thus "Christ is more than man" expresses for Luther Christ's unique power to save. There are two classes of man, he says: man for himself and the man from God. The second is a class of one, for Christ says that no one ascends to heaven but He Who descends from heaven, and thereby excludes everyone but Himself. All the children of men except the one seed of the woman are of the earth, earthy; but He Who comes from above is above all.[47] (In the nominalist logic, incidentally, this allows Luther to say both that Christ is man just like other men, and also that humanity is not predicated univocally of Christ and other men.)[48] Christ assumed real flesh from His mother Mary, but since He was begotten not by flesh but by the Spirit, His flesh is to be distinguished from all other flesh born of Adam. "By nature He is Mary's child, yet He has spiritual flesh, a true, divine, and spiritual body, in which there dwells the Holy Spirit Who begot Him and permeates His flesh with Spirit."[49] Language like this is notoriously prone to monophysite distortion—not the use of "spiritual," for Luther sees no reason why anything at all cannot be spiritual if God uses it, but the epithet "divine" applied to body is disconcerting. The suspicion is relieved, however, by his further comment that birth from above, the birth from the Spirit, is now offered to all men through faith. The two classes thus become "all men born of the flesh" and "Christ and His Christians," with no suggestion that the humanity of men is thereby annulled.[50] So also, when he calls the works of Christ "divine works" (in contrast to our human works) he is not denying that they are performed by a real man, but "whatever God does, even if it were as insignificant as a straw, is a mightier and weightier work than all heaven and earth": that is, even one human work done by God excels any and all the merely human works of other

46. 21, 234, 5; cf. 20, 540, 1; 551, 1.
47. 47, 63, 17; 169, 1.
48. 39/II, 17, 4.
49. 33, 262, 34; cf. 23, 203, 32; 39/II, 28, 7.
50. 33, 263, 5.

men.[51] So we must distinguish Christ's righteousness, life, being, and work from all other men's: "the sleep or fasting of this person, even for a moment, is worth more than all the labor and all the fasting of all the saints"; "I should rather call one single work of Christ's my own than all the works and holiness of all saints." [52] Therefore, compared with the man Christ, man is nothing; and I have missed the only path to God if I see Him only according to the flesh, a carpenter's apprentice from Nazareth, like any other man.[53]

If these formulations escape the pitfalls of Apollinarianism and monophysitism, the specter of Docetism raises its hoary head when he says, "True, Christ *took on* the form of a servant, but He *was* not in that form . . . He dispensed with the form of God in which He was, and took on a servant form in which He was not." [54] So far from being a temptation, however, a docetic denial of Christ's real humanity seems to Luther an incomprehensibly silly heresy, as we have already seen. Indeed, in the very sermon from which this quotation comes (an exposition of Phil. 2:5–11), he argues as follows: Paul's statement, "He was found in a fashion as a man," is intended to establish that Christ was more than merely a man, for applied to a mere man it would be a stupid thing to say, and Christ was indisputably a man! [55] This sermon deserves further attention for its fascinating christological suggestions.

Luther acknowledges, but does not accept, the classical interpretation of the hymn as a description of the Incarnation of the preexistent Christ. In that case, Luther says, "form of God" would refer to the divine essence and nature of Christ, and the passage would mean that Christ, though true God, humbled Himself in becoming man. Rather, Luther argues, μορφή or *forma* cannot in this context mean "essence" but must mean something visible or manifest. He suggests that its vernacular translation should be "deportment," "bearing," or "appearance." The whole passage

51. 33, 289, 2.
52. 33, 211, 26; 47, 63, 23; 33, 288, 22.
53. 33, 536, 8; 47, 153, 27.
54. 17/II, 241, 8.
55. 17/II, 242, 22

is introduced into the Epistle as the outstanding example to Christians of service and humility; and it describes how the man Christ, even though He could and did display the lordly bearing appropriate to His divine essence ("He *was* in the form of God"), nevertheless chose freely to deport Himself as humbly as the poorest of men ("He *took* the form of a servant"). It was as the man Who was God that He divested Himself of the bearing that was His by right and assumed the servant role—indeed, abased Himself to serve all men with the supreme service, the giving of His life. The hymn is about the Incarnation only so far as He had to become man in order to serve us in this way.[56]

As an account of the deportment of the incarnate Christ, then, the hymn asserts that He divested Himself—"that is, He appeared to lay aside His divinity, by divesting Himself of its benefit and glory; not that He could or did divest Himself of His divine nature, but He put aside the form of divine majesty, He did not act as the God He was." [57] Occasionally, of course, the man Christ did display the form of God, in His miracles, His words, and His actions, yet in such a way that He served us even with that divinity. Throughout, the implication is plain: as God, the man Christ might always have acted differently. "Even in His humanity He could have exalted Himself over all men and served no-one . . . He had power to avoid ordinary human vicissitudes; as God He could have behaved quite differently . . . He gave up even the respect, repute, and honor due to the servant-form which He assumed to reveal Himself." [58] Elsewhere Luther pursues the implications of this voluntary self-abasement. As the man Who alone was without sin, Christ was in no way beholden to the law, but submitted Himself to its every ordinance, and finally its curse, for our sake.[59] While in every area of His life He somewhere displayed His bearing as God, there is no area in which He did not choose to act in a purely human manner. Thus at times He revealed the form of God by knowing men's inmost thoughts, but at other times revealed the form of a servant by voluntarily

56. 17/II, 238, 28ff.
57. 17/II, 243, 3.
58. 17/II, 243, 30.
59. 25, 469, 24; 46, 630, 27.

assuming ignorance and the ordinary limitations of human knowledge.[60] He revealed His divine power by withstanding the arrogance of men, but revealed His servant form by experiencing fear and distress and the need of prayer.[61] And finally, in His suffering He was forsaken by God. "This does not mean that the divinity was separated from the humanity, for in this person Who is Christ, God's Son and Mary's, deity and manhood are so united that they can never be separated or divided; but it means that the deity withdrew and hid, so that it appeared, as an onlooker might say, that 'this is not God, but a mere man—yes, a distressed and desperate man.' The manhood was left alone, and the devil had full access to Christ; the divinity withheld its power and left the manhood to fight alone. This is what St. Paul means . . . when he says that Christ emptied Himself of the form of God. That is, He did not use His divine strength or let His almighty power be seen, but He withdrew it when He suffered." [62]

Does Christ's radical, divine freedom in all this vitiate the reality of His manhood? It might appear so, if we compared only Christ's freedom in the likeness of sinful flesh with our bondage in the reality of sinful flesh. But for Luther the integrity of Christ's manhood is maintained for two reasons: first, despite His divine freedom, His history was that of a natural man, experiencing all the necessities of ordinary mortals; and secondly, in His manhood God created a new possibility of a genuinely human life sharing in the glory and exaltation of His divinity. In the transfiguration, for example, God revealed "the future splendor and glory of our bodies. For it was a thing of wonder that Christ should be glorified while still in His mortal and passible body. By it, He showed the splendor of immortality in the very midst of mortality. What will it be, when mortality is at last taken completely away and there is nothing but immortality and splendor?!" [63] If Christ enjoyed a constant hidden spiritual com-

---

60. 10/I/1, 149, 12ff.; 447, 11ff.; 46, 765, 3ff.
61. 17/II, 244, 8; 36, 274, 22; 43, 131, 1.
62. 45, 239, 32.
63. 38, 656, 7.

munion with God during his earthly life, the same is now true of the faithful. Colossians 3:1ff. and Ephesians 2:4ff. describe the life of all Christians as hidden in heaven while apparently present only on earth.[64] So, too, now that God has highly exalted Him, "Christ has completely divested Himself of the servant-form and put it aside; henceforth He is in the form of God, and is glorified, preached, confessed, honored, and acknowledged as God"—but is still (as we have seen) true man in His exaltation; and in the last day we shall share in everything that is in God.[65]

The statement that Christ is more than man does not deny, but affirms, that the Word was made flesh. It must be admitted, however, that in some of his earlier sermons, when Luther was still (by his own account) ironing confusions out of his Christology,[66] he inadvertently failed to give sufficient weight to the role of Christ's humanity. He could describe the manhood as the "cloud or curtain" through which the light of the divinity shone[67]— which unfortunately implies not accommodation of His majesty to our grasp but a real duality inconsistent with the "communication of properties" Luther was to espouse so fervently in the pressure of the sacramental dispute. He could carelessly predicate humiliation of "the man" instead of "the person according to His manhood."[68] Even more strikingly, in 1522 he could bemoan the disciples' failure to "lift their thoughts above the humanity to the divinity"; yet at Marburg, when Johann Oecolampadius urged him to do just that, he retorted: "I neither know nor worship any other God but Him Who was made flesh, nor do I want another! There is no other god who could save us but the incarnate God. Therefore I shall not suffer His humanity to be underestimated or degraded."[69] But if there are some confusing passages in the earlier sermons, it is also clear that the main lines of Luther's position were thoroughly laid before the sacramental dispute grew fierce. One role of that dispute was to inculcate in Luther a far

64. 10/I/2, 303, 29; 20, 428, 12; 47, 55, 6.
65. 17/II, 245, 11; 20, 698, 12.
66. 10/I/1, 163, 12; 33, 155, 10.
67. 10/I/1, 233, 21.
68. 10/I/1, 150, 9.
69. 10/I/2, 84, 25; 30/III, 132, 23ff.

greater accuracy of christological predication and to eliminate some potentially misleading formulations.

Luther's most insistent emphasis on the role of Christ's manhood, and his most frequent use of the expression, "Christ is more than a mere man," both occur together in his continuous exposition of John 6, Christ's discourse on the bread from heaven.[70] This passage was the most hotly debated locus of the long pamphlet war over the sacrament. Only a few months after its culmination at the Marburg Colloquy, Luther undertook a thorough sermonic exposition, in which he drew heavily upon the foregoing debates. In this discourse, he says, Christ is not speaking (as the Sacramentarians imagine) of ordinary flesh and blood—"like you buy from the butcher . . . from which you make red sausages" —but He uses the words "*My* flesh and blood" and endues them with a far greater strength than ordinary flesh and blood can possess. His is "food indeed, a truly spiritual flesh, a divine flesh imbued with the Holy Spirit." [71] (Virtually identical words occur in the 1527 treatise, *That These Words of Christ . . . Still Stand,* etc.) [72] Luther's reading of this passage, however, was in large part formulated before the sacramental controversy broke out. In 1522 he explained John 6:55 and 63 as follows: "The man Christ, separate from and without God, would be useless, as He says Himself in the words, 'The flesh profits nothing . . . My flesh is meat indeed. Why does the flesh profit nothing, yet My flesh is the only true meat? Simply because I am not only flesh and merely man, but I am the Son of God. My flesh is meat not because it is flesh, but because it is My flesh.'" [73] Both in 1522 and in 1531 Luther is at pains to insist that this unique efficacy of Christ's flesh in no way denies its genuineness as flesh: "flesh and blood, marrow and bone, skin and hair are really there in Him"; "I have flesh and blood like other men." [74] But if it is really flesh, it is not fleshly flesh; in other words, Christ uses "flesh" in two

70. See Helmut Gollwitzer, "Zur Auslegung von Joh. 6 bei Luther und Zwingli," in W. Schauch, ed., *In Memoriam Ernst Lohmeyer* (Stuttgart, 1951), pp. 143ff.

71. 33, 183, 24; 261, 18.

72. 23, 243, 36.

73. 10/I/1, 198, 24; cf. 20, 604, 13; 42, 170, 31.

74. 33, 183, 24; 10/I/1, 199, 7.

senses, both literally (meaning His body) and as a synecdoche (meaning fallen human nature in contrast to "spirit").[75] Whenever Scripture contrasts flesh and spirit, flesh cannot mean Christ's flesh, but means the old Adam; but when Scripture speaks of Christ, flesh and spirit are one.[76] The case can be stated two ways. A human body by itself is of no avail; but a human body used by God avails as He wills. Or, carnal human nature is clearly profitless; but Christ's spiritual, sinless humanity is given to be the bread of life. (Neither alternative, we may note in passing, necessarily excludes—as Luther did—a eucharistic interpretation of John 6.) In either case what is at issue is saving faith. "He who believes that I, Who am man and have flesh and blood like other men, am the Son of God, yes, God Himself, will find true nourishment in Me, and will live. But he who believes Me to be only man is not profited by the flesh, since it is not My flesh or God's flesh to him." [77]

### The Unity of the Person

If it is true that Luther's ground lines for relating the human and the divine in Christ were laid before the sacramental controversy, it is also true that the dispute provoked him to embellish his doctrine with illustrations and elaborations designed to protect the confession for faith. The emergence of anti-Trinitarian opinion in the radical wing of the Reformation further impelled this development. Inevitably, "Luther's Christology" has come to mean these elaborations, forged in the heat of dissension—especially, of course, his use of the *communicatio idiomatum,* the communication of properties between the two natures in Christ. Luther's story here parallels that of the early Church: there is an ever-present danger that a dogmatic formula, springing originally from lively experience and proper and adequate to the task of protecting faith, may come by stages first to explain, then to interpret, and finally to replace that experience of faith.

Luther was very much aware of this danger and ardently

75. 33, 262, 5.
76. 23, 193, 34; 26, 369, 24ff.; 432, 17ff.
77. 10/I/1, 199, 6; cf. 33, 267, 22.

warned his congregation against replacing faith with dogmatic speculation.[78] It would certainly be a gross injustice to imply that Luther's own doctrine of Christ declined from the primacy of faith; but it would be equally irresponsible to overlook those elements of his technical Christology which fail to clarify the faith they are intended to express (and are therefore prone to that decline). Here, then, we have a twofold task: to discover how Luther describes the relation between the two natures in Christ, and then to ask how far, in preaching, Luther successfully applies his description to the issues of faith.

The two distinct natures of God and man are united in the undivided person of Christ. This ancient and honorable expression appears often in Luther's christological utterances:[79] since he persistently argues from the history to the fact of the two natures, the traditional statement about the union of the natures is inevitable. "Undivided" becomes his normal epithet for "person" in this context;[80] there is, of course, only one Jesus of Whom both sorts of action are predicated. Unfortunately, the traditional formula (especially as the scholastics expounded it) had gained implications which obscure rather than clarify Luther's approach, when instead of rephrasing the formula, he simply repeats it. First, it is scarcely a clear expression of Luther's order of discussion because of its long-standing association with precisely the opposite order. That is, the dogma had long been a presupposition of interpreting Scripture, rather than its result. Secondly, the *enhypostasis*, the location of the ground of the unity in the person of the Word, had implied that "person" could be used univocally of the unchanging divine *hypostasis* and of the historical figure, with resulting Apollinarian tendencies; but because the dogma was applied a priori, it had not become apparent that the scriptural testimony was explained away, rather than explained —a process against which Luther violently reacted.

Now, despite the violence of his reaction, he does not appear consciously to have isolated all the elements of scholastic Chris-

78. E.g. *46, 20, 12.*
79. E.g. *20, 603, 10; 33, 79, 19; 46, 601, 1; 47, 199, 26;* etc.
80. E.g. *26, 326, 31; 33, 232, 6; 45, 467, 33; 556, 20; 47, 52, 20;* etc.

tology that caused his disquiet. With remarkable consistency, he returns to the primitive order, maintaining the confession of the two natures on the basis of the two types of action and discourse; yet on occasion, in the midst of so doing, he accuses the heretics of abandoning "the principle of distinguishing the two types of discourse on the basis of the two natures." [81] In practice, his case against them is not (as he suggests here) that they fail to distinguish the two modes of speech, but that having done so, they will not allow one or the other to mean what it says. If we are entitled to conclude from this sort of curiosity that Luther does not fully realize how radically he has reversed the scholastic way of doing Christology, it becomes easier to see why he grapples with some traditional technicalities which strictly need not arise from his own method.

For instance, by taking over traditional formulations, Luther encounters a difficulty with the meaning of "person." His repetition of the traditional phrase, the unity of the natures in the person of Christ, makes plain his intention to espouse the orthodox view of the hypostatic union. Yet he is not entirely comfortable in it. For what it expresses depends on the meaning of "person," and Luther hints that "person" may bear more than one sense, even in christological statements.

First, we speak of the three "persons" of the Holy Trinity. The Father is one person, the Word a distinct person, and the Holy Spirit a distinct person, yet there is only one God, not three Gods.[82] "We have no alternative but to use this little word 'person' here as the Fathers also used it: it means the same thing as a *hypostasis* (an essence or substance complete in itself) that is God. There are three distinct persons, but only one God, or one single Godhead; there is but one single God." Luther is employing terminology which emerged from the Arian controversy as orthodox: "three *hypostases* in one *ousia.*" But he suspects its adequacy.[83]

81. 45, 556, 37; cf. 10/I/1, 147, 11.
82. E.g. 10/I/1, 183, 13; I/2, 294, 29; 42, 43, 39; 45, 549, 33; 612, 26; 46, 601, 16; 50, 274, 20; etc.
83. 46, 550, 16; cf. 52, 338, 5.

Luther is aware that "person" has a rather simpler sense in everyday discourse, and moreover that the source of our faith is a historical "person" in just that everyday sense. The subject of the gospel is "the person born of the Virgin Mary," "the person called Christ," "the person endowed with real flesh and blood, and crucified." All our teaching and faith are about this person, and God and His grace are found nowhere but in this one person.[84] But the referent is always the historical figure, the earthly personality named Jesus of Nazareth. On this basis we assert the unity of the two natures in one person, because it is in the person called Jesus that we find divine and human modes of action, the greatest omnipotence and the frailest weakness, side by side.[85]

Now, it is easy to see how a problem of terminology arises. Simultaneously "person" has to serve for the *hypostasis* of the Son in His divine essence, and for the lowly human figure of Christ. How can we maintain both identity and contrast between God's majesty and Christ's humility? (Not, we may say in passing, in the manner Gustaf Wingren suggests: "For Luther, it is just *majesty* that is humble." [86] Luther maintains a sharp distinction between majesty and humility.) Rejection of the gospel, Luther says, does despite to God not in His majesty but in the person and message of Christ. A few sentences later, he recasts this proposition in the form: "Whoever dishonors this Christ also blasphemes God; for He is one person of the Godhead." [87] In a contrasting approach Luther elsewhere makes a sharp distinction between "person" and "office." When Christ says, "My teaching is not Mine, but His Who sent Me," He is referring to His office and speaks "as preacher, not as God . . . The teaching Christ here proclaims applies not to the person, Who is God, but to the office." [88] The same distinction is used to explain the words, "The Father is greater than I": it is said not "of His own personal divine essence" but "of His ministry or servile state." "There is no

84. *33*, 134, 20; 176, 11; 190, 33; *45*, 481, 21; 489, 22.
85. *45*, 556, 39; *47*, 213, 39.
86. Wingren, *The Living Word*, p. 206.
87. *47*, 180, 41 to 181, 11; 182, 29.
88. *33*, 357, 41 to 358, 18.

change in His person and essence . . . but He speaks of a change of office, from His state as servant or minister to His dominion and eternal kingdom." [89]

The office of preaching (and of suffering) is a humble, human office. Is this person, Who is "one person of the Godhead," to be excepted from the state of humility involved in this office, or to be identified with it, despite the contrast between the majesty of the divine essence and the lowliness of the man? The first alternative receives much subtle support from the scholastic tradition. For instance, this was the force of the distinction between *unio* and *assumptio* in the Incarnation: the divine nature is united to the human but not assumed by it, whereas the human nature is both united to the divine and assumed by it. The person of the Word thus acts in assuming, and effects its union with the manhood without change in itself, since the process of becoming refers only to the nature passively assumed.[90] The immutability of the divine essence is preserved in this way, but at the expense of making the biblical testimony equivocal: the dominant medieval treatment of ἐγένετο in John 1:14 is the prime case in point.[91] Now, Luther's fundamental principle of exegesis is the perspicuity of Scripture, and he instinctively revolts against such equivocation, especially since it distorts the biblical picture of Christ, investing Him with an air of gross unreality. But the presumption that the divine *hypostasis* is a priori immutable and impassible continues to influence him nonetheless. Occasionally—indeed, only very occasionally—he seems to use the phrase "according to His human nature" in the Nestorian manner—namely, to deny any more than verbal predication of Christ's humiliation to the eternal Word. We have noticed instances in the course of this study: on the ground that "life cannot die," Luther asserts that Christ the Word remained alive when Christ the man died; or again, that His entering the Virgin's womb or descending into hell "really applies only to the human nature." [92] And in the last

89. *21*, 474, 32–39; *29*, 368, 19ff.
90. Thus Thomas Aquinas, ST III, q. 2, a. 8.
91. E.g. Lombard, *Sent.* III, dist. 6; Thomas Aquinas, *Comm. in Ioh.*, ad 1:14.
92. *10/I/1*, 208, 4; *47*, 56, 26.

analysis, the distinction between "person" and "office" performs
the same function in a subtler way: it seems to allow more than
merely verbal predication of Christ's history to the Word, but by
identifying everything which could impugn the Word's immutability as human and official, and everything consonant with it as
personal, essential, and divine, it effectively achieves the same result as the scholastic scheme.

Luther experiments with this distinction; but its dangers must
have become apparent to him (as to Athanasius before him, who
also propounded this notion),[93] for he is not prepared to abide
by it. It is a tentative effort to resolve a suspicion that where dogmatic tradition has used "person" univocally of the divine *hypostasis* and of the Word made flesh, the paradoxical result has been
an Apollinarian Christ. But this avenue is quite closed, for any attempt to circumvent the *enhypostasis*—to speak as if the second
person of the Trinity were not indeed the subject of Christ's
human words and actions—not only divides the person but
thereby destroys the affirmation central to Luther's gospel.[94] Because the Son is one undivided essence with the Father and the
Spirit, where we hear one person speak, we hear the entire Deity.
So when we grasp the Son of God, we grasp the Father too: the
whole Trinity is known in the person of Christ.[95] "Since Christ,
Who is one undivided person, God and man, speaks to us, we are
sure that God the Father and the Holy Spirit—that is, the whole
divine majesty—is also present and speaking. So God is entirely
comprehended in this one person, and you need not nor dare not
search elsewhere."[96] And He says to us that as He lives by the
Father's eternal begetting and indwelling—Christ in the Father
and the Father in Christ—so also in faith we live by Him and become one with Him—Christ in us and we in Christ. Thus we are
united to God as sons and coheirs like Christ, save that we are
not one natural essence with God as He is, but adopted for His
sake.[97] This chain is utterly shattered if we cannot cling to the

93. See Jaroslav Pelikan, *The Light of the World* (New York, 1962), p. 79.
94. 39/II, 117, 16.
95. 33, 135, 10; 45, 612, 26.
96. 45, 550, 22.
97. 33, 231, 23ff.; 28, 183, 7; 187, 1ff.; 33, 232, 1 and 31; 39/II, 23, 11; 46, 637, 14–38.

person of Christ Who preached and suffered and died, or if that
person is not one with the Father.[98]

## The Union of the Natures

The strongest stress in Luther's doctrine, then, is on the unity
of Christ's person. Both the rules and the illustrations which Luther employs to describe this unity have a long prehistory in the
dogmatic tradition. Curiously, they run a constant risk of misinterpretation, because Luther does not argue in the traditional categories or in the traditional order. Taken out of context, there are
illustrations which suggest that Luther avoids neither Scylla nor
Charybdis, but both separates the natures and confuses them. In
context, however, it is possible to say without special pleading
that Luther's doctrine is quite orthodox. He is guilty not of heter-
odoxy but of failure to eliminate the anomalies which arise when
old expressions are used within a new logical schema.

It is only fair to add that when he offers an illustration of the
union, he almost invariably warns that it is only an illustration, an
analogy to a phenomenon which is strictly sui generis. The conjunction of the natures is so close, he says, that there is nothing
like it in all the world. The most frequent of his illustrations is a
case in point—the analogy of the unity of body and soul in one
human being. Even though he regards this as "the closest analogy," Luther warns that it is "not adequate in every point of comparison," but a simple image for the simple.[99] A body, he says,
has one nature, a soul an entirely different nature. One without
the other does not constitute a human being, but together the two
natures constitute one human being, not two. Wherever the soul
is, the body must be also, and vice versa. As one human being,
the two natures are so closely united that we attribute to the
whole entity what affects only one of the two constituents. When
someone is bitten on the shin, we say, "The dog bit Peter." We
strike a man's body, not his soul, yet regard the whole person as
recipient of the blow.[1] A mother bears and nourishes her child's

98. 20, 606, 3ff.; 43, 582, 28.
99. 26, 333, 11; 39/II, 114, 14; 45, 558, 14; 47, 56, 10.
1. 20, 603, 19; 26, 321, 28; 333, 13; 45, 558, 11; 47, 55, 21.

body, not its soul, by means of her own body, not her soul; yet she is the child's mother.[2] "Or take a person asleep: the body is certainly sleeping, but the soul is not asleep—it reflects and moves, breathes and lives. In this way a man sleeps and simultaneously does not sleep, lives and does not live, smells and does not smell. Yet the two natures form one entity and essence, despite the distinction between the two: body and soul cannot be divorced in a living being."[3]

This set of illustrations (colorfully embellished with references to highwaymen, daggers, intellectuals, Hansel and Gretel, and a somewhat outmoded embryology) is a fascinating example of the conflict between Luther's intention and his success. On the dogmatic level his illustrations maintain clearly enough that God and man are of two different natures and by no means to be confused, yet there are not two Jesuses, but one. On the level of practical response the figure of striking the whole person when we strike only a limb, or touching the whole person when we touch only one hair, can illustrate Luther's assertion that where we meet the manhood of Christ, we meet the triune God. But Luther's listener might be forgiven for gaining a different impression from the illustration of the sleeper, which unintentionally suggests a separation of the natures, as if the divine "part" of Christ was somehow spared the earthly experiences of His human "part." "Although (so to speak) one part, the divinity, does not suffer, yet the person, Who is God, suffers in the other part, the humanity. Thus we say, 'The king's son is hurt,' when really only his leg is hurt . . . This is the way people everywhere speak."[4] Perhaps Luther's most misleading legacy from traditional Christology is the phrase, "according to the divine (or human) nature," giving rise as it does to a mental image of two "parts" of Christ, a combination of materials.

Other physical analogies equally reveal the dangers inherent in reading such a structural view of natures into Luther's doctrine of Christ, but in the opposite direction. As we saw, Luther contends that the flesh and blood which Christ offers to be our true food are

2. 45, 558, 8; 47, 55, 35; 50, 586, 16.
3. 47, 55, 28.
4. 26, 321, 26.

"more than mere flesh and blood, but are invested with greater strength by virtue of the word 'My.' " [5] Then he offers an illustration which is "clear" but "crude": a physician mixes pure water with sugar to make a syrup; when we drink it we no longer call it water, but sugar-water, because even though it actually is water, it is not pure water; but as sugar-water it possesses a new taste, a new quality, a new action. "I can no longer properly regard it as water—as indeed it was—but it is now so saturated with sugar, cinnamon, and spice that it has been transformed into a different essence." So with Christ: He has flesh and blood like us, but we are nothing but flesh and blood, whereas "a sugar was added to Christ's flesh, so that when we see the flesh and taste and drink the blood, we see God and worship God; and conversely, if we desecrate them, we crucify and dishonor God. So we eat the God-head in the humanity. Here is the parallel with the sugar-water: when I touch it, I also touch the sugar; when I drink it, I also taste, drink, or lick the sugar." [6]

Now suppose this were taken as a way of describing the relation between two substantial natures in Christ; then it would be a classic statement of the Eutychian error, locating the union in the natures and thus robbing the constituents of their integrity, making Christ a tertium quid between God and man.[7] (Luther actually speaks of the change of water's "substance and essence" when it is "boiled, cooked, and mixed" together with sugar.) [8] But here, of course, Luther is not addressing the scholastic problems of unitive Christology, and he has abandoned substantial categories. Once again, he is simply asserting that this true and natural flesh and blood, born of Mary, given and crucified for the life of the world, is unique, because it belongs to the person in Whom God alone is to be sought and found by faith. "This is a living and yet a dead flesh, a flesh that has died and through its death makes all the world alive." [9]

The undogmatic character of his use of these images is shown

5. 33, 183, 38.
6. 33, 184, 5ff.
7. Cf., e.g., Thomas Aquinas, SCG IV, 35, 8.
8. 33, 189, 3.
9. 33, 190, 26.

by his blithe juxtaposition of illustrations which, taken traditionally, would yield opposite emphases. A further illustration, he says, of the truth expressed by the sugar-water image is the old figure of glowing iron.[10] When iron is heated, it loses the qualities of iron: it glows, it burns, it bores, it brands. "Certainly it is still iron, but it is so permeated with fire that when you see or touch it, you cannot call it iron but feel only the fire." It is the fire, not the iron, which burns or brands: a cold iron cannot. "Just so the divine power is present bodily in Christ's humanity and does what God does by nature (like the fire in the iron). Only flesh and blood are visible; but faith sees a man, a flesh and blood, which is like fiery iron—it is permeated with the divine." [11] The iron and the fire, Luther assures us, is paralleled in turn by this instance: I give someone a purse full of gold pieces, but the guldens are not visible, only the purse.[12] This equation by itself reveals that the issue is not christological theory but the pouring out of God's grace for us in the man Christ, and faith's discovery of this gracious God in Him alone.

Some of these images, however, are offered as illustrations of the ancient rule of mutual predication, the *communicatio idiomatum*. Luther's use of the rule is beyond reproach; but his expositions of the rule once again leave much to be desired. His biblical writings certainly prompt the judgment that its technicalities need not have arisen for Luther. His chief treatments of it are to be found not in biblical exposition but in controversy. It is presupposed in the anti-Zwinglian polemics; it is spelled out in the academic disputations occasioned by the neo-Arianism of Caspar Schwenckfeld; and its historical roots are examined in the treatise *On the Councils and the Church*. Apart from these technical treatments, Luther mentions it only a few times in lectures or preaching; [13] and in none of these allusions does he succeed in adding anything by means of this rule which he has not said

10. Origen, *De princ.* II, vi, 6 (MPG XI, 213); John of Damascus, *De fide orthod.* III, 17 (MPG XCIV, 1069); cf. Leontius of Byzantium, *C. Nest. et Eutych.* (MPG LXXXVI/1, 1304).

11. *33*, 191, 3; cf. *40/I*, 417, 17.

12. *47*, 636, 24ff.

13. E.g. *20*, 603, 24; *45*, 556, 14ff.; *47*, 55, 11ff.; *76*, 33ff.; *86*, 3ff.; *199*, 19ff.

more clearly in terms we have already examined. On the contrary, his short digressions on the *communicatio* must have been virtually incomprehensible to the unlearned in his congregation. (The way in which he introduces the subject abruptly into a sermon, amplifies it with a string of scholastic terms, and then reverts to his previous line of thought suggests that he intends this material for his students—an academic *tour de force!*) Enough of Luther's doctrine is now before us to establish, beyond a shadow of doubt, that he has far more lucid and straightforward ways of expressing the claim he tries to protect by means of the *communicatio*—the claim, on the one hand, that we must take the perfectly human words and deeds of Christ as if they were the words and deeds of God, and on the other, that the relationship of unity and mutual indwelling in the Holy Trinity now extends to the manhood of Christ and thus also to us, His body. Luther's use of the *communicatio* is sometimes commended for its usefulness in presenting this claim; [14] but in exposition, at least, such commendations must be limited to what Luther might have done, not to what he does, with this formula. For here Luther, the model of clarity, becomes strangely turgid and abstruse. The soteriological thrust is quite obscured.

In outline his teaching is this: In the account which the faith gives of Christ, certain properties peculiar to human nature are described (such as being born, drinking milk, working, weeping, laughing, suffering, dying, being exalted), and also certain properties peculiar to God (such as creating, residing in heaven, being immortal and infinite, answering prayer, possessing all things).[15] But these attributes appear to be mutually exclusive: How can they be reconciled? God manages to reconcile them, so we must reconcile them too,[16] by this means: the two natures, the human and the divine, are inseparably united in one person. The effect of this union is that the properties of the one are attributed to the other: since the Incarnation, the properties of the divine nature are communicated to the human, and, conversely,

14. For a recent example, see Wingren, *The Living Word,* pp. 204ff.
15. *47,* 199, 39; *50,* 587, 22ff.
16. *47,* 199, 39.

the human to the divine.[17] By this means, for instance, we can explain how He Who possesses all things can be given all things. Or we can understand how Christ's human properties can be predicated of God, or divine properties predicated of this man.[18] Thus to be born and suckled is human, not divine; but because God and man are one Christ, "Mary makes broth for God," "Mary suckles God with her breasts, bathes God, rocks and carries Him; moreover, Pilate and Herod crucified and killed God"; "the infant Christ, lying in the cradle and suckled by the Virgin Mary, created heaven and earth." [19] Conversely, to be worshiped or to give eternal life is divine, not human; but because the human nature shares in the glory of all the properties which otherwise pertain to God, "to worship this man is to worship God"; "outside this man Christ, Who was born of the Virgin Mary, and Who suffered, you must not seek God or any salvation or help." [20] "Whoever has touched Christ's skin has actually touched God!" [21]

So far, this is an unexceptionable statement of Chalcedonian orthodoxy. On the one hand, both natures are predicated of one subject, so that there is no danger of Nestorianism; on the other, there is a genuinely mutual predication of the attributes of these natures, so that there is no danger of monophysitism. Furthermore, he explicitly states his concern: he is proclaiming that when we deal with the man, we are dealing with the only God.[22] What, then, has been gained by stating this concern in such complex guise, replete with physical analogies and decked out in learned phrases—"quae uni naturae conveniunt, toti personae conveniunt in concreto"; "communicatio naturarum adducit etiam communicationem idiomatum"; "propter unitam coniunctionem et unitatem duarum naturarum fit communicatio idiomatum"? [23]

Luther's discussion of "nature" is functional rather than struc-

---

17. 39/II, 98, 6; 45, 557, 7; 47, 55, 13; 72, 22; 199, 26ff.
18. 47, 201, 16; 39/II, 93, 6.
19. 50, 587, 14; 47, 200, 19; 77, 34 (cf. 87, 2).
20. 47, 201, 20 and 39.
21. 40/I, 417, 17; cf. 20, 606, 4.
22. 47, 72, 36.
23. 39/II, 98, 8; 47, 56, 28; 77, 38.

tural. He has led us to believe that "to possess human nature," "to possess divine nature," means simply "to be man," "to be God"; the conclusion that Christ is both God and man (*communicatio naturarum . . .*) rests on the observation that He acts and speaks appropriately to both. But now this same speaking and acting are called "properties" or "attributes," whose unity is said to be effected by Christ's being God and man (. . . *adducit etiam communicationem idiomatum*). Plainly, such terminology seems redundant; in fact, it escapes tautology only if content can be given to the distinction between a nature and the function of a nature. Luther certainly makes such a distinction. "Essence implies a condition, whereas its expression implies an act . . . An essence may exist without being expressed; an expression may (fraudulently) exist without the corresponding essence; or we may find an essence together with its proper expression." [24] Or against Zwingli's notion of *alloeosis:* "Even if it were valid, so that one nature could be taken for the other, the concept would still apply only to the actions or functions of the natures, but not to the essence of the natures . . . for essence is essence, each its own and not the other's." [25] But as we have seen repeatedly, Luther can give content to this distinction only a posteriori, identifying the natures by their corresponding expressions. The distinction has the minimal form, "We know Christ is (always) God in essence, because He (sometimes) acts divinely; we know He is (always) man by nature, because He (sometimes) acts humanly." Luther's use of the *communicatio,* then, is saved from tautology, but at the expense of seeming to rest upon an a priori definition of the natures. (On his own terms, for instance, there is no need for the question of abstract predication even to arise.) [26] Moreover, it not only seems to, but actually does, reverse the order Luther otherwise adopts, since he occasionally uses the rule of the *communicatio* as an a priori device for explaining Scripture's paradoxical conjunction of the divine and the human in Christ—a con-

24. 17/II, 239, 31ff.
25. 26, 325, 33.
26. 39/II, 93, 10.

junction which Luther himself insists cannot and is not to be explained but only believed.[27] He acts out of character when he adduces theory to justify the Word of God to man. It is not his wont to explain the inexplicable.

And, of course, he really does not intend to explain the mystery of the Incarnation: "After the article of the Trinity, the highest is that about the Incarnation of the Son of God, where proportion between the finite and the infinite (which is impossible) came about. This person, finite and infinite at once, became the servant of sinners, and the latest and lowest of all things—which is unbelievable, but to those who believe it, sheerest joy!" [28] God has done a new thing, and therefore a new grammar is required, new ways of talking which God Himself has given us.[29] Logic must not dictate subject matter; logic simply analyses the rules by which discourse about a given subject matter proceeds. If the subject itself already shatters all our philosophical preconceptions, how foolish to bring a philosophical logic to bear upon it. Clearly, Luther presumes that dogmatic formulations in general, and the *communicatio idiomatum* in particular, function merely as a descriptive grammar of the language of faith (in Scripture, preaching, and confession). Unfortunately, however, he takes over formulations whose previous purpose was not merely grammatical in this sense, but which arose in the course of metaphysical analyses of the hypostatic union. As a result, remnants of a philosophical logic are imported unrecognized into what Luther intends to be biblical discourse.

In short, even though Luther's presentation of the *communicatio idiomatum* is technically tenable, it creates an impression alien to his design. Fortunately, it is a minor incident in his biblical exegesis; and at most points Luther is content to confess the unity of the natures on the ground that the biblical account means what it says. He finds simple justification for the usage in the fact that Scripture itself speaks thus: "they crucify the Son of God afresh" (Heb. 6:6); "they crucified (not the *humanity* of

27. *47*, 51, 30; 52, 33; 54, 4ff.
28. 39/II, 340, 14.
29. 39/II, 98, 13; 104, 24.

glory, but) the *Lord* of glory" (I Cor. 2:8); "God sent forth His Son, born of a woman" (Gal. 4:4); "to you is born this day . . . Christ the Lord" (Luke 2:11).[30]

Luther's attitude is perhaps epitomized by his assertion that the decrees of Ephesus and Chalcedon added nothing to what was far more richly and powerfully formulated in the Gospels.[31] It is striking, too, how mildly Luther deals with both Nestorius and Eutyches. Instead of treating them as formidable heresiarchs, he presents them as otherwise faithful men whose bumbling pride and deficient learning led them into logical transgressions against the *communicatio idiomatum*.[32] In fact, Luther says, Nestorius did not teach more than one Christ, and so he could not have regarded Christ as two persons without contradicting himself. "This crude, unlearned man failed to realize that he was stating the impossible when both at once he seriously believed Christ to be God and man in one person, and yet refused to ascribe the *idiomata* of the natures to the same person of Christ." [33] The same is true of Eutyches, who was "simply another crude Nestorius" in that he did not deny that the deity had assumed humanity, and therefore his one-nature doctrine was a self-contradiction. Nestorius taught that Christ was two persons and yet only one person; Eutyches, that Christ had two natures and yet only one nature; they not only contradicted each other, but each contradicted himself! [34] Their confusion reveals that both committed similar errors regarding the *idiomata*: "Nestorius will not ascribe the *idiomata* of humanity to the divinity in Christ (even though he maintains that Christ is God and man); and Eutyches will not ascribe the *idiomata* of divinity to the humanity (though he, too, maintains that Christ is true God and true man)." [35] This delightfully simple account is perhaps more revealing of Luther's approach than of the fifth-century protagonists'. So completely has the historical

30. *20*, 603, 16; *26*, 320, 26; *47*, 77, 13; *86*, 33; *50*, 591, 28ff.

31. *50*, 591, 22; for Luther's historical sources, see esp. Cassiodorus, *Historia tripartita*, Bk. XII, 4–5 (MPL LXIX, 1204ff.).

32. *50*, 586, 9; 596, 11.

33. *50*, 589, 15.

34. *50*, 594, 3.

35. *50*, 595, 2ff.

figure of Jesus Christ preempted the definition of unity for Luther that the Nestorian extreme becomes an obvious grammatical blunder; so completely have the divine and human characteristics preempted the definition of the natures that the monophysite extreme, too, is simply bad logic. Both parties have "conceded the antecedent and denied the consequent." [36] If the apostolic testimony is admitted as faith's premise, the truth that the one Christ is God and man follows inexorably. There can be no inconsistency between being God and acting as man, or between being man and acting as God, because this is what happened.[37] " 'But,' you object, 'God cannot be crucified or suffer.' I reply: I know—while He is not yet man. From eternity He has not suffered, but since He became man, He is passible. From eternity He was not man, but now, conceived by the Holy Spirit and born of the Virgin, He becomes God and man, one person, and the same things are predicated of God and man." [38]

From our vantage point, because the figure of Christ defines the unity, Eutyches' error may seem the more plausible. For since Christ's exaltation and the laying aside of the servant role, the divine *idiomata* have taken the dominant place. Human characteristics are so eclipsed that it is easy to see why Eutyches thought only the divine nature remained.[39] Zwingli certainly thought that Luther had fallen into this trap with his doctrine of the ubiquity of Christ: his assertion that because Christ's humanity, body and soul, must be wherever His Godhead is, His flesh may be present ("locally, definitively, or repletively") however and wherever He wills. "This is My body" then tells us where Christ wills to be for us, since He may be anywhere, everywhere, or nowhere in His sovereign freedom.[40] Zwingli felt that to communicate such modes of presence (divine *idiomata*) to Christ's flesh and blood (human *idiomata*) could only mean the obliteration of the human by the divine. Luther's fierce reaction was that Zwingli had completely misunderstood the relation between Christ's person and His attri-

36. 50, 596, 19; 598, 15.
37. 39/II, 12, 6.
38. 39/II, 101, 24.
39. 50, 595, 35.
40. 26, 324, 19ff.

butes. For by the same token, in the days of His flesh Christ's self-emptying was so extreme that the human *idiomata* seemed to have eclipsed the divine.[41] (Indeed, Luther counsels, "do not listen to what anyone says about the glorified Jesus unless you have first seen the crucified Jesus.") [42]

Here, no doubt, we can see and respect the motive which impels Luther's rather misleading exposition of the *communicatio idiomatum*. His derivation of the two-nature doctrine from Christ's twofold action and discourse is liable to make nonsense of the gospel history, if it, in turn, is applied as an a priori. (This, of course, is what happened in Antiochene Christology, where a perfectly valid insistence on the integrity of the acts of the two natures became an exegetical rule of double predication.) For to say that we observe both divine and human actions in Christ is a true but incomplete account of the facts. In practice, those of His words and actions which faith apprehends as divine are still words and actions of a human being. Faith is finally bound to confess that all His words and actions—even those by which we know Him to be a man—are in the fullest sense words and actions of the person of the Word. The implications of this confession stupefy the imagination; but this is Luther's confession.

It is a confession which Luther makes with great clarity in biblical exposition: "The person of God must not be separated from the humanity of Christ"; "in this crucified God dwells all the fullness of the Godhead bodily"; "He is true man with body and soul; and yet the one Who lies in the womb, His body is the body of God Himself. As Paul says in Colossians 1, all things were created through Him and for Him, and in Him all the fullness of God was pleased to dwell. Paul means that His body is God's own, personal body. All other bodies are His, too—mine, yours— but they are not His personal, very own body, so that it is said, 'He Who lies in the womb is very God and this body is God's body' "; "What Christ does and suffers, essentially God does and suffers." [43]

41. *45*, 239, 32.
42. *Br*, 2, 425, 39; cf. *40*/III, 656, 21.
43. *20*, 605, 21; *28*, 486, 24; *41*, 481, 3; *10*/I/1, 150, 22.

Unhappily, it is a confession which is thrown into confusion by Luther's haphazard attempts at adapting inherited technicalities. The meaning of *idioma* itself is a leading case in point. In scholastic usage it had implied an essential and permanent quality. Yet in Luther it comes to mean a characteristic manifestation, expression, function, or action, which may be exercised or suspended. However, Luther cannot escape from the tradition, so in the case of the manhood he now and then attempts a further distinction between "temporal and transient *idiomata*" (physical need, passibility, circumscription) and "natural *idiomata*" (the body and soul of an ordinary human being), between "the works of the natures" and "the essence of the natures," or between what is accidental and what is natural in man.[44] In the case of the divinity (where the issue is even more pressing, because of the classical notion of God as without accident) Luther's lists of divine *idiomata* sometimes follow traditional lines—immortality, omnipotence, infinity, insusceptibility—but more authentically branch off into evangelical concerns—"the glorious divine *idiomata* such as atoning for sin, reconciling God's wrath, justifying sinners."[45] He senses but fails to identify his confusion when he writes: "I cannot find a single German word for it. *Idioma* means what is inherent in a nature, or its attribute, such as dying, suffering, weeping, talking, laughing, eating, drinking, sleeping, sorrowing, rejoicing, being born, having a mother, taking the breast, walking, standing, laboring, sitting, lying, and similar things called *idiomata naturae humanae*, that is, attributes inherent in man by nature, things he can and must do and moreover suffer. Thus *idioma* in Greek, or *proprium* in Latin, is something . . . well, for the moment, let us call it an attribute. Furthermore, an *idioma deitatis*, an attribute of the divine nature, is to be immortal, omnipotent, infinite, not to be born, and not to eat, drink, sleep, stand, walk, sorrow, weep —what more can one say?"[46] The same confusion, as we saw above, sometimes afflicts the word "person" and certainly complicates the word "essence." In use, "essence" seems to be merely a

44. 50, 596, 4; 26, 326, 24; 39/II, 371, 10.
45. 39/II, 22, 14; 40/I, 77, 20; 50, 587, 30; 597, 17.
46. 50, 587, 22–31.

periphrasis for the verb "to be"; but in technical contexts it has a disconcerting tendency to be interchanged sporadically with a series of traditional terms—nature, *hypostasis,* person. Clearly Luther creates difficulty for himself by equating "the divine essence" with "the divine majesty." [47] And when Luther, in academic disputation, entertains a distinction between "essence considered essentially" and "essence considered personally," one joins him in exclaiming, "What more can one say?" [48]

## *"Without Confusion, without Change, without Division, without Separation"*

Luther's struggles with the formal categories of christological theory arise from traditional familiarity, not from evangelical concern; and he is therefore unsuccessful in reinterpreting the old orthodoxy in terms of his new and living faith. Yet the basis for such a reinterpretation is implicit in the rich doctrine of Christ that we have reviewed in these pages—implicit, but sadly not explicit, so that his legacy (as Adolf Harnack said) was "an unspeakable confusion as regards the significance of the old dogmas in the strictest sense of the word. No bridge leads to them from his justifying, saving faith, not because this faith does not reach to them, but because those dogmas do not describe the being of God in so wonderful and comforting a way as evangelical faith is able to do from its knowledge." [49]

"Not because this faith does not reach to them . . ." Implicit in the warp and woof of Luther's faith is a dimension that could have reanimated the static product of Chalcedon—a discovery of God Himself graciously and uniquely and sufficiently in Christ, in a way that transforms Chalcedon's ἀτρέπτως. He has instructed us not to seek God "absolutely," in His incomprehensible essence, uncovered, apart from Christ. That quest is fatal not only because we cannot sustain the discovery of God as He is in Him-

47. E.g. *46,* 541, 11; 39/II, 18, 4.
48. 39/II, 370, 21.
49. Adolf Harnack, *History of Dogma, 7* (7 vols. in 5, New York, 1961: reprinted from trans. by Neil Buchanan of 3d German ed., ca. 1900), 242.

self, but because such a God is not God as He is. If only Luther had rigorously pursued his own counsel into the realm of dogma! But remnants of the philosophers' God persist, despite his radical insistence that whatever rational apprehension of God we may possess, it is to be abandoned for the lively knowledge of the God and Father of our Lord Jesus Christ. This should lead to a complete reworking of the truth enshrined in the sentence, "Christ maintained His Godhead unaltered when He became man." [50] For it should mean that even what we know of God's unchangeability is determined by what we discover of it through faith in Christ. And this God is not the almighty, incomprehensible First Cause of the schools, but a God Whose mercy is from everlasting to everlasting. "Since that day God speaks to us Himself through His Son and Holy Spirit. Now we hear a fatherly voice proclaiming sheer unfathomable, ineffable love and mercy, uttering nothing but blessing, nothing but goodness, sweetness, and love. *For that is what it means to be God.*" [51] The God Who dwells in unapproachable light, the creator and preserver of all, has poured Himself out for us in the person of Jesus Christ, with all that He is, has, and does.[52]

For Luther knew that that truth about Jesus Christ, and therefore the truth about God, must be expressed in terms of the salvation He came first to proclaim and then to accomplish: "Who for us men and for our salvation came down from heaven, and was incarnate . . . and was made man." The unchangeability of God must never be determined by our profoundest metaphysics or our loftiest speculations, but only by what God has revealed. And He has revealed Himself in utter humility and obedience, as one Who was rich, yet for our sakes became poor, that we, through His poverty, might be rich.

"The heretical Manichaeans, such knaves were they, were offended at the assertion that the Son of God had become man; and to embellish their error, they feigned great wisdom and piety, saying that it was an outrage to the divine majesty to claim

50. *47*, 55, 6.
51. *33*, 149, 36.
52. *17*/II, 205, 35.

that He had been born from poor and sin-corrupted, unclean, mortal flesh, and a woman's flesh at that—yes, impossible, they said, that the divine purity, which is brighter than the sun, should submerge itself in this vile slime . . . But we believe the Holy Scripture . . . Until His thirty-fourth year He ate and drank, was angry, prayed, grew sad, wept, and accomplished the task to which He was sent from the Father: He suffered persecution and finally death at the hands of His own people. Thus the Jews crucified the true Son of God, the lord of glory: and we saw His blood shed and flowing to the ground." [53]

The twofold movement of being sent from the Father and going to the Father—of descent and ascent—informs all Luther's exposition of the history of Christ. He was sent by the Father into the world. If we are to take this statement with the seriousness that Luther (and his text) would have us take it, can we persist in any qualification which suggests that the transcendent Word is thereby unaffected? Again, Luther instructs us that Christ's going to the Father through suffering and death is the sole possibility of our salvation. To accomplish it, He became a curse and sin for us. "The love of the Son of God is so great toward us that the greater the filth and stench upon us, the more He gives Himself to us, cleanses us, and takes all our sin and wretchedness, lifts them off our shoulders, and lays them on His own back . . . What does it mean that the Son of God should be my servant, and so utterly debase Himself that He should take the burden of my misery and sin—yes, the whole world's sin and death? He says to me, "You are no longer a sinner, but I am. I step into your place—you have not sinned, but I have. The whole world is in sin, but you are not in sin—I am. All your sins are to lie on Me and not on you.'" [54] If it was not the very God Himself Who became sin for us, what hope of life is left?

Luther's biblical faith could equally have breathed life into Chalcedon's "without confusion . . . without division." Because of his freedom from metaphysical preconceptions, he can retain equally the biblical truths behind the Antiochene stress on the

53. *46*, 633, 21; 634, 7 and 26.
54. *46*, 680, 31.

moral character of the union (its grounding in the gracious good-pleasure of God) and the Alexandrian stress on its natural character (its grounding in the being and act of God). This double stress is illustrated by Luther's fondness for St. Bernard's dream, with its motif of Christ's twofold claim on heaven, by desert and by nature.[55] Moreover, his account of the relation among person, nature, and attribute, once freed from inherited impediments, holds rich potential for the discovery of God in Christ. He implies that the person of Christ, in His complete freedom, could exercise or omit to exercise the attributes of this nature or that as He willed. This freedom is both human and divine. As a human freedom, it was exercised in the total obedience of Christ, by which He became the beloved, God's elect, the head of the new creation; as divine freedom, it was the outpouring of eternal love and mercy and life on sinful men. The concurrence in Christ of the human obedience with the divine love made His humanity such a perfect instrument of the Godhead that in the fullest sense the acts of this man must be called the acts of God, and furthermore, that the eternal dominion of God as God is accomplished in this human will and body.

Luther's gospel without these affirmations would be nothing. They are his doctrine of Christ. Luther has scant interest in relating the two natures speculatively, and his essays in this field are not intrinsic to his evangelical concerns. As P. T. Forsyth says, in words which could have been Luther's, "The mighty thing in Christ is His grace and not His constitution." [56] It is this emphasis in Luther that Dietrich Bonhoeffer wants to maintain when he says that the person of Jesus Christ is His work.[57] Yet for all that, Luther does find value in dogmatic Christology as protector of the unequivocal truth of the Word of God. "I have noticed and observed in all the histories of the whole of Christendom that all those who have correctly held and maintained the chief article of Jesus Christ have remained safe and secure in right Christian

55. See above, p. 187.
56. P. T. Forsyth, *The Person and Place of Jesus Christ* (London, 1910), p. 10.
57. Dietrich Bonhoeffer, "Christologie," in his *Gesammelte Schriften*, ed. Eberhard Bethge, 3 (München, 1960), 176ff.

faith." [58] Luther's own preaching of the words and saving deeds of Christ evokes a new apprehension of God's unchangingness, of the constant and unwavering being of God in Jesus Christ—an apprehension that preserves and transmits and revitalizes the truth enshrined in the christological dogma, and points the way to the discovery that God the Son, in His very essence, is for us, to the glory of God the Father.

58. *50*, 266, 32.

# 7.   Christ Named, Preached, and Pictured

I t is characteristic of a good preacher," Luther says, "that he can address himself to his subject, briefly encompass it and sum it up in two or three words, and then, if need be, also spell it out and make it clear with epigrams and illustrations, and out of one flower make a whole meadow—just as a goldsmith fashions the same piece of silver together into a solid lump, or else he can beat it flat, fluted, curled, or into thin foil." [1]

The precious metal of Luther's doctrine of Christ is now before us; it remains only to examine the ornamental detail of his craftsmanship, the more and less skillful intricacies of his wrought-work. Some of Luther's descriptions of Christ are drawn immediately from the Gospels or elsewhere in the Scriptures; some of them he has borrowed or adapted from the Fathers; and some are the fruit of his own homiletic genius. But Luther himself adds one warning about embellishing the gospel: "The Christian Church, and the Holy Spirit Himself, abide by what Christ said and commanded: they may make more of it—that is, spell it out in length and breadth—but not make anything different of it. For Christ's words, 'I have yet many things to say to you,' mean that we drive home one point in manifold ways, yet always one and the same thing." [2] This is Luther's rubric: "Even though Christ is named, preached, and pictured in sundry ways, He is ever the same Christ." [3]

1. 21, 376, 11.
2. 21, 375, 38.
3. 45, 507, 22.

## Shepherd and Bishop

In Christ's portrait of Himself as the good shepherd Luther
sees an epitome of Christ's office as preacher. In the early days of
the Reformation, Luther turns often to the exposition of John 10,
conscious of tragic contrasts between the preaching of Christ and
the doctrine of the contemporary Church. In this passage he finds
Christ's own criterion for authentic Christian ministry, a parable
of who is, and who is not, a true pastor of Christ's flock. Those
who snatch Christians away from the uniqueness of Christ are
thieves or wolves; those who drive people to the gospel by
preaching the law, or who abandon their duty under pressure, are
merely porters or hirelings; but only those deserve to be called
true pastors who by their words and actions maintain unalloyed
the ministry of Christ, Who is the only true and good shepherd.[4]

Christ's own mission, we recall, was to direct men to Himself
by His preaching, so that accepting Him as the unique and perfect spokesman of God, they could cling to Him in His going to
the Father, and by His sacrifice escape the power of the tyrants.
Luther finds all the elements of his "circular motif" in this discourse. Christ is the door of the sheep—that is, the words of His
preaching are the only access to the knowledge of God's grace.[5]
The words of His preaching are words of consolation and forgiveness, for Christ the shepherd is called "good"—that is, comforting
and helping and tending the sheep, going before them, caring for
the weak, the sick, the scabby, binding the wounded, seeking the
lost, rejecting none, and finally, giving His life when the wolves
come, so that the sheep will not be torn and scattered.[6] To know
a gracious God, then, we must recognize the shepherd's voice.
"Sheep, of course, are extraordinarily silly and stupid animals—
if we want to say someone is stupid, we say, 'He's a sheep!'—
but they have this trait over all other animals, they soon learn to
heed their shepherd's voice." [7] "As soon as the sheep recognizes

4. E.g. 10/I/2, 243, 17ff.; 21, 323, 22f.; 498, 20ff.
5. 21, 502, 34 to 503, 3.
6. 10/I/2, 243, 18; 12, 534, 7ff.; 21, 322, 31.
7. 12, 531, 17; cf. 51, 277, 3.

its shepherd, as it does by instinct, it is quite unafraid, but runs up to him with complete trust and goes along before him in perfect reliance. Indeed, it has only to hear his voice for it to bleat and to run after him, not stopping until it reaches him. Theirs is a simple, natural affection and mutual love; they have only one heart and mind toward each other, so that if the lamb could speak and pour out its heart, it would have no desire but the shepherd, who in turn has no other care or concern but how he may find the precious pet that has strayed away from him." [8] Christ's sheep have a very sharp ear, Luther says, and hear their shepherd calling, "My lamb, My lamb." [9] And Christ's sheep are known by their shepherd, too, for Christ "looks at the sheep, not the wool": He looks not at their condition but at whether they are really sheep (that is, at their faith).[10]

The effect of the good shepherd's tending (and "what He does not tend is not kept") [11] is that the sheep are led forth into the luxuriant green pastures of God's Word, not into the desert and the foul, noxious waters of the law. In God's pleasure-ground the sheep go in and out. This is an image of our Christian liberty; for we are no longer penned in by anxiety under the law or by fear of wolves and thieves.[12] "The only true shepherd does not allow the sheep to struggle with the wolf (for if it came to that, they would immediately fall into its jaws)." Instead, He lays down His life for the sheep and thereby overthrows devil and death, proving Himself "a good, sweet, lifegiving shepherd, Who makes our conscience free." [13] For this shepherd, foretold so long ago by the prophets, is a shepherd far different from Moses. He is appointed shepherd so that He may break down the obstacles and make a pathway for the sheep in His cross and feed them by His Word.[14]

We may identify true pastors and true preaching, then, by

8. 36, 290, 14.
9. 37, 73, 23; 21, 503, 11.
10. 12, 539, 6; 48, 165: 214.
11. 12, 530, 8.
12. 21, 504, 24ff.; 51, 280, 33.
13. 21, 327, 31 (cf. 51, 275, 30); 36, 172, 2.
14. 51, 273, 39; 13, 313, 27; 341, 15.

whether they direct us to the right place—that is, to the shepherd Who lays down His life for the sheep.[15] External pomp and circumstance do not make a shepherd or a bishop: a bishop is not a bishop unless he points to Christ, "the shepherd and bishop of your souls." [16] Extending this idea, Luther calls Christ "our abbot and bishop," Whose words are worth more than all the cowls and pilgrimages of monasticism; for He is not a judge, but a true pope, a faithful guardian and true bishop of souls, a teacher and loyal pastor, Whom we must recognize, as sheep their own shepherd, by His voice saying, "Be unafraid." [17]

## Leader and Guide

"We are just like someone with vertigo, who, when he has to climb a high tower, or cross a bridge with deep water flowing under it, has to be blindfolded, and have a coat hung over his head, and be led and carried across, or else he falls from the tower and breaks his neck, or falls in the water and drowns. So we, too, if we are to be saved, must follow our leader—then we are safe. We must simply close our eyes and follow the guide, the divine Word, and say, 'I will let myself be swathed in wrappings, and have a cloak thrown over my head, and be led to the point where I believe and do not see; and there I will live and die.' We shall never make it by another means, even if we tear ourselves apart over it. Many fret to have it and yearn to be certain where our resting place and destination will be when we die, where we will be led; and many great men have gone mad because they could not discover where man goes when he leaves this life. This is the source of the proverb:

'I live, but do not know my span;
I die, but have no inkling when;
I pass beyond—but beyond what?
My cheer's astounding, is it not?'

15. 10/III, 173, 17ff.; 15, 533, 25ff.
16. 10/I/2, 246, 29; 10/III, 174, 18; 12, 388, 11; 46, 588, 2.
17. 46, 580, 4ff.; 47, 15, 1ff.; 21, 315, 26; 33, 83, 7; 41, 195, 36; 47, 100, 9; 45, 475, 31.

And it is true that a non-Christian can know absolutely nothing, but a Christian must adopt another attitude. He has a faithful leader for the crossing; and he follows this leader and guide, Christ, Who tells him what he should do." [18]

Luther cheerfully rewrites the proverb, as he expands this theme at great length in his exposition of "the way, the truth, and the life":

> I live, and well I know my span;
> I die, and know just how and when (namely,
>     every day and hour before the world!);
> I go beyond to where I know;
> Then what have I to grieve me so? [19]

Christ is the beginning, middle, and end of the way to God; there is no other road or way to travel. "Turn a deaf ear to all other ways and paths that claim to lead to that life, for all others are most certainly false ways and no ways at all, that lead through thickets and briars, over stumps and stones, yes, that bruise your feet, tear your nose and mouth, break your legs, and finally your neck." [20] There are spiritual, as well as physical, will-o'-the-wisps! [21] Those who try to make their own way to heaven by their works and piety have made themselves "a bridge and stairway of spider webs," but we have a bridge that is stronger than stone and iron. "There is no other way, no other safe, reliable, and certain highway, no other firm bridge or path, no other haven or crossing, than this Christ alone." [22] Despite all the obstacles strewn on our way—law, Satan, death, and hell—we burst through into life after Christ, our leader. [23] The papists, Turks, sects, and fanatics want to seek God without this path, ladder, and lantern; but Christ alone is the ladder by which we ascend to heaven. He must be the first, middle, and the last rung of the ladder. [24] He is the only door that opens into heaven—a narrow

18. *47, 34, 2.*
19. *45, 501, 23.*
20. *1, 275, 1; 45, 508, 3; 496, 2.*
21. *45, 496, 7–14.*
22. *45, 492, 34 to 493, 25; 506, 26.*
23. *13, 313, 29.*
24. *33, 82, 1; 43, 582, 20; 45, 504, 37.*

door—and we must be small to enter it. Those who are bedecked and laden with their own works can never get through it.[25] He wants our heart and our trust to rest wholly upon Him when we come to depart this life. And He promises to bear us safely across and bring us to the Father, if we but hold fast to Him.[26]

## Book and Letter

As we cling to Christ, we come to love and trust God, for we discover that Christ did all things at His Father's behest: "We discover that Christ is the true letter, the golden book, in which we read and learn how He kept the Father's will ever before Him . . . This is the true guidebook from which we learn the will of the eternal Father." [27]

We have seen already how Luther connects the image of a letter with the "sealing" of Christ by the Father.[28] As Christ is God's letter, so we are His letters. "Jesus Christ is the true writer: in His pen (that is, in His preaching office) He has not ink, but the Holy Spirit and His gifts, as we read in I Cor. 12. The ink is the sermon which He writes through the apostles, and which the Holy Spirit has written through us. Christ is the writer Who writes in our hearts, not in ink, but in the beautiful letters of the Holy Spirit which are faith and hope—they flow out as fiery and living letters . . . aglow with love." [29]

## Sun of Righteousness

The imagery of conflict between light and darkness is one of the most ancient motifs in biblical, as in nonbiblical, religion. Luther handles it with typical freshness and color. Christ, he says, is a quickening light that shines brilliantly forever and ever.[30] Luther regards the Neoplatonic handling of this theme as not so

25. *10/III*, 165, 17.
26. *45*, 502, 1.
27. *1*, 274, 41.
28. See above, p. 92.
29. *47*, 183, 24.
30. *46*, 566, 28.

much mistaken as beside the point. He insists he does not differ from Augustine's doctrine that even the natural light of reason has its source in Christ—of course it does, for Christ is God—but that is not the subject of the gospel. For the light of reason has been perverted by separation from its source; so another light, the light of grace, has shone into our darkness. This light is the human history of the man Christ, through which the divine light shines. Specifically, it is the preaching of Christ, by which we may know that Christ Himself is the light of men: outside is utter darkness.[31] (Luther comments on the circularity of this statement that simply because "darkness rules wherever He is not," He had to identify Himself as the light; He had to sing His own praise, "like the cuckoo who sings its own name.")[32] The "coming day" of Malachi's prophecy is the time of the gospel: "everything else is night and darkness, for Christ Himself is the sun."[33]

The world is full of horrible darkness, and outside this light there is not even the faintest gleam. Yet the world hates the light; it wants to shine well before other men, but it cannot stand the light of Christ, for its deeds are evil. It is a blind world that prefers hell to heaven.[34] Despite this darkness, the light continues to shine in the "dispensation of the gospel, the light of the present day that radiates from Christ, from the sun of righteousness, shining and enlightening the whole world."[35]

Christ's coming by the Word of the gospel is the dawn of Hosea's prophecy (Hos. 6:3), with its showers and spring rains.[36] "If the Holy Spirit is to glorify Christ, He must eclipse many other lights with His radiancy, just as when the dear sun rises in the sky all other fires, lights, and stars are eclipsed by its brightness."[37] The moon and the stars shine too; but they derive their light from the sun and reflect only a fraction of its light. Besides, even though they also shine, it is the sun alone that fash-

31. 10/I/1, 202, 2ff.; 46, 562, 8ff.; 10/I/1, 225, 15; 239, 7.
32. 33, 514, 26.
33. 13, 703, 3.
34. 33, 527, 27; 47, 108, 3ff.; 10/III, 167, 22; 21, 495, 30; 47, 111, 27.
35. 17/II, 236, 12; cf. 40/III, 615, 2.
36. 13, 28, 1.
37. 46, 66, 2; cf. 22, 242, 3.

ions the day.[38] Luther identifies these lesser lights with the testimony to the coming light of grace throughout the Old Testament
Scriptures, to the promises or the law or the prophets; [39] but now
"Christ has lit the brightest torch, which shines with unprecedented brilliance." [40] This sun has eclipsed them all; even though
they glistened in beauty, they now pale like a wax candle in the
daylight. One sun now streams into all hearts, bringing spring,
not winter: it brings beauty and joyfulness, health, liveliness, and
hilarity. The crucified Christ is the source of the gospel day: "He
creates this day with its light and splendor." [41] He is not only the
sun but the day itself; and His kingdom is a glorious overarching
vault where sheer grace and forgiveness shine, and our sin is a
mere spark against an all-illumining sea of light.[42]

## Brood Hen

"The sun of righteousness shall rise with healing in its wings."
These words of Malachi evoke a series of biblical associations for
Luther, notably Psalm 91 and Christ's lament over Jerusalem
(Matt. 23:37), and give rise to his most delightful and intimate
image of Christ's mediation—the picture of the brood hen shel-
tering her chicks beneath her wings. "Such is the kingdom of
Christ that He Himself is the mediator and protector, just as a
hen protects her chickens from the hawk. So let the man who
wishes to be safe from that wrath and judgment of God which
the law urges flee beneath the wings of Christ." [43] Luther says he
knows of no more beautiful passage of Scripture than Christ's picture of what He does for believers: "Look at the hen and her
chickens, and you will see Christ and yourself painted and depicted better than any painter could picture them!" [44] This
image applies to both parts of Christ's work of grace—His cloak-

38. *46*, 586, 31.
39. *33*, 520, 25; *46*, 562, 34ff.
40. *46*, 565, 36.
41. *33*, 445, 18; *9*, 669, 7; *13*, 635, 9ff.; *10/I/2*, 9, 17; *31/I*, 175, 31.
42. *33*, 449, 14; *29*, 572, 34.
43. *13*, 701, 22.
44. *10/I/1*, 280, 11ff.

ing us to cover our sin and shame, and His nourishing us with His strength, as a hen feeds her chickens and warms them with her own body. "I have grievously broken God's commandments, but I creep under the wings of this dear hen (my dear lord Christ), and believe that . . . He covers me with His innocence and gives me His righteousness." [45] There is no wrath beneath the wings of this brood hen: God has placed all His love on no one but the Son, so that only under the wings of the brood hen is there shelter from wrath: outside we should be snatched away by the marauding hawks. We must stay as close to Him as chicks to their mother hen.[46] For "the spirits of Satan are more subtle in robbing us of our souls than the hawks are in stealing chickens!" We must put our reliance nowhere else—not even upon the Fathers and their writings—but creep like chickens beneath our brood hen's wings. For "faith, if it is true faith, is such that it does not trust its possessor, or even faith itself, but clings to Christ and finds refuge under His righteousness. It lets His righteousness be its shield and protection, just as the little chicken never trusts its own life or efforts, but takes shelter under the body and wings of the hen." [47] Even our weak, imperfect life and works are pleasing to God under these wings. "Whoever believes in Him, and takes refuge under this brood hen, shall be saved. Under these wings alone there is salvation, and there is no salvation besides: he who will not stay here must perish. Christ is a noble hen, a fine brood hen. To the man who creeps beneath He promises salvation, eternal life, and forgiveness of sins—he will lack nothing." [48]

## Lamb of God

Christ's mediatorial role was consummated in His sacrifice for our sakes. Naturally, Luther makes free use of Old Testament sac-

45. *45*, 153, 33; *21*, 329, 28.
46. *46*, 775, 29; *47*, 102, 10; 198, 9; 99, 20.
47. *10/I/1*, 281, 4; *46*, 770, 20; *10/I/1*, 281, 11.
48. *21*, 505, 35; *33*, 522, 6.

rificial types in describing the atonement, and chief among them is the Johannine image of "the Lamb of God."

The paschal lamb of the old covenant was a type of Christ's innocence and spotlessness, a mime to point the people forward to the true Lamb of God.[49] Now, however, the paschal festival and its lamb have been abolished by Christ, and in its place He Himself has become our passover and our Easter Lamb. We observe our passover daily when we eat and sacrifice Christ, the Lamb of God—that is, believe that He was offered up for us.[50] For though He was innocent, a lamb without spot or blemish, His innocence was loaded down with the weight of all our sins, past, present, and future, and He bore them away. God ordained Him as the lamb to be sacrificed and roasted on the cross for the sins of the whole world.[51]

Not only the paschal rite but all the offerings of the old covenant have been abolished in the new. "We have one sacrament which fulfills them all—Christ, Who gave Himself on the cross. He is the bull calf, the ox, the goat, the cereal, the wine." [52] We may permissibly read the ordinances of the abrogated Mosaic cult as figures and allegories of Christ's eternal sacrifice. For example, when we read in Numbers 19 of the slaughter of the red heifer outside the camp, we may say, "Christ is the red heifer," and recall, as Hebrews 13 does, that like the guiltless heifer, Christ was condemned to suffering and death for the sins of others, not His own.[53]

## The Bait and the Hook

Luther's imagery in describing Christ's work of atonement borrows from some of the more startling patristic metaphors, particularly those that picture the devil's deception in the death of

49. *12, 292, 22; 46, 676, 39.*
50. *31/I, 396, 25; 35, 444, 13; 14, 663, 22.*
51. *40/I, 435, 13; 46, 677, 21.*
52. *25, 411, 12.*
53. *25, 469, 1ff.*

Christ. Perhaps because they are so startling, it is easy to gain the impression that Luther uses them far more often than he does. As a matter of fact, such images are rather few in number.

The best known of these is the grotesque figure, elaborated originally by Gregory of Nyssa,[54] of the bait and the hook. Luther presents it in this form: "The hook, which was the divinity of Christ, was hidden under the earthworm. The devil swallowed it with his jaws when Christ died and was buried; but it ripped his belly so that he could not hold it down but had to disgorge it. He ate his own death, and it is our great consolation: for as the devil could not hold Christ in death, neither can he hold us who trust in Christ." [55] "Christ died, and death swallowed the Son of God; but in so doing it swallowed a thorn and had to disgorge it—it was impossible that death should hold Him. For this person is God; and since both God and man, in one individual person, entered the belly of death and the devil, death took a bait that ripped his belly open." Christ's title is "the person Whom death could not devour." [56] As we saw above, Luther follows Augustine in the notion that Christ's innocence convicted the devil of injustice in condemning Him: "The law burnt its fingers, death soiled itself, and devil, death, and sin all overreached themselves and became guilty." [57] "He wants to devour Me, and I shall submit to him. But he will find his belly torn asunder by it, for he has no rights over Me—I owe him nothing! . . . He will have to strain at this bait until he chokes on it." [58]

In another place Luther conflates this image with the biblical metaphor of the gnat and the camel (Matt. 23:24): "I want to attach you to Me and Me to you, and then you can find comfort and reliance in Me. In this way both great and small, rich and poor, will be linked and more than equal to the great monster Behemoth. If he tries to swallow and devour you like a little gnat, I will be a great camel in his throat and rip out of his belly until he

54. Gregory of Nyssa, *Or. cat.* 22–24 (MPG XLV, 59).
55. 46, 556, 34.
56. 47, 80, 14; 45, 585, 3.
57. 44, 697, 24.
58. 45, 635, 14.

bursts and must return you whole, like it or not." [59] Another variation on the same theme is this: "Even if the devil swallows and devours us, his belly will burst with his everlasting mockery and mischief, and disgorge us alive, for he will certainly have to leave undevoured the lord Who dwells in us." [60]

## Serpent

Even though this sort of preaching is full of color, Luther actually finds it less congenial than biblical imagery. And on the theme of atonement the biblical image of the bronze serpent receives more attention from Luther than the extrabiblical image of the bait and the hook. "Christ is our serpent of salvation, symbolized for us by that earlier bronze serpent. For after Adam and Eve disobeyed, we, too, were stung by the poisonous serpent in paradise . . . he injected his poison for which there is no cure, and Adam died. By nature we are mortal and must die—there is no help or remedy . . . Jesus Christ, God's Son born of a virgin, became like us in our condemnation, and hung on the cross like a poisonous, evil and hurtful worm—yes, like the serpent which deceived us in paradise, the devil." [61] The pole is the cross; the bronze serpent, Christ; the fiery serpents, sin, death, an evil conscience, and Satan.[62] Christ has the form and appearance of a sinner, but He has become my salvation. His death is my life, since He atones for my sin and removes the Father's wrath from me. "The living, fiery serpent is in me, for I am a sinner, but He never committed a sin." [63] He is a healing serpent, without venom: "He has only the form of a serpent, and in this guise possesses a power greater than any ointment, for He heals and saves mankind from sin, death, and condemnation." [64]

Moses' action in the wilderness, then, has a threefold signifi-

59. *46*, 106, 15.
60. *45*, 607, 13.
61. *47*, 66, 33 to 68, 7.
62. *25*, 477, 3.
63. *10/I/2*, 305, 39.
64. *25*, 477, 27; *47*, 69, 5.

cance for Luther. First, "it symbolizes that God would allow His Son to come down from heaven and be nailed to the cross, where He hangs like a serpent or a worm, an object of scorn and contumely (as Christ Himself laments in Psalm 22). But he who believes in this crucified Christ will not be lost and perish but have everlasting life, just as those who looked at the bronze serpent in the wilderness did not die, but were preserved." [65] Secondly, Luther undertakes a short excursus about the retention of Moses' serpent in the ark, and how the Jews were wrong to imagine that it still possessed its efficacy. It was not the metal snake that cured them but the Word associated with it in the wilderness. But now the Word tells us that we must not only look at our serpent but must believe in Him.[66] Lastly, this looking seemed such a useless, paltry thing in the wilderness—"even a cow could look at a serpent!" [67]—and so, too, faith seems to amount to nothing. "But whoever wishes to gain unfailing help and salvation against sin and eternal death must head and follow this amazing counsel of God." For "there is no cure outside Christ the lord, Who in the form of a cursed and vile worm would redeem and eternally save men from death, sin, and the devil's power." [68]

## Death's Poison: The Medicine of Immortality

Luther combines the imagery of the bait and the serpent into a notion of what, today, we should call antivenene. Christ is "a little pill the devil will gleefully devour, but which will create such a rumbling in his belly and in the world! . . . He will be death's venom." [69] Christ addresses death in Hosea 13:14: "I, Christ, will labor unceasingly through My Resurrection to slay you. I will be your plague, death, and your disease, hell!" He is the fatal illness which carries off death and our old Adam.[70]

65. *47*, 67, 16.
66. *47*, 73, 32ff.; cf. 20, 617, 9.
67. *47*, 75, 1.
68. *21*, 551, 8; *47*, 71, 22.
69. *47*, 80, 21 and 37.
70. *13*, 63, 21 and n.; 31/II, 139, 27; 40/I, 273, 24.

It was a wonderful strife
When death and life embattled:
The victory belongs to life,
Death's power has it toppled.
Holy Writ predicted this—
Death by death devoured is:
Death has become derision!
        Hallelujah.[71]

In this paradoxical manner Christ becomes our remedy. "God so loved the world that He gave us a potent plaster, remedy, and potion against sin, death, devil, and hell, so that the person who applies it over his heart will not perish." [72] It is unthinkable but true that the Spirit of life flows from the death of Christ. "For whoever would have hoped for a life-giving Spirit from dead and buried flesh?" [73]

Christ is not only remedy but physician. "If you have sin, He has righteousness; if you have an oppressed or wounded conscience, He is its health, an almighty physician Who can surely cure you. Even if you are sick and at the point of death, He will restore you to health and life." [74] His kingdom is a hospital for curing sins. He is our good and faithful physician, the only physician for that most dreadful disease, our evil inclinations.[75] Luther describes the forty days after the Resurrection as a period when Christ "doctored" the disciples with all sorts of strengthening medicines, until He gave them "the proper strong drink, the Holy Spirit." [76]

In particular, Christ is a "medicine of immortality." The ancient idea of the φάρμακον ἀθανασίας [77] was historically applied to the Eucharist. Luther takes over the motif but gives it no eucharistic content. Its physical realism is in no way diminished,

---

71. 35, 444, 5.
72. 47, 84, 10.
73. 14, 634, 21.
74. 33, 242, 3.
75. 17/I, 463, 3; 32, 491, 1; 40/II, 290, 25.
76. 49, 157, 21.
77. Ignatius of Antioch, *Ephesians* XX, 2 (MPG V, 661).

but the application is exclusively to the eating which is faith.[78]
Christ calls Himself the bread of life: "This bread is to be a pre-
servative against death, just as if a physician or apothecary were
to say to a sick man, 'I will give you some *Aquavitae*, a potion or
purgative that will make you immune from death.'" This is no ordinary, natural bread. "Here we have the bread of life from heav-
en—he who eats of this will never die." [79]

Luther embellishes the life-giving nourishment of this heavenly
food with a series of amusing associations. "God has set His seal
on the Son, Who is man. He is the food, but also the grain mer-
chant, the baker, the waiter, and the storehouse." [80] With the
words, "which the Son of Man will give you," Christ "tears all our
hearts and eyes away from all bakeries and granaries, from all
cellars, shops, fields, and purses, yes, from any labor at all, and
points them to Himself. He says He is an excellent baker, and
will give us what neither field nor purse can procure." Christ
wants to be "the farmer, the victualler, the baker, the brewer, the
cook, the butler, the waiter, the food, the bread, the dish, and the
plate that gives us imperishable food." [81] But our sole concern
must be to eat and drink—that is, to believe, for Christ is drink
and food for our souls when He is preached to us in the gospel.[82]

## One Cake

Luther has inherited from German idiom yet another culinary
term, "one cake" (*ein Kuchen*). It means "one entity": "to bake
together into one cake" means to unite disparate elements into a
single thing. Luther uses the expression to describe each link in
the chain of indwelling, unity, and coinherence. Christ and the
Father are "one cake" in their words and actions toward us. Divinity and humanity are "one cake" in Christ.[83] Christ and His
Christians have been made "one cake" in order that good fruits

78. 17/II, 433, 28; 33, 182, 25.
79. 33, 57, 40 (cf. 10/I/2, 432, 9); 33, 175, 31.
80. 33, 17, 10.
81. 33, 11, 26; 15, 32; 24, 4.
82. 25, 415, 26; 33, 16, 18.
83. 45, 521, 21; 33, 232, 19.

may result (in this instance an illustration of the abiding of the branches in the true vine).[84] For we are being transformed from glory to glory as Christ's own glory is reflected in our hearts: we are being changed into "one cake" with Him.[85] All those who preach the Word of the gospel and are joined to Christ in His holy supper are all "one cake" as we are united with Him as His body and His members. This oneness is not just concord—even the world knows what concord is—but Christ prays that "they may be one" with Himself and the Father—that is, "one body, one thing, one cake" with the almighty God Himself.[86] In short, "When you see Me risen from the grave and death, and ascending up into heaven to the Father, and you preach this concerning Me, then you will learn and discover, through the Holy Spirit and your own experience, that I am in the Father and the Father in Me, and moreover I in you. Thus we shall be 'one cake' with each other." [87]

*Bridegroom*

The closest biblical parallel to the expression "one cake" is "one flesh"; and Luther finds St. Paul's mystery of the Church as the bride of Christ immensely congenial. The theme of the sharing of all things between Christ and His Christians, so that what we may say of the one is true of the other, is central to Luther's concerns, as we have repeatedly seen; and the image of Christ the bridegroom is the perfect expression of this theme.

"The true Christian Church is one body with Christ through faith. She is His bride, His very own possession; He is her bridegroom and her head. It is the bridegroom's desire that the bride should partake by faith of all His goods—for example, His eternal righteousness, holiness, and bliss—and so that she may be glorious and great before God, He has adorned and beautified her with heavenly wisdom and strength." [88] A bride possesses every-

84. *45*, 667, 32 (cf. *28*, 184, 15).
85. *10/III*, 425, 21.
86. *12*, 486, 1 (II); *45*, 525, 29; *Tr*, 3, 671: 3868; *46*, 98, 7; *28*, 184, 13.
87. *45*, 586, 23.
88. *46*, 712, 31.

thing her bridegroom has, even his own body.[89] The Baptist's description of Christ as bridegroom is especially fitting, "because a groom and a bride have everything in common. The husband confides all his secrets to his wife; she has become part of his body, and she bears the keys at her side. In just this way Christ is the bridegroom, and flesh of our flesh." [90]

This is a union of great joy and assurance, since as bride and wife of the lord of all, Christendom is His empress in heaven and on earth, sitting exalted above all sin, death, and hell.[91] The bride cannot rest or be satisfied until she has only her beloved; and Christ, too, will have His bride only, and none beside. Yet it is a very unequal union. The bride is an impure bride, a dirty, old, withered hag; the groom is an exceedingly beauteous youth, the eternal wisdom, light, and truth. But because this is a marriage and a union, the bride and the groom become one flesh, cleave to each other, and embrace. We bring nothing but our sorrows and misfortunes, our sins and our death; He gives us Himself, whole and entire, with all His wisdom, love, righteousness, and life. "The bride says, 'I am yours, you must have me.' So Christ has to take all my misfortune upon Himself, and my sins become eternal righteousness, my death eternal life, my hell heaven. For sin and righteousness, hell and heaven, cannot exist together, and since we have come together, the one must consume and obliterate the other so that we may be joined as one. But His righteousness is immeasurably stronger than my sins, and His life than my death (for He is life itself, and the source of life), and therefore my death is swallowed up in His life, my sins in His righteousness, my condemnation in His salvation." [92] This is the washing and adorning of His bride that Christ has accomplished by His death: He Himself is the holy wedding-garment we put on in baptism, our laver of regeneration.[93]

Christ is the only bridegroom permitted to the Church. "This

89. *12*, 307, 23.
90. *47*, 164, 24; cf. *7*, 55, 24.
91. *22*, 335, 19ff.
92. *10*/III, 416, 14 to 418, 28.
93. *10*/III, 419, 11; *12*, 287, 24; *40*/I, 541, 33.

bridegroom Christ must be alone with his bride in His private chamber—even the family and the household must all be hustled away." [94] Everything is commendable and good in its place, but to put a shoe on your head is stupidity. God created the eye as a beautiful and valuable member, but if it were on the kneecap it would be terrifying. No matter how fine the fabric, it is senseless to try and make a coat out of a sleeve. If the maid tries to reform the mistress, or the pupil to teach the schoolmaster, it would be intolerable. If a woman is ever so pretty and a whore, she is not fitted for marriage. "John the Baptist can say, 'I am the greatest of those born of woman, but I am not entitled to sleep with the bride.' That is, no one else can teach the Church how it should be saved." [95] There is no room for a second bridegroom: nothing has any place here but the bride alone with Christ in the nuptial chamber.[96] But the pope and the tyrants and the heretics would flirt and dally with the Church. Some rape her; some indulge in amorous dalliance, trying to seduce her into harlotry; some (the worst of all) delude her by impersonating the bridegroom's voice and creeping into the bridal bed.[97] "Cling to the Word of God. Ignore every other word, whether it is without Christ, in the name of Christ, or against Christ, or however else it comes. No one must sleep with the bride or know her or make her pregnant but the one lord Christ alone—if He does not teach or preach or make souls pregnant, all is lost." [98] But where the Word is received and held firm, the result is "joy, the voice of the bridegroom and the bride." [99]

*Friend, Guest, and Parent*

Luther's language expressing the intimacy of the Christian's relationship to Christ overflows with warmth and passion. It is a re-

94. *25,* 18, 4; *40/*I, 241, 12.
95. *47,* 152, 13 to 153, 35; 154, 6.
96. *36,* 278, 24 and 35.
97. *47,* 164, 41.
98. *47,* 167, 20.
99. *40/*II, 117, 24.

lationship of deep friendship. When we know Christ as the Gospels portray Him, we yearn for Him as the best friend our hearts could choose, and then love follows.[1] Christ says He is not our judge, hangman, or jailer, but our loving brother and good friend.[2] He not only proves Himself the friend above all friends, but He made the Father our friend too. He reveals Himself as pure love and friendship, so that we may be comforted.[3] This is not a friendship such as the world knows: "In the world 'friendship' means something different from His. To call someone a friend means that you seek something for yourself, and expect to receive some benefit from him, not that he is unable to serve, give, help, or benefit you. But here Christ calls those His friends who never did Him any good, indeed never knew Him, but are poor, wretched sinners, yes, God's enemies, whose sins and death He takes on His own shoulders."[4] With such a friend, what have I to fear from the world's hostility? If Christ is my friend, let the devil and the world—if they will not smile!—rant and rage to their heart's content: I have all I want.[5]

Again, Christ comes to us as our guest. Because He promises that His Father will love us and that He will make His abode with us, "we are sure that Christ will remain our guest and we His inn and dwelling . . . They shall not rob us of this guest, even if they deprive us of life and limb and everything we have."[6] This means that "God and man will cleave together as friends, for the Holy Spirit Himself will prepare man's heart and consecrate it as a holy house and dwelling, a temple and tabernacle of God. What a glorious, noble, loving and exalted guest and lodger and house companion man receives there—God the Father and the Son!"[7]

More intimately still, Christ deals with us as a parent with a child. He has a true, fatherly, divine heart full of ineffable and

1. 10/III, 164, 14.
2. 33, 85, 16.
3. 45, 691, 29; 22, 430, 13.
4. 45, 697, 15.
5. 45, 605, 6; 21, 291, 13; 472, 29.
6. 45, 607, 7.
7. 21, 457, 16.

boundless love toward us, and He shows it by the gentleness with which He adapts His speech to us, as a father with his children, even taking delight in our childish patter and our faltering attempts to learn.[8] Scripture richly describes the maternal mercy of Christ, in which He cherishes and bears us just as a mother cherishes her tiny child and caresses it.[9] "A mother's heart and love cannot forget her children—it is against nature. She would go through fire for her children. See how much labor women expend on making food, giving milk, keeping watch over a child. God compares Himself to that passion. 'I will not desert you, for I am the womb that bore you, and I cannot let you go!'"[10] Christ wants us to stay as close to Him as children cling to their parents. "Even if you are feeble and soil yourself like an infant or an invalid, He will not summarily cast you away, but He will always clean you and improve you . . . Ask for what you want unconcernedly, as a child with its father, who is pleased with everything the child does, so long as it comes to him."[11]

Within the Church, Christ rules as the father in a household or a prince in his realm.[12] "An emperor cannot allow another governor beside himself in his territory. The judge from Kemburg has no jurisdiction here in Wittenberg. Nor can any man rule in my household unless I give him the authority; but if someone tries to play householder here and does what he likes, we should judge that his scheme will collapse, because he has not received that authority. If this is the case in home, city, and realm, how much more in the Church?"[13] Christ desires to be master in His house, prince in His castle, God in His Church. For this house of God is not of wood or stone, fashioned by the hands of men, but a new creation of God Himself: a people that loves Christ and keeps His Word.[14]

8. *21*, 456, 36; *45*, 631, 6; *46*, 100, 17.
9. *13*, 508, 16.
10. *31*/II, 405, 1.
11. *47*, 99, 20; *45*, 679, 16.
12. *47*, 779, 14.
13. *47*, 151, 7.
14. *21*, 460, 12 and 35.

*Rock and Cornerstone*

God's new creation is built upon the foundation of Christ.[15] He is the living stone which bears up the whole edifice, a choice and exceedingly precious stone in God's sight. God, the true builder, chose Him for the cornerstone of the foundation on which all Christendom stands. "Christ is called the rock because all of us who are Christians rest upon Him. He alone is the firm foundation on which we can depend." [16] The gospel builds faith and confidence only on this rock, and warns us not to let go of Christ in our hearts as the only sure foundation, the cornerstone of our salvation and bliss. For if Christ were not our bulwark, we could not stand for a moment.[17]

But God's cornerstone was rejected by men, and Christ became a rock against which the greatest and best of men stumble and fall. "Christ is set as savior. He cannot yield or change. But the arrogant are willful and stubborn, and will not abandon their pride, so they run headlong at Christ, and one or the other has to break and fall. But Christ must stand—He cannot fall. He is rock, not sand, and He is not merely tossed down or carelessly laid, but most firmly founded against all assault." [18] When kings and nations and the whole world set themselves against Him, they are mere dust, but Christ is a huge mountain.[19] The rejected cornerstone alone can bring us salvation and make us to stand. He alone is the temple where God will be found.[20]

*Treasure and Consolation*

Christ is God's greatest gift and treasure, our only savior and the consolation of the world.[21] In heaven above we have a treasure which far outweighs everything in our life in this world—one,

15. *10*/III, 167, 4; *31*/I, 214, 1; *46*, 65, 37; 787, 24.
16. *12*, 305, 18; 306, 4; *31*/I, 172, 20; *13*, 583, 1 (cf. *12*, 310, 23ff.).
17. *17*/II, 74, 3; *32*, 534, 2; *40*/II, 513, 23.
18. *10*/I/1, 396, 11; *31*/II, 164, 26.
19. *40*/II, 208, 33.
20. *31*/I, 174, 32; *46*, 762, 7.
21. *10*/III, 157, 31; *47*, 93, 16; *46*, 588, 3.

indeed, Who holds all this world in the hollow of His hand.[22] What, then, can Satan do to harm us if we have Him as our own possession?[23] We must accept Him as our comfort, reliance, trust, and our all.[24] When we have the conviction in our hearts that He is our treasure and savior, our life and our consolation, then our hearts rejoice, and love to Him and to God will surely follow.[25] We even find Christ the judge to be our consolation, for He will judge as a merciful savior and deliverer.[26] But to rely on one's own piety is to forbid Christ to be the only consolation.[27] Faith takes hold of nothing but Christ, its jewel.[28]

Luther's preaching abounds in expressions of deeply moved emotion at the freedom of conscience and blessed hope that is ours in Christ. "May I not call my Lord Jesus Christ . . . my heart's crown, my heart's joy, my ruby?"[29] Christ preached by the Word is "an inestimable and most joyful treasure."[30] To seek Him is "to seek help, grace, life, consolation, bliss, and deliverance from death, sin, devil, and hell."[31] And to find Him is to possess all; "for He is sheer righteousness, life, and everlasting bliss, and the lord over death. Christ is without spot or blemish. He is eternal life, joy, righteousness, and blessedness—a treasure that is all mine in Christ, for He is all, without flaw, and lacking nothing."[32] Christ is the greatest joy man's heart can possess.[33]

### Fountainhead

Finally, Christ is the eternal spring, source, and fountainhead of all that we can need or desire, and infinitely more than we can

22. 29, 573, 22.
23. 12, 559, 8.
24. 45, 480, 9.
25. 22, 427, 1; 45, 595, 22.
26. 33, 540, 17; 541, 1.
27. 33, 560, 32.
28. 40/I, 167, 24.
29. 18, 141, 12.
30. 13, 525, 6.
31. 33, 574, 6.
32. 33, 163, 36.
33. 12, 520, 31; 21, 293, 11.

desire.[34] He is the inexhaustible fountain of living waters.[35] He is unique. He is the all-sufficient one. With this image Luther is at the heart of his faith and the kernel and marrow of all his preaching and doctrine of Christ.

"If we would glory, then we must glory in this, that we receive from the fullness of the Lord Christ, that by Him we are enlightened, receive forgiveness of sins, and become God's children. For this is the heart of the matter: whoever wishes to be safe from the devil's power—to escape sin and death—must draw from this fountain, Christ, from Whom all salvation and bliss flow. This fountain is inexhaustible; it is full of grace and truth before God; it never runs dry, if we draw from it as much as we will. Even if we all keep drawing from it without pause, it cannot be exhausted, but remains an endless spring of all grace and truth, an unfathomable fountain and eternal spring. The more we draw from it, the more richly it gives—a water, St. John says, that springs up to eternal life. The precious sun is not dimmed or darkened because it gives so much light; yes, it supplies the whole world with its shining, brilliant beams, yet it retains its light quite whole. It loses nothing, it is a measureless light that could light ten more worlds. Or again, you could kindle a hundred thousand lamps from one lamp, and yet that one lamp, which ignited and kindled so many other lamps or tapers, would not lose any of its own brilliance. A learned man, too, can make a thousand others learned without sacrificing any of his own skill—indeed, the more he shares, the more he has. So Christ our lord, to Whom we must flee and from Whom we must ask for everything, is an endless well and fountainhead of all grace, truth, righteousness, wisdom and life, without measure, end, or limit." [36]

34. 21, 483, 27; 33, 81, 23; 45, 525, 19.
35. 10/I/2, 430, 36; 13, 87, 8.
36. 46, 652, 29.

# Epilogue

At the outset the reader was forewarned against expecting from
Luther a closely knit, dogmatic exposition of the doctrine of
Christ. He simply does not offer one. If we had attempted to
structure the materials in this book by asking the questions of
classical Christology and scouring Luther for the answers, the result would have been indeed "glaring omissions or tantalizing
loose ends"—or worse, misrepresentation of the Reformer's concern by finding, as orthodoxy often did, answers where no answer
was intended. Here, come what may, my purpose has been to
allow Luther's own range of concerns to dictate both the themes
and the limits of the inquiry. In the Introduction I sketched some
of my extrinsic reasons for adopting this inductive approach;
here, in conclusion, let me suggest that there are essential and intrinsic reasons why this method is appropriate to Luther's doctrine of Christ. For Luther's own choice of an unsystematic approach is not arbitrary or whimsical. Rather, it is part and parcel of his conception of the theological task. From it we may
learn much that is salutary if the Church is to be faithful in its
proclamation of Christ.

Luther's task was undertaken at a time when the Church's will
to faithfulness in its preaching was at low ebb, when it had sub-
stituted for its commission a formidable array of alternative sum-
monses: to pious occasions for self-righteousness, to crusading
zeal against the infidel foes of Christendom, to submissive venera-
tion of the spiritual élite, to ecclesiastically sanctioned commuta-
tions of guilt, to the imposing doctrinal disquisitions of the
schools, and to maudlin inspirational sentiment or urbane moral-
ism. In the face of all this Luther insisted that the Church could

be true to its commission in only one way: the Church's faithfulness consisted in preaching the gospel of Christ. The essence of Luther's reforming task was not so much that he asserted this but that he practiced it. Anything other than the gospel of Christ, however worthy in itself, was a lie in the mouth of the Church, since it was sent to preach the Word of God, and that Word was the gospel.

Luther early discovered that the Church could perpetrate this lie not only by preaching false gospels but by substituting theology for the gospel. It could be faithless not only by changing the content but also by changing the modality of its commission. He recognized with extraordinary clarity that while the gospel confers meaning upon theology, theology does not constitute the meaning of the gospel. Doctrine is not some higher or more articulate form of what is roughcast in the rudiments of the gospel, as if grasping the gospel waited upon its translation into an intelligible system. Rather, the *viva vox evangelii* is the norm of the Church's doctrine, of its faithfulness, and of its authority. (Indeed, in Luther's vocabulary "theology" becomes a synonym for "the language of faith" rather than "the language of doctrine.")

It is in this sense that I have questioned whether Luther "has a Christology" at all. The mode of his preaching Christ is determined by the character of God's living voice in the gospel. First, that living voice addresses man not in a speculative or abstract way but in a specific and concrete way. In securing conviction it relies not upon analysis and argument but upon its graphic and dramatic power of portrayal. Its content is a history—the life of Jesus of Nazareth. This history is not related in a detached chronicle of events. It is couched in a rhetoric which discloses the identity both of the speaker and of the hearer. It is a rhetoric of promise, in which God identifies Himself as the God Who in the history of Jesus has taken away the middle wall of alienation and will be gracious to His people, and in which man is identified as the one for whom this mercy and this liberation were achieved.

We have already seen how strikingly Luther underlines these characteristics in his account of Christ the Preacher, Whose authority and identity were disclosed both by the message and the mode of His preaching. Luther is equally convinced that the preacher in the Church must indicate the source of his own authority and identity, as one sent by Christ, by conforming both the content and character of his discourse to the gospel. He, too, must faithfully portray the man Christ as the unique and sufficient revelation of the Father, and in such a way that the *pro nobis* of this history is always heard. Only then does the living Word evoke within its hearer a recognition that what it describes is his own identity and destiny, and the voice of the gospel grafted in his consciousness becomes the language of faith.

Save for purposes of abstract analysis, form and substance are no more separable here than they are in the ministry of Christ. "God does not trifle with empty names." If in any measure we have succeeded in our object—"to learn Christ aright" by Luther's precept and example—let us heed his precept in this respect also, and be confident that to grasp the doctrine of Christ, God and man, is not to have arduously attained the key to some deep and recondite theorem but to name, preach, and picture Christ with hope and joy.

# Bibliography

## BIBLIOGRAPHICAL WORKS

Aland, Kurt, *Hilfsbuch zum Lutherstudium*, 2. Aufl., Gütersloh, 1957.
Commission Internationale d'Histoire Ecclésiastique Comparée au sein du Comité Internationale des Sciences Historiques, *Bibliographie de la Réforme 1450–1648: Ouvrages Parus de 1940 à 1955: Allemagne-Pays Bas*, 2ième edition Leiden, 1961; *Belgique-Norvège-Danemark-Irlande-États-Unis d'Amerique*, Leiden, 1960; *Italie-Espagne-Portugal*, Leiden, 1961.

## LUTHER'S WORKS

*D. Martin Luthers Werke, Kritische Gesamtausgabe*, Weimar, 1883–     .
*Dr. Martin Luthers sämmtliche Schriften*, herausgegeben von Joh. Georg Walch, St. Louis, 1880–1910.
*Dr. Martin Luthers sämmtliche Werke*, Erlangen, 1826–57.
*Luther's Works, American Edition*, ed. Jaroslav J. Pelikan and Helmut T. Lehmann, St. Louis and Philadelphia, 1955ff.
*D. Martin Luthers Evangelien-Auslegung*, herausgegeben von Erwin Mülhaupt, 5 vols. Göttingen, 1951–54.
*Luther's Works, Standard Edition*, ed. John Nicholas Lenker, Minneapolis, 1903ff.

## OTHER PRIMARY SOURCES

Anselm, *Cur Deus homo*, in Vol. 2 of *S. Anselmi opera omnia*, ed. F. S. Schmitt, 6 vols. Edinburgh, 1946–61.
Aristotle, *Nichomachean Ethics*, in *The Ethics of Aristotle*, ed. John Burnet, London, 1900.
Athanasius, *Oratio de incarnatio Verbi*, in MPG XXV, 95–198.
Augustine, *Contra Faustum*, in MPL XLII.
———— *De civitate Dei*, in MPL XLI.
———— *De doctrina christiana*, in MPL XXXIV.
———— *De libero arbitrio*, in MPL XXXII.

———— *De trinitate,* in MPL XLII.
———— *Enarrationes in Psalmos,* in MPL XXXVI.
———— *In Iohannis evangelium tractatus,* in MPL XXXV.
———— *Sermones,* in MPL XXXVIII and XXXIX.
Bernard of Clairvaux, *Sermones in cantici canticorum* in Vol. 1/2 of *S. Bernardi opera omnia,* ed. Joannes Mabillon, 2 vols. in 4, Paris, 1839, 2665ff.
Bonaventura, *Opera theologica selecta: Commentaria in IV libros Sententiarum,* 4 vols. Florence, 1941.
Bucer, Martin, *In sacra qvatvor evangelia, Enarrationes perpetvae,* Basel, 1536.
Calvin, John, *Institutes of the Christian Religion,* ed. John T. McNeil, trans. Ford Lewis Battles, Library of Christian Classics 20 and 21, London, 1961.
———— *Commentary on the Gospel according to St. John,* trans. T. H. L. Parker, chaps. 1–10, Edinburgh, 1959; chaps. 11–21 and 1 John, Edinburgh, 1961.
Cassiodorus, *Historia tripartita,* in MPL LXIX.
Eusebius of Caesarea, *Historia ecclesiastica,* in MPG XX, 45–906.
Gerhard, Johann, *Loci theologici,* Jena, 1610–22.
Gregory Nazianzus, *Epistolae,* in MPG XXXVII, 21–388.
Gregory of Nyssa, *Oratio catechetica magna,* in MPG XLV, 9–116.
Hollaz, David, *Examen theologicum acroamaticum,* Rostock and Leipzig, 1707.
Ignatius of Antioch, *Epistolae,* in MPG V, 643–728.
Irenaeus, *Adversus haereses,* in MPG VII/1, 437–1224.
Jacobus de Voragine, *Legenda aurea,* in Granger Ryan and Helmut Ripperger, trans., *The Golden Legend of Jacobus de Voragine,* New York, 1941.
John of Damascus, *De fide orthodoxa,* in MPG XCIV, 790–1228.
Leontius of Byzantium, *Contra Nestorianos et Eutychianos,* in MPG LXXXVI, 1267–1396.
Origen, *De principiis,* in MPG XI, 111–414.
Osiander, Andreas, *An filius dei incarnandus, si peccatum non introivisset in mundum. Item de imagine dei, quid sit,* Monteregio, 1550.
———— *Von dem einigen Mittler Jhesu Christo und Rechtfertigung des Glaubens,* Königsberg, 1551.
Peter Lombard, *Libri quatuor sententiarum,* 2d. ed., 2 vols. Quaracchi, 1916.
Quenstedt, Johann Andreas, *Theologia didactico-polemica sive Systema theologicum,* Wittenberg, 1685–91.
Schwartz, Eduard, ed., *Acta conciliorum oecumenicorum,* 4 vols. in 21, Berlin and Leipzig, 1914ff.
Thomas Aquinas, *Summa theologiae,* in *Sancti Thomae opera omnia,* 25 vols. reprinted New York, 1948–50.
———— *Summa contra Gentiles,* trans. A. C. Pegis, 5 vols. New York, 1955.

Thomas Aquinas, *Catena aurea in Joannis evangelium,* in Vol. 12 of *Sancti Thomae opera omnia,* 25 vols. reprinted New York, 1948–50.

Usingen, Bartholomaeus Arnoldi von, *Libellus F. Bartholomei de usingen augustiniani In quo respondet confutationi fratris Egidii mechlerii monachi franciscani sed exiticii larvati et coniugati. Nitentis tueri errores et perfidiam Culsameri. qui illi clitellas suas archabicas imposuit cum ipse amplius possit nihil quia sub sarcina fatescens defecit. Contra Lutheranos,* Erfurt, 1524.

### SECONDARY WORKS

Althaus, Paul, *Die Theologie Martin Luthers,* Gütersloh, 1962.

Atkinson, James, "Luthers Einschätzung des Johannesevangeliums," in Vilmos Vajta, ed., *Lutherforschung Heute* (Berlin, 1958), 49–56.

Aulén, Gustaf, *Christus Victor: An Historical Study of the Three Main Types of the Idea of the Atonement,* trans. A. Gabriel Hebert, New York, 1961.

———— *Eucharist and Sacrifice,* Philadelphia, 1958.

Barth, Karl, *Church Dogmatics,* ed. Geoffrey Bromiley and Thomas F. Torrance, 4 vols. in 12, Edinburgh, 1936ff.

Bizer, Ernst, *Fides ex auditu: Eine Untersuchung über die Entdeckung der Gerechtigkeit Gottes durch Martin Luther,* 2., erweiterte Aufl., Neukirchen, 1961.

———— "Glaube und Demut in Luthers Vorlesung über den Römerbrief," in Vilmos Vajta, ed., *Luther and Melanchthon* (Philadelphia, 1961), 63–72.

Bonhoeffer, Dietrich, "Christologie," in Vol. 3 of his *Gesammelte Schriften,* ed. Eberhard Bethge, 4 vols. München, 1958–61.

Bornkamm, Heinrich, *Luther und das Alte Testament,* Tübingen, 1948.

———— *Luther's World of Thought,* St. Louis, 1958.

———— "Justitia Dei in der Scholastik und bei Luther," *ARG, 39* (1942), 30–62.

———— "Zur Frage der Iustitia Dei beim jungen Luther," *ARG, 52* (1961), 16–29; 53 (1962), 1–60.

Boismard, M.-E., "Constitué Fils de Dieu," *Revue Biblique, 60* (1953), 5–17.

Brilioth, Yngve, *Eucharistic Faith and Practice, Evangelical and Catholic,* reprinted London, 1956.

Brunner, Emil, *The Christian Doctrine of Creation and Redemption,* Philadelphia, 1952.

Brunner, Peter, "Luther and the World of the Twentieth Century," in *Martin Luther Lectures,* Vol. 5: *Luther in the 20th Century* (Decorah, Iowa, 1961), 3–79.

Bultmann, Rudolf, *Theology of the New Testament,* 2 vols. New York, 1951–55.

———— *Das Evangelium des Johannes (Meyers Kommentar über das Neue Testament),* 2. Aufl., Göttingen, 1950.

Carlson, Edgar M., *The Reinterpretation of Luther*, Philadelphia, 1948.

Cranz, F. Edward, *An Essay on the Development of Luther's Thought on Justice, Law, and Society*, Harvard Theological Studies, *19*, Cambridge, Mass., 1959.

Crouse, Robert D., "The Augustinian Background of St. Anselm's Concept *Justitia*," *Canadian Journal of Theology*, 4, No. 2 (1958), 111–119.

Cullmann, Oscar, *The Christology of the New Testament*, Philadelphia, 1959.

Diem, Harald, *Luthers Lehre von den zwei Reichen*, München, 1938.

Dietz, Phillip, *Wörterbuch zu Dr. Martin Luthers Deutschen Schriften, 1* and *2/1*, Hildesheim, 1961.

Ebeling, Gerhard, *Evangelische Evangelienauslegung: Eine Untersuchung zu Luthers Hermeneutik*, München, 1942.

——— *Luther: Einführung in sein Denken*, Tübingen, 1964.

——— *Word and Faith*, Philadelphia, 1963.

——— "Die Anfänge von Luthers Hermeneutik," *Zeitschrift für Theologie und Kirche, 48* (1951), 172–230.

Elert, Werner, *The Shape of Lutheranism*, trans. Walter A. Hansen, St. Louis, 1962.

Ellwein, Eduard, *Summus Evangelistica: Die Botschaft des Johannesevangeliums in der Auslegung Luthers*, München, 1960.

Ernesti, Johann August, "De Officio Christ triplici," in *Opuscula Theologica* (Leipzig, 1773), 412–438.

Fairweather, Eugene, "Incarnation and Atonement: An Anselmian Response to Aulén's Christus Victor," *Canadian Journal of Theology, 7*, No. 3 (1961), 167–175.

——— "Introduction to Anselm of Canterbury," in *A Scholastic Miscellany: Anselm to Ockham*, Library of Christian Classics 10 (London, 1956), 47–62.

Fischer-Galati, S. A., *Ottoman Imperialism and German Protestantism 1521–1555*, Harvard, 1959.

Forck, Gottfried, *Die Königsherrschaft Jesu Christi bei Luther*, Berlin, 1959.

Forsyth, P. T., *The Person and Place of Jesus Christ*, London, 1910.

Gerrish, Brian, *Grace and Reason*, Oxford, 1962.

Gogarten, Friedrich, *Die Verkündigung Jesu Christi: Grundlagen und Aufgabe*, Heidelberg, 1948.

Gollwitzer, Helmut, "Zur Auslegung von Joh. 6 bei Luther und Zwingli," in W. Schauch, ed., *In Memoriam Ernst Lohmeyer*, Stuttgart, 1951.

Grillmeier, Aloys, *Christ in Christian Tradition*, New York, 1965.

Gyllenkrok, Axel, *Rechtfertigung und Heiligung in der frühen evangelischen Theologie Luthers*, Uppsala and Weisbaden, 1952.

Harnack, Adolf, *History of Dogma*, trans. Neil Buchanan from 3d German ed., 7 vols. in 4, reprinted New York, 1961.

Harnack, Theodosius, *Luthers Theologie, mit besonderer Beziehung auf seine Versöhnungs- und Erlösungslehre*, 2 Bde, neue Ausg., München, 1927.

Headley, John, *Luther's View of Church History*, Yale Publications in Religion, 6, London and New Haven, 1963.

Heppe, Heinrich, *Reformed Dogmatics*, London, 1950.

Hermann, Rudolf, *Die Gestalt Simsons bei Luther*, Berlin, 1952.

Heyer, George, "Rectitudo in the Theology of St. Anselm," doctoral dissertation, Yale University, 1963; University Microfilms, 1963.

———— "St. Anselm on the Harmony between God's Mercy and God's Justice," in Robert E. Cushman and Egil Grislis, eds., *The Heritage of Christian Thought: Essays in Honor of Robert Lowry Calhoun* (New York, 1965), 31–40.

Hirsch, Emanuel, *Hilfsbuch zum Studium der Dogmatik. Die Dogmatik der Reformatoren und der altevangelischen Lehrer quellenmässig belegt und verdeutscht*, Berlin and Leipzig, 1951.

———— *Lutherstudien*, 2 Bde, Gütersloh, 1954.

———— *Die Theologie des Andreas Osiander und ihre geschichtliche Voraussetzungen*, n.p., 1919.

Holl, Karl, *Gesammelte Aufsätze zur Kirchengeschichte*, 3 Bde, 7. Aufl., Tübingen, 1948.

Jansen, John, *Calvin's Doctrine of the Work of Christ*, London, 1956.

Kattenbusch, Ferdinand, *Luthers Stellung zu den ökumenischen Symbolen*, Giessen, 1883.

Köhler, Walther, *Zwingli und Luther. Ihr Streit über das Abendmahl nach seinen politischen und religiösen Beziehungen*, 2 Bde, Leipzig, 1924; Gütersloh, 1953.

Kooiman, Willem Jan, *Luther and the Bible*, Philadelphia, 1961.

Krause, Gerhard, *Studien zu Luthers Auslegung der Kleinen Propheten*, Tübingen, 1962.

Lau, Franz, *Luthers Lehre von den beiden Reichen*, Berlin, 1952.

———— "Erstes Gebot und Ehre Gottes als Mitte von Luthers Theologie," *ThLZ*, 73 (1948), 719–30.

Lerch, David, *Isaaks Opferung christliche gedeutet*, Tübingen, 1950.

Lilje, Hanns, *Luthers Geschichtsanschauung*, Berlin, 1932.

Link, Wilhelm, *Das Ringen Luthers um die Freiheit der Theologie von der Philosophie*, München, 1940.

Loewenich, Walther von, *Luthers Theologia Crucis*, München, 1954.

———— *Luther als Ausleger der Synoptiker*, München, 1954.

———— *Luther und das johanneische Christentum*, München, 1935.

———— *Luthers evangelische Botschaft*, 2. Aufl., München, 1948.

———— *Die Eigenart von Luthers Auslegung des Johannes-Prologes*, München, 1960.

Lohse, Bernhard, *Ratio und Fides. Eine Untersuchung über die ratio in der Theologie Luthers*, Göttingen, 1958.

McIntyre, John, *St. Anselm and His Critics*, Edinburgh, 1954.

Möller, Wilhelm, *Andreas Osianders Leben und ausgewählte Schriften*, Elberfeld, 1870.

Nygren, Anders, "Luthers Lehre von den zwei Reichen," *ThLZ*, 74 (1949), 1–8.

Oberman, Heiko, *Forerunners of the Reformation: The Shape of Late Medieval Thought Illustrated by Key Documents*, New York, 1966.

——— *The Harvest of Medieval Theology: Gabriel Biel and Late Medieval Nominalism*, Harvard, 1963.

Østergaard-Nielsen, Harald, *Scriptura Sacra et Viva Vox: Eine Lutherstudie*, München, 1957.

Pelikan, Jaroslav, *Luther the Expositor: Introduction to the Reformer's Exegetical Writings* (companion volume to *Luther's Works, American Edition*), St. Louis, 1959.

——— *The Light of the World*, New York, 1962.

Polman, A. D. R., *The Word of God According to St. Augustine*, Grand Rapids, 1961.

Prenter, Regin, *Spiritus Creator*, trans. John M. Jensen, Philadelphia, 1953.

——— "Luther on Word and Sacrament," in *Martin Luther Lectures*, Vol. 2: *More About Luther* (Decorah, Iowa, 1958), 65–122.

Preus, James Samuel, *From Shadow to Promise: Old Testament Interpretation from Augustine to the Young Luther*, Harvard, 1969.

Ritschl, Albrecht, *The Christian Doctrine of Justification and Reconciliation*, 3 vols. Edinburgh, 1872–1902.

Rupp, E. Gordon, *Luther's Progress to the Diet of Worms*, London, 1951.

——— *The Righteousness of God*, London, 1953.

——— "Ernst Bizer: Fides ex auditu," book review, *ZKG*, 71 (1960), 351–55.

Saarnivaara, Uuras, *Luther Discovers the Gospel*, St. Louis, 1951.

Sasse, Hermann, *This Is My Body: Luther's Contention for the Real Presence in the Sacrament of the Altar*, Minneapolis, 1959.

Schleiermacher, Friedrich, *The Christian Faith*, trans. of 2d ed., reprinted Edinburgh, 1960.

Schmid, Heinrich, *Doctrinal Theology of the Evangelical Lutheran Church*, Philadelphia, 1876.

Schwarz, Werner, *Principles and Problems of Biblical Interpretation*, Cambridge, 1955.

Seeberg, Erich, *Luthers Theologie*, Vol. 1: *Die Gottesanschauung bei Luther* Göttingen, 1929; Vol. 2: *Christus Wirklichkeit und Urbild*, Stuttgart, 1937.

——— *Luthers Theologie in ihren Grundzügen*, Stuttgart, 1950.

Stange, Carl, *Der johanneische Typus der Heilslehre Luthers im Verhältnis zur paulinischen Rechtfertigungslehre*, Gütersloh, 1949.

Stange, Carl, "Das Heilswerk Christi nach Luther," *Zeitschrift für syste-matische Theologie*, *21* (1950), 112–27.

Stendahl, Krister, "The Apostle Paul and the Introspective Conscience of the West," *Harvard Theological Review*, *56* (1963), 199–215.

Tillich, Paul, *Systematic Theology*, 3 vols. Chicago, 1951ff.

Törnvall, Gustaf, *Geistliches und weltliches Regiment bei Luther*, München, 1947.

Vignaux, Paul, "Sur Luther et Ockham," *Franziskanische Studien*, *32* (1950), 21–30.

Vogelsang, Erich, *Die Anfänge von Luthers Christologie*, Berlin, 1933.

Watson, Philip S., *Let God Be God!*, London, 1958.

————— "Luther und die Heiligung," in Vilmos Vajta, ed., *Lutherforschung Heute* (Berlin, 1958), 75–84.

Wingren, Gustaf, *Luther on Vocation*, Philadelphia, 1957.

————— *The Living Word*, Philadelphia, 1960.

Wolf, Ernst, *Peregrinatio: Studien zur reformatorischen Theologie und zum Kirchenproblem*, München, 1954.

————— "Asterisci und Obelisci zum Thema: Athanasius und Luther," *Evangelische Theologie*, *18* (1958), 481–490.

# Register of Luther Citations

10/III, 129, 32                  122
10/III, 129, 35                   46
10/III, 130, 23                  171
10/III, 130, 24                  153
10/III, 133,  9                  145
John 15:26–16:4, on the consolation of the Holy Spirit in persecution, June 1
10/III, 136,  2                  114
10/III, 137, 27                  110
John 14:23–31, Pentecost, June 8
10/III, 149,  3                   45
10/III, 149,  8                   46
10/III, 154, 16                  161
John 3:16–21, Pentecost Monday,
June 9
10/III, 155,  2 ff.               46
10/III, 155,  6                   45
10/III, 155,  8                  106
10/III, 157, 14                   55
10/III, 157, 31                  264
10/III, 157, 32 f.               142
10/III, 158, 27                  198
10/III, 158, 27 ff.              115
10/III, 158, 30 ff.              115
10/III, 159, 29                  132
John 10:1–11, on the preaching
office, Pentecost Tuesday, June
10
10/III, 161, 11                  126
10/III, 161, 11                  149
10/III, 161, 14 & 16             116
10/III, 161, 21                  113
10/III, 162,  1                  205
10/III, 162, 11                  126
10/III, 163, 22 ff.              123
10/III, 164,  1                  123
10/III, 164, 14                  262
10/III, 165, 17                  249
10/III, 167,  4                  264
10/III, 167, 22                  250
10/III, 168, 12                  106
10/III, 168, 15                  107
10/III, 168, 19 ff.              161
10/III, 169, 15                  162
Luke 16:19–31, on the damned
rich man and the blessed pauper
Lazarus, June 22

10/III, 171, 15                   76
10/III, 173, 17 ff.              247
10/III, 174, 18                  247
10/III, 175, 17                   71
Luke 15:1–10, July 6
10/III, 191, 17                   22
Matthew 1:1–17, on the lineage
of Mary, the Mother of God,
September 8
10/III, 221,  8                   89
10/III, 221, 11                   38
Matthew 5:12 & 22: 1–14, All
Saints', November 1 & 2
10/III, 327,  1                   34
John 4:47–54, on the sign of
Jonah, November 9
10/III, 404,  6 to 19             36
10/III, 416, 14 ff.              260
10/III, 417, 20                  153
10/III, 419, 11                  260
10/III, 425, 21                  259
10/III, 426, 16                   44
Sermons of 1523
John 6:55 ff., June 19
11, 126,  9                      150
John 1:1 ff., December 27
11, 226,  8                       14
On Temporal Authority, 1523
11, 249, 27                      184
11, 258, 13                       51
On Ordering the Ministry of the
Church, 1523
12, 188, 20 ff.                   41
12, 191, 12                       51
To the Knights of the Teutonic Order,
To Avoid False Chastity, 1523
12, 235, 24                       71
The First Epistle of St Peter, 1523
12, 259,  5                       73
12, 266,  1                      116
12, 267, 33                      115
12, 268, 21                      168
12, 275, 16                       22
12, 285, 27                       52
12, 285, 27                       56
12, 285, 27                       70
12, 285, 29                       51
12, 287, 21                      156

| | |
|---|---|
| 13, 299, 11 | 175 |
| 13, 312, 24 | 24 |
| 13, 312, 24 | 173 |
| 13, 313, 27 | 246 |
| 13, 313, 29 | 248 |
| 13, 317, 13 | 24 |
| 13, 320, 37 | 193 |
| 13, 320, 37 | 206 |
| 13, 324, 12 | 20 |
| 13, 324, 29 | 24 |
| 13, 324, 29 | 173 |
| 13, 324, 32 | 25 |
| 13, 341, 15 | 246 |

Nahum, June/July, 1525

| | |
|---|---|
| 13, 354, 22 | 20 |

Habakkuk, July/August, 1525

| | |
|---|---|
| 13, 426, 29 | 27 |
| 13, 432, 35 | 173 |
| 13, 440, 16 ff. | 25 |
| 13, 441, 16 | 20 |

Zephaniah, August, 1525

| | |
|---|---|
| 13, 480, 2 | 173 |
| 13, 480, 4 | 26 |
| 13, 503, 32 ff. | 186 |
| 13, 508, 16 | 263 |

Haggai, September, 1525

| | |
|---|---|
| 13, 525, 6 | 265 |
| 13, 540, 27 | 173 |
| 13, 541, 1 | 177 |

Zechariah, late 1525/early 1526

| | |
|---|---|
| 13, 551, 18 | 66 |
| 13, 570, 16 | 1 |
| 13, 572, 6 | 24 |
| 13, 572, 6 | 206 |
| 13, 572, 20 | 26 |
| 13, 572, 30 | 25 |
| 13, 581, 6 | 26 |
| 13, 583, 1 | 264 |
| 13, 593, 15 | 25 |
| 13, 595, 23 | 173 |
| 13, 608, 25 | 177 |
| 13, 609, 1 | 25 |
| 13, 615, 25 | 26 |
| 13, 621, 3 | 20 |
| 13, 626, 1 | 176 |
| 13, 626, 21 | 36 |
| 13, 627, 24 | 30 |
| 13, 635, 9 ff. | 251 |

| | |
|---|---|
| 13, 647, 38 | 76 |
| 13, 649, 28 | 24 |
| 13, 658, 28 | 183 |

Malachi, 1526

| | |
|---|---|
| 13, 694, 23 | 183 |
| 13, 701, 1 | 173 |
| 13, 701, 22 | 251 |
| 13, 703, 3 | 250 |

2 Peter and Jude, January/March, 1523 (published 1524)

| | |
|---|---|
| 14, 27, 15 | 77 |
| 14, 27, 16 | 94 |
| 14, 27, 22 ff. | 83 |
| 14, 27, 22 ff. | 185 |
| 14, 30, 13 | 125 |

Deuteronomy, 1523/24 (published 1525)

| | |
|---|---|
| 14, 547, 20 | 71 |
| 14, 561, 17 | 19 |
| 14, 582, 25 | 154 |
| 14, 634, 21 | 257 |
| 14, 663, 22 | 253 |
| 14, 675, 11 | 63 |
| 14, 676, 29 ff. | 53 |
| 14, 676, 36 | 63 |
| 14, 677, 3 | 64 |
| 14, 677, 12 | 63 |
| 14, 678, 21 ff. | 64 |
| 14, 679, 10 | 63 |

Sermons of 1524

John 6:25–42, March 8

| | |
|---|---|
| 15, 467, 16 | 157 |
| 15, 467, 17 | 150 |
| 15, 467, 24 | 92 |
| 15, 470, 14 | 113 |

John 13:1 ff., on the fruit of the Sacrament, Christian love, March 24

| | |
|---|---|
| 15, 497 to 506 | 37 |
| 15, 497, 22 ff. | 163 |
| 15, 499, 7 | 163 |
| 15, 502, 22 | 162 |
| 15, 505, 6 | 45 |
| 15, 506, 9 | 181 |
| 15, 506, 10 | 85 |
| 15, 506, 12 | 182 |
| 15, 506, 13 | 181 |
| 15, 506, 14 | 177 |

21, 211, 31                    136
Mark 16:1–8, Easter Day, 1538
  21, 214, 6 & 19              168
Acts 10:34–43, Easter Monday
  21, 216, 19                  110
  21, 217, 29                  138
  21, 218, 30                  107
  21, 218, 37                  135
Luke 24:13–35, Easter Monday,
1534
  21, 224, 31                  172
  21, 231, 12                  203
  21, 233,  6                   21
  21, 234,  5                  215
  21, 234, 17                  130
Luke 24:36–47, Easter Monday,
1534
  21, 245,  4                   67
  21, 259,  9                  130
  21, 259,  9 ff.              134
  21, 261, 26                  183
  21, 264, 27                  135
Colossians 3:1–7, Easter Wednes-
day, 1534
  21, 267, 29
1 John 5:4–12, Sunday after
Easter, 1537
  21, 286, 33                   73
John 20:19–31, Sunday after
Easter, 1523
  21, 291, 13                  262
  21, 292, 30 to 37            123
  21, 293, 11                  265
  21, 293, 25 & 31             143
  21, 295,  1                   50
  21, 295,  7                  177
  21, 296, 17                  194
1 Peter 2:20–25, 2nd Sunday
after Easter, 1537
  21, 300, 26 ff.              163
  21, 315, 26                  247
John 10:12–16, 2nd Sunday after
Easter
  21, 317, 23                  190
  21, 317, 28                   76
  21, 318, 38                  189
  21, 320, 37                   53
  21, 320, 37                   76

21, 321, 31                    187
21, 322, 31                    245
21, 323, 22 ff.                245
21, 327, 31                    246
21, 329, 28                    114
21, 329, 28                    252
21, 330, 27 ff.                 76
21, 336, 21                     46
21, 336, 32 ff.                124
21, 336, 33                    124
21, 337,  8                    181
21, 337, 21                     44
21, 337, 21                     45
1 Peter 2:11–20, 3rd Sunday
after Easter, 1539
  21, 340,  8                  152
John 16:5–15, 4th Sunday after
Easter
  21, 353, 24                   55
  21, 358, 37                   55
  21, 359,  1                   55
  21, 359, 10                  153
  21, 359, 27 ff.              123
  21, 358, 34                  130
  21, 361, 30                  150
  21, 362, 31                  153
  21, 363, 10                   56
  21, 363, 10                  151
  21, 363, 14                  130
  21, 363, 14                  153
  21, 363, 15                   55
  21, 363, 20                  117
  21, 363, 20                  121
  21, 364,  5 ff.               77
  21, 364, 16 ff.              158
  21, 364, 24                   40
  21, 365,  4                  153
  21, 365, 10                  153
  21, 365, 28                  122
  21, 365, 28 f.               123
  21, 368,  1                  157
  21, 368, 10                  184
  21, 368, 17                  185
  21, 368, 24                  169
  21, 369, 16 ff.              182
  21, 371, 13                  178
  21, 371, 29                  143
  21, 371, 35                  183

John 1:1 ff., December 27

John 17: The Prayer of Christ, August/October, 1528

John 6 to 8 (*continued*)

| | | | |
|---|---|---|---|
| 33, | 17, | 9 | 92 |
| 33, | 17, | 10 | 258 |
| 33, | 17, | 33 | 78 |
| 33, | 19, | 16 | 92 |
| 33, | 19, | 20 ff. | 86 |
| 33, | 19, | 20 ff. | 94 |
| 33, | 19, | 34 | 77 |
| 33, | 20, | 21 | 125 |
| 33, | 20, | 25 | 101 |
| 33, | 21, | 28 to 38 | 92 |
| 33, | 24, | 4 | 258 |
| 33, | 24, | 32 | 78 |
| 33, | 24, | 35 | 78 |
| 33, | 27, | 35 | 95 |
| 33, | 28, | 27 | 178 |
| 33, | 28, | 34 | 187 |
| 33, | 29, | 14 ff. | 147 |
| 33, | 30, | 15 ff. | 148 |
| 33, | 31, | 11 | 148 |
| 33, | 34, | 5 | 56 |
| 33, | 35, | 27 | 97 |
| 33, | 36, | 29 | 61 |
| 33, | 36, | 30 | 58 |
| 33, | 37, | 3 ff. | 189 |
| 33, | 37, | 22 | 148 |
| 33, | 40, | 8 | 42 |
| 33, | 48, | 31 | 124 |
| 33, | 52, | 17 | 124 |
| 33, | 52, | 32 | 29 |
| 33, | 53, | 1 | 22 |
| 33, | 54, | 4 | 125 |
| 33, | 54, | 13 | 92 |
| 33, | 56, | 26 | 36 |
| 33, | 57, | 31 | 36 |
| 33, | 57, | 40 | 258 |
| 33, | 77, | 3 | 155 |
| 33, | 78, | 25 | 103 |
| 33, | 79, | 18 | 210 |
| 33, | 79, | 19 | 205 |
| 33, | 79, | 19 | 222 |
| 33, | 81, | 23 | 266 |
| 33, | 82, | 1 | 248 |
| 33, | 83, | 7 | 247 |
| 33, | 85, | 6 to 22 | 114 |
| 33, | 85, | 16 | 262 |
| 33, | 85, | 19 | 124 |
| 33, | 86, | 7 | 145 |

| | | | |
|---|---|---|---|
| 33, | 86, | 12 | 146 |
| 33, | 88, | 15 | 116 |
| 33, | 96, | 32 | 155 |
| 33, | 101, | 33 | 117 |
| 33, | 102, | 28 | 103 |
| 33, | 103, | 26 | 102 |
| 33, | 103, | 34 | 60 |
| 33, | 104, | 10 | 102 |
| 33, | 104, | 13 | 103 |
| 33, | 107, | 8 | 144 |
| 33, | 107, | 8 | 145 |
| 33, | 109, | 18 | 107 |
| 33, | 110, | 1 | 102 |
| 33, | 111, | 14 ff. | 182 |
| 33, | 112, | 1 ff. | 171 |
| 33, | 112, | 28 | 171 |
| 33, | 112, | 40 | 172 |
| 33, | 113, | 22 | 172 |
| 33, | 114, | 12 ff. | 183 |
| 33, | 114, | 18 | 168 |
| 33, | 115, | 4 | 206 |
| 33, | 115, | 8 | 205 |
| 33, | 115, | 13 | 206 |
| 33, | 115, | 26 | 199 |
| 33, | 116, | 26 | 9 |
| 33, | 116, | 33 | 43 |
| 33, | 119, | 27 | 78 |
| 33, | 119, | 31 | 78 |
| 33, | 125, | 8 | 212 |
| 33, | 124, | 9 | 212 |
| 33, | 125, | 11 | 211 |
| 33, | 125, | 21 | 210 |
| 33, | 128, | 30 | 194 |
| 33, | 135, | 10 | 226 |
| 33, | 131, | 11 | 59 |
| 33, | 131, | 20 | 74 |
| 33, | 134, | 20 | 224 |
| 33, | 134, | 28 | 60 |
| 33, | 141, | 18 | 59 |
| 33, | 147, | 23 ff. | 78 |
| 33, | 141, | 34 | 59 |
| 33, | 149, | 36 | 240 |
| 33, | 141, | 37 | 60 |
| 33, | 153, | 19 | 72 |
| 33, | 153, | 20 | 77 |
| 33, | 154, | 4 | 32 |
| 33, | 155, | 10 | 219 |
| 33, | 158, | 15 | 75 |

| | |
|---|---|
| 33, 158, 32 | 40 |
| 33, 160, 10 | 194 |
| 33, 160, 10 | 195 |
| 33, 160, 11 | 195 |
| 33, 161, 39 ff. | 140 |
| 33, 163, 21 | 190 |
| 33, 163, 36 | 265 |
| 33, 165, 21 | 147 |
| 33, 165, 32 | 198 |
| 33, 166, 20 | 197 |
| 33, 167, 21 | 42 |
| 33, 171, 13 | 161 |
| 33, 172, 6 | 77 |
| 33, 173, 13 | 33 |
| 33, 173, 16 | 166 |
| 33, 175, 9 ff. | 42 |
| 33, 175, 31 | 258 |
| 33, 176, 11 | 224 |
| 33, 176, 42 | 197 |
| 33, 177, 29 | 32 |
| 33, 178, 38 | 44 |
| 33, 182, 25 | 258 |
| 33, 183, 14 | 88 |
| 33, 183, 24 | 220 |
| 33, 183, 38 | 229 |
| 33, 184, 5 ff. | 229 |
| 33, 186, 3 | 154 |
| 33, 187, 19 | 95 |
| 33, 189, 1 | 201 |
| 33, 189, 3 | 229 |
| 33, 190, 26 | 229 |
| 33, 190, 33 | 224 |
| 33, 191, 3 | 230 |
| 33, 191, 27 | 204 |
| 33, 192, 12 ff. | 95 |
| 33, 201, 3 | 201 |
| 33, 211, 26 | 149 |
| 33, 211, 26 | 216 |
| 33, 212, 27 | 149 |
| 33, 219, 13 | 187 |
| 33, 224, 19 | 149 |
| 33, 225, 12 | 45 |
| 33, 225, 18 | 150 |
| 33, 225, 20 | 153 |
| 33, 225, 25 | 155 |
| 33, 228, 14 | 150 |
| 33, 230, 25 | 150 |
| 33, 230, 30 | 153 |

| | |
|---|---|
| 33, 231, 8 | 69 |
| 33, 231, 14 | 196 |
| 33, 231, 23 ff. | 226 |
| 33, 231, 29 | 170 |
| 33, 231, 32 | 198 |
| 33, 232, 1 & 31 | 226 |
| 33, 232, 6 | 222 |
| 33, 232, 19 | 258 |
| 33, 235, 16 | 198 |
| 33, 237, 4 & 9 | 71 |
| 33, 240, 38 | 150 |
| 33, 241, 1 | 155 |
| 33, 242, 3 | 257 |
| 33, 244, 35 | 40 |
| 33, 244, 35 | 69 |
| 33, 245, 2 | 40 |
| 33, 251, 40 ff. | 43 |
| 33, 251, 40 | 199 |
| 33, 252, 40 | 42 |
| 33, 254, 1 | 201 |
| 33, 254, 1 | 207 |
| 33, 256, 6 | 198 |
| 33, 261, 18 | 220 |
| 33, 262, 5 | 221 |
| 33, 262, 34 | 215 |
| 33, 263, 5 | 215 |
| 33, 267, 22 | 221 |
| 33, 281, 13 ff. | 135 |
| 33, 283, 37 | 120 |
| 33, 288, 18 | 45 |
| 33, 288, 18 | 155 |
| 33, 288, 22 | 216 |
| 33, 289, 2 | 216 |
| 33, 291, 33 | 194 |
| 33, 295, 31 | 43 |
| 33, 300, 36 | 43 |
| 33, 309, 39 | 123 |
| 33, 310, 3 | 101 |
| 33, 310, 3 | 123 |
| 33, 310, 15 | 117 |
| 33, 310, 15 | 117 |
| 33, 310, 15 | 118 |
| 33, 310, 19 | 50 |
| 33, 310, 24 & 32 | 177 |
| 33, 310, 31 | 30 |
| 33, 311, 14 | 119 |
| 33, 317, 35 | 163 |
| 33, 330, 10 | 43 |

John 6 to 8 (*continued*)

| | | |
|---|---|---|
| 33, 331, 3 | 76 | |
| 33, 343, 35 | 41 | |
| 33, 346, 1 ff. | 32 | |
| 33, 350, 25 | 41 | |
| 33, 352, 3 | 41 | |
| 33, 357, 41 | 52 | |
| 33, 357, 41 ff. | 54 | |
| 33, 357, 41 ff. | 224 | |
| 33, 358, 1 | 71 | |
| 33, 358, 1 | 203 | |
| 33, 358, 18 | 54 | |
| 33, 359, 30 | 44 | |
| 33, 362, 10 | 57 | |
| 33, 366, 11 | 75 | |
| 33, 369, 17 | 78 | |
| 33, 369, 38 | 55 | |
| 33, 387, 37 | 69 | |
| 33, 389, 12 ff. | 59 | |
| 33, 390, 8 ff. | 58 | |
| 33, 390, 25 | 92 | |
| 33, 392, 1 | 85 | |
| 33, 393, 25 | 68 | |
| 33, 393, 33 | 124 | |
| 33, 394, 20 to 37 | 72 | |
| 33, 394, 22 | 58 | |
| 33, 394, 22 | 72 | |
| 33, 395, 5 | 59 | |
| 33, 396, 3 | 52 | |
| 33, 398, 13 | 147 | |
| 33, 402, 28 | 52 | |
| 33, 407, 29 | 163 | |
| 33, 412, 38 | 31 | |
| 33, 413, 36 | 56 | |
| 33, 413, 36 | 58 | |
| 33, 423, 7 | 188 | |
| 33, 428, 17 | 31 | |
| 33, 431, 10 | 68 | |
| 33, 431, 27 | 68 | |
| 33, 431, 40 ff. | 68 | |
| 33, 433, 29 | 72 | |
| 33, 433, 33 | 63 | |
| 33, 436, 26 & 37 | 72 | |
| 33, 436, 26 ff. | 143 | |
| 33, 436, 29 | 72 | |
| 33, 438, 6 | 73 | |
| 33, 438, 12 | 73 | |
| 33, 445, 4 | 52 | |
| 33, 445, 18 | 251 | |

| | |
|---|---|
| 33, 447, 30 | 93 |
| 33, 448, 9 | 101 |
| 33, 449, 14 | 251 |
| 33, 451, 6 | 36 |
| 33, 451, 11 | 32 |
| 33, 462, 8 | 102 |
| 33, 463, 4 ff. | 69 |
| 33, 467, 33 | 69 |
| 33, 469, 12 ff. | 194 |
| 33, 469, 24 | 69 |
| 33, 471, 38 | 101 |
| 33, 473, 38 ff. | 69 |
| 33, 473, 40 ff. | 29 |
| 33, 474, 1 | 28 |
| 33, 476, 5 | 147 |
| 33, 495, 28 | 184 |
| 33, 505, 29 | 184 |
| 33, 505, 31 | 67 |
| 33, 507, 38 ff. | 67 |
| 33, 508, 17 | 53 |
| 33, 508, 17 | 64 |
| 33, 508, 23 | 67 |
| 33, 509, 6 ff. | 67 |
| 33, 509, 13 | 183 |
| 33, 509, 18 | 182 |
| 33, 510, 12 | 183 |
| 33, 512, 1 ff. | 77 |
| 33, 512, 9 | 76 |
| 33, 514, 26 | 250 |
| 33, 518, 1 | 57 |
| 33, 520, 25 | 251 |
| 33, 521, 30 | 78 |
| 33, 521, 33 | 78 |
| 33, 522, 6 | 252 |
| 33, 522, 39 | 159 |
| 33, 522, 39 | 162 |
| 33, 527, 2 | 103 |
| 33, 527, 27 | 250 |
| 33, 529, 13 | 106 |
| 33, 531, 1 ff. | 156 |
| 33, 531, 17 | 155 |
| 33, 533, 35 | 52 |
| 33, 533, 35 | 76 |
| 33, 534, 1 | 57 |
| 33, 534, 29 ff. | 52 |
| 33, 536, 8 | 216 |
| 33, 538, 17 | 155 |
| 33, 539, 5 | 53 |
| 33, 540, 3 | 186 |

| | |
|---|---|
| 41, 123, 34 | 177 |
| 41, 149, 9 | 55 |
| 41, 149, 24 | 117 |
| 41, 168, 17 | 50 |
| 41, 173, 26 | 118 |
| 41, 182, 19 ff. | 25 |
| 41, 183, 18 | 118 |
| 41, 183, 29 | 118 |
| 41, 183, 29 ff. | 119 |
| 41, 185, 27 ff. | 118 |
| 41, 191, 18 | 117 |
| 41, 192, 35 | 118 |
| 41, 194, 20 | 113 |
| 41, 195, 8 | 119 |
| 41, 195, 36 | 247 |
| 41, 216, 18 | 182 |
| 41, 231, 24 | 30 |
| 41, 235, 22 | 177 |

Sermon on the Holy Trinity, May 23, 1535

| | |
|---|---|
| 41, 272, 16 | 193 |
| 41, 273, 5 | 192 |
| 41, 273, 27 ff. | 194 |
| 41, 274, 36 ff. | 194 |
| 41, 273, 38 | 193 |
| 41, 275, 2 | 193 |

Sermons of 1535
Romans 8:18 ff., June 20

| | |
|---|---|
| 41, 317, 12 | 185 |

Luke 2:1 ff., December 25

| | |
|---|---|
| 41, 477 ff. | 34 |
| 41, 480, 25 | 34 |
| 41, 480, 29 | 34 |
| 41, 481, 3 | 237 |

Sermons of 1536
John 20:19 ff., April 23

| | |
|---|---|
| 41, 541, 20 ff. | 175 |

Ephesians 5:22 ff., April 24

| | |
|---|---|
| 41, 554, 20 | 153 |

John 16:16 ff., May 7

| | |
|---|---|
| 41, 573, 17 | 45 |
| 41, 573, 17 | 200 |
| 41, 574, 9 | 168 |
| 41, 574, 14 | 169 |
| 41, 575, 3 | 168 |

Lectures on Genesis, 1535/45

| | |
|---|---|
| 42, 13, 34 | 14 |
| 42, 14, 10 | 14 |

| | |
|---|---|
| 42, 14, 8 | 196 |
| 42, 14, 18 | 14 |
| 42, 14, 18 | 196 |
| 42, 43, 39 | 223 |
| 42, 44, 30 | 18 |
| 42, 44, 34 | 19 |
| 42, 59, 12 | 21 |
| 42, 80, 2 | 71 |
| 42, 109, 28 | 19 |
| 42, 109, 30 | 23 |
| 42, 141, 34 | 21 |
| 42, 143, 1 | 140 |
| 42, 144, 19 | 21 |
| 42, 146, 38 ff. | 133 |
| 42, 147, 3 ff. | 143 |
| 42, 162, 33 | 18 |
| 42, 163, 33 | 27 |
| 42, 170, 31 | 220 |
| 42, 174, 6 | 153 |
| 42, 195, 3 ff. | 2 |
| 42, 243, 36 | 18 |
| 42, 272, 16 | 2 |
| 42, 294 to 296 | 81 |
| 42, 294, 36 ff. | 83 |
| 42, 356, 23 | 65 |
| 42, 358, 33 | 2 |
| 42, 413, 34 | 188 |
| 42, 452, 17 | 158 |
| 42, 452, 23 | 147 |
| 42, 457, 29 | 94 |
| 42, 514, 31 | 80 |
| 42, 537 ff. | 128 |
| 42, 537, 35 | 118 |
| 42, 538, 1 | 118 |
| 42, 539, 34 | 131 |
| 42, 540, 32 | 118 |
| 42, 545, 23 | 118 |
| 42, 564, 30 | 158 |
| 42, 565, 12 | 66 |
| 42, 566, 10 | 66 |
| 42, 567, 8 | 66 |
| 42, 567, 25 | 22 |
| 42, 568, 1 | 17 |
| 42, 597, 17 | 2 |
| 42, 612, 25 | 64 |
| 42, 612, 27 | 63 |
| 42, 612, 29 | 107 |
| 42, 637, 29 | 66 |

| | | |
|---|---|---|
| 45, 480, 4 | 39 |
| 45, 480, 9 | 265 |
| 45, 480, 13 | 198 |
| 45, 481, 9 ff. | 83 |
| 45, 481, 17 to 26 | 91 |
| 45, 481, 20 | 85 |
| 45, 481, 21 | 224 |
| 45, 481, 33 | 59 |
| 45, 482, 1 | 84 |
| 45, 482, 2 | 88 |
| 45, 483, 7 ff. | 181 |
| 45, 483, 16 & 25 | 84 |
| 45, 483, 25 | 122 |
| 45, 483, 25 | 124 |
| 45, 484 to 488 | 185 |
| 45, 488, 9 | 190 |
| 45, 488, 9 | 198 |
| 45, 489, 18 | 43 |
| 45, 489, 18 | 44 |
| 45, 489, 22 | 224 |
| 45, 490, 21 | 78 |
| 45, 491, 17 | 124 |
| 45, 491, 18 ff. | 46 |
| 45, 492, 34 ff. | 248 |
| 45, 494, 12 | 71 |
| 45, 496, 7 to 14 | 248 |
| 45, 496, 2 | 248 |
| 45, 497, 11 | 160 |
| 45, 497, 24 ff. | 77 |
| 45, 497, 24 | 78 |
| 45, 497, 33 | 162 |
| 45, 499, 14 | 123 |
| 45, 501, 23 | 248 |
| 45, 501, 36 | 104 |
| 45, 502, 1 | 249 |
| 45, 502, 6 | 164 |
| 45, 504, 32 | 164 |
| 45, 504, 35 | 190 |
| 45, 504, 37 | 248 |
| 45, 505, 10 | 171 |
| 45, 505, 33 | 169 |
| 45, 506, 26 | 248 |
| 45, 507, 9 | 171 |
| 45, 507, 22 | 10 |
| 45, 507, 22 | 244 |
| 45, 508, 2 | 190 |
| 45, 508, 3 | 248 |
| 45, 509, 6 ff. | 143 |

| | | |
|---|---|---|
| 45, 510, 7 | 71 |
| 45, 511, 4 | 107 |
| 45, 511, 4 | 1 |
| 45, 511, 16 | 45 |
| 45, 511, 24 | 84 |
| 45, 513, 28 | 95 |
| 45, 514, 1 | 95 |
| 45, 514, 5 | 78 |
| 45, 514, 6 | 78 |
| 45, 515, 8 | 85 |
| 45, 515, 10 | 85 |
| 45, 515, 11 | 89 |
| 45, 515, 19 | 89 |
| 45, 515, 28 | 85 |
| 45, 516, 2 | 37 |
| 45, 516, 21 | 90 |
| 45, 518, 21 | 94 |
| 45, 519, 29 ff. | 91 |
| 45, 519, 32 | 123 |
| 45, 519, 32 | 138 |
| 45, 520, 2 ff. & 16 ff. | 91 |
| 45, 520, 32 | 94 |
| 45, 520, 38 | 38 |
| 45, 521, 2 | 85 |
| 45, 521, 4 ff. | 53 |
| 45, 521, 21 | 71 |
| 45, 521, 21 | 258 |
| 45, 521, 34 | 71 |
| 45, 522, 11 | 43 |
| 45, 522, 26 | 85 |
| 45, 522, 38 | 54 |
| 45, 523, 29 | 101 |
| 45, 525, 12 | 94 |
| 45, 525, 19 | 266 |
| 45, 525, 29 | 259 |
| 45, 527, 11 ff. | 198 |
| 45, 527, 14 | 43 |
| 45, 527, 23 ff. | 90 |
| 45, 528, 5 | 194 |
| 45, 528, 7 | 102 |
| 45, 528, 10 | 122 |
| 45, 528, 15 ff. | 43 |
| 45, 530, 27 | 58 |
| 45, 531, 20 | 43 |
| 45, 531, 27 ff. | 188 |
| 45, 532, 4 | 188 |
| 45, 532, 9 | 183 |
| 45, 532, 32 | 42 |

John 14 to 16 (*continued*)

| | | |
|---|---|---|
| 45, 535, 17 | 188 | |
| 45, 537, 25 | 39 | |
| 45, 538, 8 to 38 | 182 | |
| 45, 538, 28 | 39 | |
| 45, 543, 7 | 206 | |
| 45, 543, 14 | 201 | |
| 45, 543, 21 | 192 | |
| 45, 543, 31 | 123 | |
| 45, 543, 35 | 206 | |
| 45, 544, 30 ff. | 195 | |
| 45, 544, 35 ff. | 71 | |
| 45, 545, 32 | 208 | |
| 45, 546, 22 | 192 | |
| 45, 548, 10 | 113 | |
| 45, 548, 10 | 2 | |
| 45, 548, 17 | 205 | |
| 45, 548, 23 | 206 | |
| 45, 549, 14 | 198 | |
| 45, 549, 29 to 32 | 84 | |
| 45, 549, 30 | 193 | |
| 45, 549, 31 | 85 | |
| 45, 549, 33 | 85 | |
| 45, 549, 33 | 223 | |
| 45, 550, 3 | 123 | |
| 45, 550, 13 | 79 | |
| 45, 550, 15 | 90 | |
| 45, 550, 22 ff. | 79 | |
| 45, 550, 22 | 226 | |
| 45, 551, 6 | 40 | |
| 45, 551, 30 | 198 | |
| 45, 554, 4 | 125 | |
| 45, 555, 1 | 117 | |
| 45, 555, 2 | 117 | |
| 45, 555, 32 ff. | 209 | |
| 45, 556, 14 ff. | 230 | |
| 45, 556, 20 | 222 | |
| 45, 556, 27 | 201 | |
| 45, 556, 37 | 223 | |
| 45, 556, 39 | 37 | |
| 45, 556, 39 | 224 | |
| 45, 557, 7 | 232 | |
| 45, 558, 8 | 228 | |
| 45, 558, 11 | 227 | |
| 45, 558, 14 | 227 | |
| 45, 559, 17 | 214 | |
| 45, 559, 19 | 214 | |
| 45, 567, 23 | 72 | |

| | | |
|---|---|---|
| 45, 567, 28 | 117 | |
| 45, 571, 16 | 116 | |
| 45, 581, 22 ff. | 53 | |
| 45, 585, 3 | 254 | |
| 45, 586, 23 | 259 | |
| 45, 586, 31 | 194 | |
| 45, 587, 19 ff. | 198 | |
| 45, 587, 37 ff. | 60 | |
| 45, 588, 35 | 89 | |
| 45, 589, 1 | 79 | |
| 45, 589, 25 | 142 | |
| 45, 589, 25 | 85 | |
| 45, 589, 26 | 102 | |
| 45, 589, 31 | 153 | |
| 45, 589, 31 | 90 | |
| 45, 589, 31 | 89 | |
| 45, 589, 39 ff. | 153 | |
| 45, 589, 41 | 55 | |
| 45, 590, 1 | 153 | |
| 45, 592, 17 | 123 | |
| 45, 594, 29 | 103 | |
| 45, 594, 34 | 190 | |
| 45, 595, 22 | 124 | |
| 45, 595, 22 | 265 | |
| 45, 599, 10 | 123 | |
| 45, 601, 6 | 114 | |
| 45, 602, 36 | 176 | |
| 45, 603, 7 | 176 | |
| 45, 604, 11 | 124 | |
| 45, 605, 6 | 262 | |
| 45, 607, 7 | 262 | |
| 45, 607, 13 | 255 | |
| 45, 607, 26 | 176 | |
| 45, 612, 8 | 75 | |
| 45, 612, 26 to 34 | 72 | |
| 45, 612, 26 | 223 | |
| 45, 612, 26 | 226 | |
| 45, 614, 35 | 158 | |
| 45, 615, 13 ff. | 155 | |
| 45, 616, 3 | 156 | |
| 45, 616, 14 | 155 | |
| 45, 617, 22 | 158 | |
| 45, 626, 3 | 43 | |
| 45, 629, 6 | 183 | |
| 45, 629, 7 | 178 | |
| 45, 629, 29 | 196 | |
| 45, 629, 29 | 198 | |
| 45, 631, 6 | 263 | |

John 1 and 2 (*continued*)

| | |
|---|---|
| 46, 637, 30 | 86 |
| 46, 637, 37 | 187 |
| 46, 639, 19 | 93 |
| 46, 639, 22 | 93 |
| 46, 639, 28 | 95 |
| 46, 640, 5 | 96 |
| 46, 640, 33 | 38 |
| 46, 641, 35 ff. | 158 |
| 46, 645, 14 | 42 |
| 46, 646, 25 | 41 |
| 46, 647, 17 | 28 |
| 46, 648, 9 | 63 |
| 46, 649, 7 | 76 |
| 46, 649, 23 | 152 |
| 46, 649, 36 | 153 |
| 46, 650, 1 | 103 |
| 46, 650, 7 | 68 |
| 46, 650, 7 | 72 |
| 46, 652, 26 f. | 124 |
| 46, 652, 29 | 266 |
| 46, 653, 11 | 144 |
| 46, 655, 1 to 5 | 152 |
| 46, 655, 8 | 124 |
| 46, 655, 23 | 116 |
| 46, 656, 34 | 152 |
| 46, 656, 37 | 153 |
| 46, 663, 25 | 53 |
| 46, 665, 36 ff. | 89 |
| 46, 666, 14 | 82 |
| 46, 667, 7 | 80 |
| 46, 667, 10 ff. | 79 |
| 46, 667, 10 | 82 |
| 46, 668, 11 ff. | 80 |
| 46, 669, 1 ff. | 80 |
| 46, 671, 32 | 87 |
| 46, 672, 2 | 29 |
| 46, 672, 17 | 77 |
| 46, 672, 24 | 81 |
| 46, 672, 26 | 80 |
| 46, 673, 20 | 106 |
| 46, 675, 9 | 28 |
| 46, 676, 4 | 102 |
| 46, 676, 32 ff. | 129 |
| 46, 676, 39 | 253 |
| 46, 677, 21 | 253 |
| 46, 677, 27 | 132 |
| 46, 678, 21 | 132 |

| | |
|---|---|
| 46, 679, 9 | 129 |
| 46, 679, 19 | 135 |
| 46, 679, 22 ff. | 129 |
| 46, 679, 25 | 131 |
| 46, 679, 28 | 131 |
| 46, 679, 35 | 131 |
| 46, 679, 36 | 132 |
| 46, 680, 1 | 131 |
| 46, 680, 31 ff. | 137 |
| 46, 680, 31 | 241 |
| 46, 680, 35 | 39 |
| 46, 682, 1 | 136 |
| 46, 682, 18 | 131 |
| 46, 683, 8 | 132 |
| 46, 683, 24 | 131 |
| 46, 683, 28 | 132 |
| 46, 683, 32 | 135 |
| 46, 685, 14 | 93 |
| 46, 688, 20 | 28 |
| 46, 693, 26 | 123 |
| 46, 697, 12 | 194 |
| 46, 699, 23 f. | 123 |
| 46, 699, 28 | 29 |
| 46, 699, 38 | 123 |
| 46, 699, 38 | 28 |
| 46, 700, 2 | 172 |
| 46, 700, 2 | 173 |
| 46, 700, 9 | 30 |
| 46, 700, 14 | 29 |
| 46, 700, 36 | 28 |
| 46, 701, 3 ff. | 182 |
| 46, 710, 8 ff. | 50 |
| 46, 710, 14 | 174 |
| 46, 712, 1 | 52 |
| 46, 712, 31 | 153 |
| 46, 712, 31 | 187 |
| 46, 712, 31 | 259 |
| 46, 713, 11 ff. | 185 |
| 46, 714, 33 | 188 |
| 46, 718, 38 ff. | 115 |
| 46, 718, 40 | 76 |
| 46, 723, 4 | 52 |
| 46, 723, 9 | 40 |
| 46, 724, 1 ff. | 40 |
| 46, 727, 3 ff. | 52 |
| 46, 727, 12 | 42 |
| 46, 730, 23 | 29 |
| 46, 730, 23 | 176 |

John 3 and 4 (*continued*)

| | | |
|---|---|---|
| 47, | 66, 18 | 17 |
| 47, | 66, 21 | 189 |
| 47, | 66, 33 ff. | 255 |
| 47, | 67, 16 | 256 |
| 47, | 67, 19 | 46 |
| 47, | 69, 5 | 255 |
| 47, | 69, 38 | 124 |
| 47, | 71, 16 | 46 |
| 47, | 71, 22 | 256 |
| 47, | 71, 36 | 207 |
| 47, | 71, 38 | 201 |
| 47, | 72, 12 | 204 |
| 47, | 72, 22 | 232 |
| 47, | 72, 36 | 232 |
| 47, | 73, 32 ff. | 256 |
| 47, | 75, 1 | 256 |
| 47, | 76, 21 | 207 |
| 47, | 76, 31 | 207 |
| 47, | 76, 33 ff. | 230 |
| 47, | 77, 13 | 235 |
| 47, | 77, 34 | 232 |
| 47, | 77, 38 | 232 |
| 47, | 78, 7 | 207 |
| 47, | 80, 14 | 254 |
| 47, | 80, 21 & 37 | 256 |
| 47, | 80, 30 | 88 |
| 47, | 80, 31 | 90 |
| 47, | 81, 31 | 141 |
| 47, | 81, 36 | 125 |
| 47, | 82, 10 | 125 |
| 47, | 84, 10 | 257 |
| 47, | 84, 34 | 132 |
| 47, | 86, 3 ff. | 230 |
| 47, | 86, 33 | 235 |
| 47, | 87, 2 | 232 |
| 47, | 87, 12 | 201 |
| 47, | 88, 35 | 125 |
| 47, | 88, 35 | 164 |
| 47, | 88, 39 | 164 |
| 47, | 89, 1 | 194 |
| 47, | 89, 32 | 88 |
| 47, | 90, 38 ff. | 83 |
| 47, | 90, 38 | 84 |
| 47, | 93, 16 | 264 |
| 47, | 97, 10 | 160 |
| 47, | 97, 39 | 55 |
| 47, | 98, 31 | 93 |
| 47, | 98, 37 | 59 |
| 47, | 99, 15 & 30 | 59 |
| 47, | 99, 20 | 252 |
| 47, | 99, 20 | 263 |
| 47, | 100, 3 | 116 |
| 47, | 100, 9 | 124 |
| 47, | 100, 9 | 247 |
| 47, | 100, 10 | 124 |
| 47, | 102, 10 | 252 |
| 47, | 102, 13 f. | 124 |
| 47, | 102, 14 | 53 |
| 47, | 103, 1 | 186 |
| 47, | 104, 33 | 133 |
| 47, | 105, 1 ff. | 132 |
| 47, | 105, 6 | 123 |
| 47, | 105, 6 | 133 |
| 47, | 105, 6 & 28 | 140 |
| 47, | 105, 30 ff. | 124 |
| 47, | 105, 30 | 102 |
| 47, | 105, 42 | 123 |
| 47, | 106, 12 | 110 |
| 47, | 106, 19 | 123 |
| 47, | 108, 3 ff. | 250 |
| 47, | 108, 15 | 76 |
| 47, | 108, 16 | 113 |
| 47, | 110, 4 | 124 |
| 47, | 110, 10 | 123 |
| 47, | 111, 27 | 250 |
| 47, | 111, 28 | 123 |
| 47, | 112, 4 | 191 |
| 47, | 113, 34 to 42 | 212 |
| 47, | 113, 38 | 135 |
| 47, | 113, 38 | 152 |
| 47, | 114, 1 ff. | 158 |
| 47, | 115, 24 | 124 |
| 47, | 115, 31 | 131 |
| 47, | 118, 6 | 102 |
| 47, | 129, 23 | 67 |
| 47, | 129, 31 to 36 | 67 |
| 47, | 130, 5 | 67 |
| 47, | 131, 31 | 69 |
| 47, | 131, 31 | 199 |
| 47, | 133, 38 | 69 |
| 47, | 143, 9 | 67 |
| 47, | 143, 12 ff. | 155 |
| 47, | 144, 25 | 29 |

| | | | |
|---|---|---|---|
| 47, 144, 30 | 21 | 47, 180, 25 | 69 |
| 47, 145, 28 | 21 | 47, 180, 37 | 56 |
| 47, 145, 34 ff. | 31 | 47, 180, 41 ff. | 224 |
| 47, 145, 41 | 31 | 47, 181, 12 | 195 |
| 47, 146, 17 | 190 | 47, 182, 29 | 224 |
| 47, 146, 38 | 132 | 47, 183, 24 | 249 |
| 47, 147, 19 | 21 | 47, 185, 8 | 149 |
| 47, 150, 12 | 155 | 47, 185, 11 | 146 |
| 47, 151, 7 | 263 | 47, 185, 26 | 69 |
| 47, 152, 6 | 214 | 47, 185, 39 | 56 |
| 47, 152, 13 ff. | 261 | 47, 187, 12 | 42 |
| 47, 153, 27 | 216 | 47, 187, 12 ff. | 43 |
| 47, 154, 6 | 261 | 47, 187, 29 | 28 |
| 47, 154, 28 | 102 | 47, 187, 30 | 28 |
| 47, 154, 36 | 104 | 47, 190, 27 | 127 |
| 47, 155, 15 | 28 | 47, 191, 27 ff. | 57 |
| 47, 160, 22 | 94 | 47, 193, 10 | 57 |
| 47, 162, 30 | 63 | 47, 193, 41 | 57 |
| 47, 163, 11 | 190 | 47, 194, 4 | 31 |
| 47, 164, 24 | 260 | 47, 194, 18 | 64 |
| 47, 164, 41 | 261 | 47, 194, 20 | 28 |
| 47, 167, 11 | 31 | 47, 194, 21 | 57 |
| 47, 167, 20 | 261 | 47, 194, 22 | 57 |
| 47, 169, 1 | 215 | 47, 194, 31 | 189 |
| 47, 172, 9 to 21 | 125 | 47, 194, 37 ff. | 57 |
| 47, 172, 15 | 126 | 47, 194, 38 | 190 |
| 47, 172, 15 | 142 | 47, 195, 11 & 16 ff. | 70 |
| 47, 172, 17 | 127 | 47, 195, 13 | 125 |
| 47, 172, 18 | 151 | 47, 196, 13 | 69 |
| 47, 172, 32 | 102 | 47, 196, 13 | 76 |
| 47, 172, 34 | 153 | 47, 196, 15 | 85 |
| 47, 172, 34 | 101 | 47, 196, 15 to 20 | 150 |
| 47, 173, 23 | 103 | 47, 196, 20 | 190 |
| 47, 173, 24 | 150 | 47, 196, 21, 29 & 36 | 72 |
| 47, 175, 7 | 201 | 47, 197, 10 | 84 |
| 47, 175, 7 | 211 | 47, 197, 11 | 104 |
| 47, 177, 5 | 28 | 47, 197, 29 | 128 |
| 47, 177, 38 | 39 | 47, 198, 9 | 252 |
| 47, 178, 1 | 174 | 47, 198, 14 f. | 95 |
| 47, 178, 3 | 62 | 47, 198, 14 | 97 |
| 47, 178, 8 & 10 | 62 | 47, 198, 24 | 95 |
| 47, 178, 11 | 125 | 47, 198, 25 & 30 | 116 |
| 47, 178, 18 | 50 | 47, 198, 26 | 124 |
| 47, 179, 28 | 127 | 47, 198, 29 & 16 to 23 | 189 |
| 47, 180, 1 | 54 | 47, 198, 34 | 117 |
| 47, 180, 19 & 25 | 58 | 47, 198, 39 ff. | 84 |
| 47, 180, 24 & 35 | 46 | 47, 198, 40 ff. | 178 |

# Index